UNSEEN WARFARE

also translated by
E. Kadloubovsky and G. E. H. Palmer

*

WRITINGS FROM THE PHILOKALIA ON
PRAYER OF THE HEART

UNSEEN WARFARE

being the SPIRITUAL COMBAT *and*
PATH TO PARADISE *of* LORENZO SCUPOLI
as edited by NICODEMUS OF THE HOLY MOUNTAIN
and revised by THEOPHAN THE RECLUSE

translated into English from
THEOPHAN'S *Russian text*
by E. Kadloubovsky
and G. E. H. Palmer

with a history of the work by
H. A. Hodges, M.A., D.Phil.
Professor of Philosophy
in the University of Reading

FABER AND FABER LIMITED
24 Russell Square
London

CONTENTS

7

CONTENTS

CONTENTS

FOREWORD

TO THE RUSSIAN VERSION

4th Edition, Moscow 1904

*In the original text of this book it is said on the title page that the book is written by another, a certain wise man, and that Staretz Nicodemus only revised, corrected and amended it, and supplemented it with commentaries and extracts from the holy fathers. So the book belongs to Staretz Nicodemus rather in the spirit than in the letter. In translating the book, it was thought best to incorporate the commentaries and testimonies of the fathers into the text, and for this and other reasons it was sometimes necessary to alter the text to make it read smoothly. Therefore this book should be regarded as a free rendering rather than as a literal translation.

---

* This Foreword to the Russian version is presumably by the translator, Bishop Theophan.

FOREWORD*

BY STARETZ NICODEMUS

This book, which profits the soul, is justly named 'Unseen Warfare'. Many holy and divinely-inspired books of the Old and New Testaments have received their titles from the subjects they deal with (for instance, Genesis is so called because it tells of the creation and right ordering of all existence out of non-existence; Exodus—because it describes the exodus of the children of Israel from Egypt; Leviticus—because it contains the sacred statutes for the Levites; the books of Kings—because they tell of the lives and activities of kings; the Gospels—because they 'bring . . . good tidings of great joy . . . For unto you is born . . . a Saviour, which is Christ the Lord' [Luke ii. 10, 11] and show to all a sure way to salvation and the inheritance of life in eternal bliss). Therefore who will dispute that the title of this book should be 'Unseen Warfare', according to its content and the subjects it deals with?

For it teaches not the art of visible and sensory warfare, and speaks not about visible, bodily foes but about the unseen and inner struggle, which every Christian undertakes from the moment of his baptism, when he makes a vow to God to fight for Him, to the glory of His divine Name, even unto death. (It is of this warfare that the book of Numbers speaks allegorically: 'Wherefore it is said in the book of the wars of the Lord' [Numbers xxi. 14].) It speaks of invisible and incorporeal foes, which are the varied passions and lusts of the flesh, and of the evil demons who hate men and never cease to fight against us, day and night, as the divine Paul says: 'For we wrestle not against flesh and blood,

* Added by Staretz Nicodemus to the manuscript he was using. (Footnote in the original.)

but against principalities, against powers, against the rulers of the darkness of this world, against spiritual wickedness in high places' (Eph. vi. 12).

This book teaches that the warriors who take part in this unseen war are all who are Christians; and their commander is our Lord Jesus Christ, surrounded and accompanied by His marshals and generals, that is, by all the hierarchies of angels and saints. The arena, the field of battle, the place where the fight actually takes place is our own heart and all our inner man. The time of battle is our whole life.

With what weapons are warriors armed for this unseen warfare? Listen. Their helmet is total disbelief in themselves and complete absence of self-reliance; their shield and coat of mail—a bold faith in God and a firm trust in Him; their armour and cuirass—instruction in the passion of Christ; their belt—cutting off bodily passions; their boots—humility and a constant sense and recognition of their powerlessness; their spurs—patience in temptations and repudiation of negligence; their sword, which they hold ever in one hand, is prayer whether with the lips or within—in the heart; their three-pronged spear, which they hold in the other hand, is a firm resolve in no way to consent to the passion which assails them, but to repulse it with anger and wholehearted hatred; their pay and food, sustaining them in their resistance to the enemy, is frequent communion with God, both through the mystery of the Holy Eucharist, and inwardly; the clear and cloudless atmosphere, which enables them to see the enemy from afar, is a constant exercising of the mind in the knowledge of what is right in the eyes of the Lord, and a constant exercising of the will in desiring only what is pleasing to God, peace and quiet of the heart.

It is here,—here in this 'Unseen Warfare' (that is, in this book) or rather in the 'Wars of the Lord', that Christ's warriors learn to discern the various forms of prelest,* the different wiles, the

* Прелесть. The nearest English equivalent seems to be 'beguilement' (cf. 'The serpent beguiled me, and I did eat' [Gen. iii. 13]). But the meaning of prelest is both wider and more technical. It has seemed best therefore to leave the word untranslated throughout the book.

Прелесть in general translates the Greek word πλάνη; the latter literally means 'wandering' or 'going astray' (cf. πλάνος, deceiver, impostor). Prelest is the resulting state in the soul which wanders away from Truth.

If we may paraphrase Bishop Ignatiy Brianchaninov (d. 1867), we could define prelest as the corruption of human nature through the acceptance by man of mirages mistaken for truth; we are all in prelest.

16

incredible subterfuges and military ruses, which our invisible foes use against us through the senses, through fantasy, through loss of the fear of God, and in particular through the four suggestions, which they introduce into the heart at the moment of death—I mean suggestions of unbelief, despair, vainglory, and of the demons themselves assuming the aspect of angels of light. But in learning to discern all this, men learn at the same time how to frustrate these wiles of the enemy and to resist them. They learn how to find out what tactical moves to make and what laws of war they must follow in each particular case, and the courage needed to enter into battle. In brief, I would say that every man, who desires salvation, will learn through this book how to conquer his invisible foes, in order to acquire the treasure of true and divine virtues and to be rewarded with an incorruptible crown and a token of eternity, which is union with God, both in this life and in the future.

So, Christ-loving readers, accept this book graciously and gladly, and learning from it the art of 'Unseen Warfare', strive not merely to fight, but to fight according to the law, to fight as you should, so that you may be crowned. For, according to the Apostle, 'If a man also strive for masteries, yet is he not crowned, except he strive lawfully' (II Tim. ii. 5). Arm yourselves, as this book shows you how, so as to strike down your inner and invisible foes, which are the soul-destroying passions and their originators and instigators—the demons. 'Put on the whole armour of God, that ye may be able to stand against the wiles of the devil' (Eph. vi. 11). Remember how at holy Baptism you vowed to renounce Satan and all his works, all service of him, and all his pride, that is, love of lust, love of glory, love of money and other passions. So strive with all your might to turn him back, to put him to shame and to overcome him with every perfection.

And what of the rewards which await you in this victory? They are many and great. Hear of them from the lips of the Lord Himself, Who makes you this promise in the holy Revelation: 'To him that overcometh will I give to eat of the tree of life, which is in the midst of the paradise of God' (Rev. ii. 7). 'He that overcometh shall not be hurt of the second death' (Rev. ii. 11). 'To him that overcometh will I give to eat of the hidden manna' (Rev. ii. 17). 'And he that overcometh, and keepeth my works unto the end, to him will I give power over the nations ... and I will give him the morning star' (Rev. ii. 26, 28). 'He that overcometh, the same shall be clothed in white raiment . . . I will confess his name before my Father, and before his angels' (Rev. iii. 5). 'Him that overcometh will I make a pillar in the temple of my God' (Rev. iii. 12). 'To him that overcometh will I grant to sit with me in my throne' (Rev. iii. 21). 'He that overcometh shall inherit all things; and I will be his God, and he shall be my son' (Rev. xxi. 7).

See, what gifts! See, what rewards! See this eight-fold many-coloured incorruptible crown, or rather, these crowns prepared for you, brethren, if you overcome the devil! So now take up this aim, take up this work, and abstain from all things 'that no man take thy crown' (Rev. iii. 11). For it is indeed most shameful that those, who compete in games, in physical and external feats of valour, abstain from all things five times more strictly in order to get a perishable wreath of wild olive, or of palm, or fig, or laurel, or myrtle, or of some other plant. But you, who can receive an incorruptible crown, spend your life in negligence and carelessness. Cannot even the word of St. Paul make you awake from your sleep, when he says: 'Know ye not that they which run in a race run all, but one receiveth the prize? So run, that ye may obtain. And every man that striveth for the mastery is temperate in all things. Now they do it to obtain a corruptible crown; but we an incorruptible' (I Cor. ix. 24, 25).

If, inspired by zeal, you gain this victory and this radiant crown, do not forget, my brethren, to pray the Lord for the remission of sins of him, who had helped you to acquire such blessings by means of this book. But above all do not forget to raise your eyes to heaven and to give thanks and praise to the first Source and Cause of your victory, our God and Leader Jesus Christ, saying to Him like Zorobabel: 'From thee cometh victory . . . and thine is the glory, and I am thy servant' (I Esdras iv. 59), and repeating the words of David: 'Thine, O Lord, is the greatness, and the power, and the glory, and the victory, and the majesty' (I Chron. xxix. 11) for ever and ever. Amen.

PART ONE

PART ONE

CHAPTER ONE

*What is Christian perfection?—Warfare is necessary
to acquire it—Four things indispensable
to success in this warfare*

We all naturally wish, and are commanded to be perfect. The
Lord commands: 'Be ye therefore perfect, even as your Father
which is in heaven is perfect' (Matt. v. 48). And St. Paul admon-
ishes: 'In malice be ye children, but in understanding be men'
(I Cor. xiv. 20). In another place he says: 'Stand perfect and complete in all the will of God' (Col. iv. 12); and again: 'Let us go
on unto perfection' (Heb. vi. 1). The same commandment is also
found in the Old Testament. Thus God says to Israel in Deuter-
onomy: 'Thou shalt be perfect with the Lord thy God' (Deut.
xviii. 13). And David advises his son Solomon: 'And thou, Solomon my son, know thou the God of thy father, and serve him with
a perfect heart and with a willing mind' (I Chron. xxviii. 9). After
all this we cannot fail to see that God demands from Christians
the fullness of perfection, that is, that we should be perfect in
all virtues.

But if you, my reader beloved in Christ, wish to attain to such
heights, you must first learn in what Christian perfection consists. For if you have not learnt this, you may turn off the right
path and go in a totally different direction, while thinking that
you make progress towards perfection.

I will tell you plainly: the greatest and most perfect thing a
man may desire to attain is to come near to God and dwell in
union with Him.

There are many who say that the perfection of Christian life
consists in fasts, vigils, genuflexions, sleeping on bare earth and
other similar austerities of the body. Others say that it consists
in saying many prayers at home and in attending long services in
Church. And there are others who think that our perfection consists entirely in mental prayer, solitude, seclusion and silence.
But the majority limit perfection to a strict observance of all the
rules and practices laid down by the statutes, falling into no excess

or deficiency, but preserving a golden moderation. Yet all these virtues do not by themselves constitute the Christian perfection we are seeking, but are only means and methods for acquiring it.

There is no doubt whatever that they do represent means and effective means for attaining perfection in Christian life. For we see very many virtuous men, who practise these virtues as they should, to acquire strength and power against their own sinful and evil nature,—to gain, through these practices, courage to withstand the temptations and seductions of our three main enemies: the flesh, the world and the devil; and in and by these means to obtain the spiritual supports, so necessary to all servants of God, and especially to beginners. They fast, to subdue their unruly flesh; they practise vigils to sharpen their inner vision; they sleep on bare earth, lest they become soft through sleep; they bind their tongue by silence and go into solitude to avoid the slightest inducement to offend against the All-Holy God; they recite prayers, attend Church services and perform other acts of devotion, to keep their mind on heavenly things; they read of the life and passion of our Lord, for the sole purpose of realising more clearly their own deficiency and the merciful loving-kindness of God,—to learn and to desire to follow the Lord Jesus Christ, bearing their cross with self-denial, and to make more and more ardent their love of God and their dislike of themselves.

On the other hand, these same virtues may do more harm than their open omission, to those who take them as the sole basis of their life and their hope; not from their nature, since they are righteous and holy, but through the fault of those, who use them not as they should be used; that is, when they pay attention only to the external practice of those virtues, and leave their heart to be moved by their own volitions and the volitions of the devil. For the latter, seeing that they have left the right path, gleefully refrains from interfering with their physical endeavours and even allows them to increase and multiply their efforts, in obedience to their own vain thought. Experiencing with this certain spiritual stirrings and consolations, such people begin to imagine that they have already reached the state of angels and feel that God Himself is present in them. And at times, engrossed in the contemplation of some abstract and unearthly things, they imagine that they have completely transcended the sphere of this world and have been ravished to the third heaven.

22

However, anyone can see clearly how sinfully such people behave and how far they are from true perfection, if he looks at their life and character. As a rule they always wish to be preferred to others; they love to live according to their own will and are always stubborn in their decisions; they are blind in everything relating to themselves, but are very clear-sighted and officious in examining the words and actions of others. If another man is held by others in the same esteem, which in their opinion they enjoy, they cannot bear it and become manifestly hostile towards him; if anyone interferes with them in their pious occupations and works of asceticism, especially in the presence of others,—God forbid! —they immediately become indignant, boil over with wrath and become quite unlike themselves.

If, desirous of bringing them to self-knowledge and of leading them to the right path of perfection, God sends them afflictions and sickness, or allows them to be persecuted, by which means He habitually tests His true and real servants, this test immediately shows what is hidden in their hearts, and how deeply they are corrupted by pride. For whatever affliction may visit them, they refuse to bend their necks to the yoke of God's will and to trust in His righteous and secret judgments. They do not want to follow the example of our Lord Jesus Christ, Son of God, Who humbled Himself and suffered for our sakes, and they refuse to be humble, to consider themselves the lowest of all creatures, and to regard their persecutors as their good friends, the tools of the divine bounty shown to them and helpers in their salvation.

Thus it is clear that they are in great danger. Their inner eye, that is their mind, being darkened, they see themselves with this and see wrongly. Thinking of their external pious works and deeming them good, they imagined that they have already reached perfection and, puffing themselves up, begin to judge others. After this it is impossible for any man to turn such people, except through God's special influence. An evident sinner will turn towards good more easily than a secret sinner, hiding under the cloak of visible virtues.

Now, having seen clearly and definitely that spiritual life and perfection do not only consist in these visible virtues, of which we have spoken, you must also learn that it consists in nothing but coming near to God and union with Him, as was said in the beginning. With this is connected a heartfelt realisation of the

23

goodness and greatness of God, together with consciousness of our own nothingness and our proneness to every evil; love of God and dislike of ourselves; submission not only to God but also to all creatures, for the sake of our love of God; renunciation of all will of our own and perfect obedience to the will of God; and moreover desire for all this and its practice with a pure heart to the glory of God (I Cor. x. 31), from sheer desire to please God and only because He Himself wishes it and because we should so love Him and work for Him.

This is the law of love, inscribed by the finger of God Himself in the hearts of His true servants! This is the renunciation of ourselves that God demands of us! This is the blessed yoke of Jesus Christ and His burden that is light! This is the submission to God's will, which our Redeemer and Teacher demands from us both by His word and by His example! For did not our Master and the Author of our salvation, our Lord Jesus Christ, tell us to say when praying to the heavenly Father: 'Our Father . . . Thy will be done in earth, as it is in heaven' (Matt. vi. 10)? And did not He Himself exclaim on the eve of His passion: 'Not my will, but thine, be done' (Luke xxii. 42)! And did not He say of His whole work: 'For I came down from heaven, not to do mine own will, but the will of him that sent me' (John vi. 38)?

Do you now see what this all means, brother? I presume that you express your readiness and are longing to reach the height of such perfection. Blessed be your zeal! But prepare yourself also for labour, sweat and struggle from your first steps on the path. You must sacrifice everything to God and do only His will. Yet you will meet in yourself as many wills as you have powers and wants, which all clamour for satisfaction, irrespective of whether it is in accordance with the will of God or not. Therefore, to reach your desired aim, it is first of all necessary to stifle your own wills and finally to extinguish and kill them altogether. And in order to succeed in this, you must constantly oppose all evil in yourself and urge yourself towards good. In other words, you must ceaselessly fight against yourself and against everything that panders to your own wills, that incites and supports them. So prepare yourself for this struggle and this warfare and know that the crown—attainment of your desired aim—is given to none except to the valiant among warriors and wrestlers.

But if this is the hardest of all wars—since in fighting against

24

ourselves it is in ourselves that we meet opposition—victory in it is the most glorious of all; and, what is the main thing, it is most pleasing to God. For if, inspired by fervour, you overcome and put to death your unruly passions, your lusts and wills, you will please God more, and will work for Him more beautifully, than if you flog yourself till you draw blood or exhaust yourself by fasts more than any ancient hermit of the desert. Even if you redeem hundreds of Christian slaves from the infidels and give them freedom, it will not save you, if with this you remain yourself a slave to your own passions. And whatever work you may undertake, however glorious, and with whatever effort and sacrifice you may accomplish it, it will not lead you to your desired aim, if you leave your passions without attention, giving them freedom to live and act in you.

Finally, after learning what constitutes Christian perfection and realising that to achieve it you must wage a constant cruel war with yourself, if you really desire to be victorious in this unseen warfare and be rewarded with a crown, you must plant in your heart the following four dispositions and spiritual activities, as it were arming yourself with invisible weapons, the most trustworthy and unconquerable of all, namely: (*a*) never rely on yourself in anything; (*b*) bear always in your heart a perfect and all-daring trust in God alone; (*c*) strive without ceasing; and (*d*) remain constantly in prayer.

CHAPTER TWO

One should never believe in oneself or trust oneself in anything

Not to rely on oneself is so necessary in our struggle, my beloved brother, that without this, be assured, not only will you fail to gain the desired victory, but you will be unable to resist the smallest attack of the enemy. Engrave this deeply in your mind and heart.

Since the time of the transgression of our forefather, despite the weakening of our spiritual and moral powers, we are wont to think very highly of ourselves. Although our daily experience

25

very effectively proves to us the falseness of this opinion of ourselves, in our incomprehensible self-deception we do not cease to believe that we are something, and something not unimportant. Yet this spiritual disease of ours, so hard to perceive and acknowledge, is more abhorrent to God than all else in us, as being the first offspring of our self-hood and self-love, and the source, root and cause of all passions and of all our downfalls and wrong-doing. It closes the very door of our mind or spirit, through which alone Divine grace can enter, and gives this grace no way to come and dwell in a man. And so it withdraws from him. For how can grace, which comes to help and enlighten us, enter that man, who thinks of himself that he is something great, that he himself knows everything and needs no outside help?—May God preserve us from this disease and passion of Lucifer!—God severely reprimands those who are stricken with this passion of vainglory and self-esteem, saying through the prophet: 'Woe unto them that are wise in their own eyes, and prudent in their own sight' (Isaiah v. 21). And the Apostle tells us: 'Be not wise in your own conceits' (Rom. xii. 16).

While God abhors this evil conceit in us, there is nothing He loves and desires to see in us more than a sincere consciousness of our nothingness and a firm and deep-felt conviction that any good we may have in our nature and our life comes from Him alone, since He is the source of all good, and that nothing truly good can ever come from ourselves, whether a good thought or a good action. Therefore He takes care to plant this heavenly seed in the hearts of His beloved friends, urging them not to value themselves and not to rely on themselves. Sometimes He does this through the action of grace and inner illumination, or sometimes through external blows and tribulations, sometimes through unexpected and almost unconquerable temptations, and sometimes by other means, not always comprehensible to us.

Yet, although expecting no good from ourselves and not relying on ourselves is the work of God in us, we on our side must make every effort to acquire this disposition, doing all we can, all within our power. And so, my brother, I offer you here four activities, by means of which, with God's help, you may end by acquiring disbelief in yourself, and learn never to rely on yourself in anything.

(a) Realise your nothingness and constantly keep in your mind the fact that by yourself you can do nothing good which is worthy

26

of the kingdom of heaven. Listen to the words of the wise fathers: Peter of Damascus assures us that 'nothing is better than to realise one's weakness and ignorance, and nothing is worse than not to be aware of them' (Philokalia). St. Maximus the Confessor teaches: 'The foundation of every virtue is the realisation of human weakness' (Philokalia). St. John Chrysostom says: 'He alone knows himself in the best way possible who thinks of himself as being nothing.'

(b) Ask for God's help in this with warm and humble prayers; for this is His gift. And if you wish to receive it, you must first implant in yourself the conviction that not only have you no such consciousness of yourself, but that you cannot acquire it by your own efforts; then standing daringly before the Almighty God, in firm belief that in His great loving kindness He will grant you this knowledge of yourself when and how He Himself knows, do not let the slightest doubt creep in that you will actually receive it.

(c) Accustom yourself to be wary and to fear your innumerable enemies whom you cannot resist even for a short time. Fear their long experience in fighting us, their cunning and ambushes, their power to assume the guise of angels of light, their countless wiles and nets, which they secretly spread on the path of your life of virtues.

(d) If you fall into some transgression, quickly turn to the realisation of your weakness and be aware of it. For God allows you to fall for the very purpose of making you more aware of your weakness, so that you may thus not only yourself learn to despise yourself, but because of your great weakness may wish to be despised also by others. Know that without such desire it is impossible for this beneficent self-disbelief to be born and take root in you. This is the foundation and beginning of true humility, since it is based on realisation, by experience, of your impotence and unreliability.

From this, each of us sees how necessary it is for a man, who desires to participate in heavenly light, to know himself, and how God's mercy usually leads the proud and self-reliant to this knowledge through their downfalls, justly allowing them to fall into the very sin from which they think they are strong enough to protect themselves, so as to make them see their weakness and prevent them from relying foolhardily on themselves either in this or in anything else.

This method, although very effective, is also not without danger, and God does not always use it, but only when all the other means we have mentioned, which are easier and more natural, fail to lead a man to self-knowledge. Only then does He finally let a man fall into sin, great or small, in accordance with the degree of his pride, conceit and self-reliance. So that where conceit and self-reliance are absent, instructive failures do not occur. Therefore, if you happen to fall, run quickly in your thought to humble self-knowledge and a low opinion and sense of yourself and implore God by persistent prayer to give you true light, so as to realise your nothingness and confirm your heart in disbelief in yourself, lest you again fall into the same or even worse and more destructive sin.

I must add that not only when a man falls into some sin, but also when he is afflicted by some ill-fortune, tribulation or sorrow, and especially a grievous and long-drawn bodily sickness, he must understand that he suffers this in order to acquire self-knowledge, namely the knowledge of his weakness—and to become humble. With this purpose and to this end God allows us to be assailed by all kinds of temptations from the devil, from men and from our own corrupted nature. St. Paul saw this purpose in the temptations he suffered in Asia, when he said: 'But we had the sentence of death in ourselves, that we should not trust in ourselves, but in God which raiseth the dead' (II Cor. i. 9).

And I shall add another thing: if a man wants to realise his weakness from the actual experience of his life, let him, I do not say for many days but even for one day, observe his thoughts, words and actions—what he thought, what he said, what he did. He will undoubtedly find that the greater part of his thoughts, words and actions were sinful, wrong, foolish and bad. This experiment will make him understand in practice how inharmonious and weak he is in himself. And if he sincerely wishes himself well, this understanding will make him feel how foolish it is to expect anything good from himself or to rely on himself alone.

CHAPTER THREE

On hope in God alone and on confidence in Him

Although, as we have said, it is very important not to rely on our own efforts in this unseen warfare, at the same time, if we merely give up all hope of ourselves and despair of ourselves without having found another support, we are certain to flee immediately from the battlefield or to be overcome and taken prisoner by our enemies. Therefore, together with complete renunciation of ourselves, we should plant in our heart a perfect trust in God and a complete confidence in Him. In other words we should feel with our whole heart that we have no one to rely on except God, and that from Him and Him alone can we expect every kind of good, every manner of help, and victory. Since we are nothing, we can expect nothing from ourselves, except stumblings and falls, which make us relinquish all hope of ourselves. On the other hand, we are certain always to be granted victory by God, if we arm our heart with a living trust in Him and an unshakable certainty that we will receive His help, according to the psalm: 'My heart trusted in him, and I am helped' (Ps. xxviii. 7).

The following thoughts will help you to be grounded in this hope and, thereby, to receive help:

(*a*) that we seek help from God, Who is Omnipotent and can do all that He chooses, and therefore can also help us.

(*b*) that we seek it from God, Who, being Omniscient and Wise, knows all in the most perfect manner, and therefore knows fully what is best for the salvation of each one of us.

(*c*) that we seek help from God, Who is infinitely Good and Who comes to us with ineffable love, always desirous and ready from hour to hour and from moment to moment to give us all the help we need for complete victory in the spiritual warfare which takes place in us, as soon as we run with firm trust to the protection of His arms.

And how is it possible that our good Shepherd, Who for three years went in search of sheep that had gone astray, calling so loudly that His throat became parched, and following ways so hard and thorny that He shed all His blood and gave up His life; how is it possible, I repeat, that now, if His sheep follow Him,

29

turn to Him with love and call for His help with hope, He should fail to turn His eyes to the lost sheep, take it into His divine arms and, placing it among the heavenly angels, make a welcoming feast for its sake? If our God never ceases to search diligently and lovingly for the blind and deaf sinner (like the woman for the piece of silver in the Gospels), how is it possible to suppose that He would abandon him now when, like a lost sheep, he cries out calling for his Shepherd? And who will ever believe that God, Who, according to the Revelation, constantly stands at the door of a man's heart, and knocks, wishing to come in and sup with him (Rev. iii. 20), and bestow His gifts upon him, who will believe that this same God should remain deaf and refuse to enter if a man opens to Him the door of his heart and invites Him in?

(d) And the fourth method of bringing to life a firm trust in God and of attracting His speedy help is to review in our memory all the instances of speedy divine help described in the Scriptures. These instances, which are so numerous, show us clearly that no one, who put his trust in God, was ever left confounded and without help. 'Look at the generations of old', says the wise Sirach, 'and see; did ever any trust in the Lord, and was confounded?' (Ecclesiasticus ii. 10).

Armed with these four weapons, enter the battle with courage, my brother, and wage war watchfully with the full conviction that victory will be granted you. For with their help you will most certainly acquire perfect trust in God, and this trust will never fail to attract God's help and invest you with unconquerable power. These two together will in the end make complete distrust of yourself deeply rooted in you. I omit no occasion in this chapter of reminding you to distrust yourself, for I know no one who has no need to be reminded of it. Self-esteem is so deeply rooted in us and so firmly enmeshed in us, making us think that we are something, and something not unimportant, that it always hides in our heart as a subtle and imperceptible movement, even when we are sure that we do not trust ourselves and are, on the contrary, filled with complete trust in God alone. In order to avoid this conceit of the heart and act without any self-reliance, led only by your trust in God, take care always to preserve an attitude in which the consciousness and feeling of your weakness always precede in you the contemplation of God's omnipotence, and let both alike precede your every action.

30

CHAPTER FOUR

How to recognise whether a man acts without self-reliance and with perfect trust in God

It often happens that self-reliant men think that they have no self-reliance whatever, but put all their trust in God and rest confidently in Him alone. But in practice it is not so. They can ascertain it for themselves, if they judge by what is in them and what happens to them if they fall down. If, when they grieve at their downfall, reproaching and abusing themselves for it, they think: 'I shall do this and that, the consequences of my downfall will be effaced and all will be well once more,' this is a sure sign that before the downfall they trusted themselves, instead of trusting God. And the more gloomy and disconsolate their grief, the more it shows that they relied too much on themselves and too little on God; and therefore the grief caused by their downfall is not tempered by any comfort. If a man does not rely on himself but puts his trust in God, when he falls he is not greatly surprised and is not overcome with excessive grief, for he knows that it is the result of his own impotence, and, above all, of the weakness of his trust in God. So his downfall increases his distrust of himself and makes him try all the harder to increase and deepen his humble trust in God. And further, hating the vile passions which caused his downfall, he thereupon endures peacefully and calmly the labours of penitence for having offended God; and armed with still more trust in God, he thereupon pursues his enemies with the greatest courage and resoluteness, even unto death.

I should like some people to reflect on what I have said above, for, although they think themselves virtuous and spiritual, when they fall into some transgression, they are overcome with anguish and torment and find no peace anywhere. Exhausted by this grief and anguish, which they suffer for no other reason but self-esteem, they run, again urged by self-esteem, to their spiritual father, to be freed of this burden. Yet they should have done this immediately after the downfall and for no other reason but a desire to wash away as quickly as possible the filth of sin which has offended God, and acquire new strength to fight against themselves through the most holy sacrament of repentance and confession.

CHAPTER FIVE

On the wrong opinion of those who deem excessive grief a virtue

It is wrong to regard as a virtue the excessive grief, which men feel after committing a sin, not realising that it is caused by pride and a high opinion of themselves, based on the fact that they rely too much on themselves and their own powers. For by thinking that they are something important they undertake too much, hoping to deal with it by themselves. When the experience of their downfall shows them how weak they are, they are astounded, like people, who meet with something unexpected, and they are cast into turmoil and grow faint-hearted. For they see, fallen and prone on the ground, that graven image which is themselves, upon which they put all their hopes and expectations. This does not happen to a humble man who trusts in God alone, expecting nothing good from himself. Therefore, when he falls into some transgression, he also feels the weight of it and grieves, but is not cast into turmoil and is not perplexed, for he knows that it happened through his own impotence, to experience which in downfalls is nothing unexpected or new to him.

CHAPTER SIX

Some indications on the scope and limits of disbelief in oneself and of complete trust in God

Since all the strength by which our enemies are overcome is born in us from disbelief in ourselves and from trust in God, it is necessary for you, my brother, to acquire exact knowledge of this, in order always to have this strength and to preserve it with the help of God. Know then, and never forget, that neither all our capacities and good features, whether natural or acquired, nor all the gifts freely given us, nor the knowledge of all the Scriptures, nor the fact that we have for long worked for God and have acquired experience in these labours, nor all this together will

32

enable us to do God's will rightly, if at every good deed pleasing to God, which we are about to undertake, at every affliction we wish to avoid, at every cross we have to bear according to God's will, if, I say, on all these and similar occasions a special divine help does not inspire our heart and does not give us strength to accomplish it, as the Lord said: 'Without me ye can do nothing' (John xv. 5). So for the duration of our life, every day and at every moment, we must keep unchanged in our heart the feeling, conviction and disposition, that on no occasion can we allow ourselves to think of relying on ourselves and trusting ourselves.

As regards trust in God, I will add the following to what I have said in the third chapter: know that nothing is easier for God than to give you victory over your enemies, whether they be few or many, whether they be old and strong or new and weak. Yet He has His own time and order for everything. Therefore if a soul be overburdened with sins, if it be guilty of all the crimes in the world, if it be defiled beyond imagination;—if, at the same time, to the extent of its desire and strength, it uses every means and endeavour to become free of sin and turn to the path of good, but cannot get stable in anything right, however small, and, on the contrary, sinks ever deeper and deeper into evil; even if it is all that, it must not weaken in its trust of God or fall away from Him. It must not abandon its spiritual weapons and strivings but must fight and fight, struggling with itself and with its enemies with all its courage and untiring efforts. For know and understand, that in this unseen war all are losers except a man who never ceases to struggle and keep his trust in God; for God never abandons those who fight in His armies, although at times He lets them suffer wounds. So fight, everyone, and do not give ground; for the whole thing is in this unceasing struggle. God is always ready with remedies for those struck down by the enemies and with help for overcoming them, which He sends to His warriors in due time, if they seek Him and firmly hope in Him. At some hour when they least expect it they will see their proud enemies vanish, as is written: 'The mighty men of Babylon have forborn to fight' (Jer. li. 30).

CHAPTER SEVEN

On how we should exercise our mind, lest it be sick with the disease of ignorance

If disbelief in oneself and trust in God, so indispensable in our spiritual warfare, remain alone in us, not only shall we never gain victory, but we shall fall into still greater evil. For in addition and accompanying them we must practise works of a special kind and perform exercises in spiritual instruction.

First among these must be exercises of mind and will.

The mind should be freed and guarded from ignorance, which is most harmful, for it darkens the mind and prevents it from knowing the truth, which is its proper object and the aim of its aspirations. For this reason it should be exercised, to make it clear and lucid, able to discern correctly what we need to purify our soul from passions and to adorn it with virtues.

There are two means by which we can acquire such clarity of mind: the first and most necessary is prayer, by which we must implore the Holy Spirit to pour His divine light into our hearts. This He will surely do, if we truly seek God alone and sincerely strive to obey His will in everything, willingly submitting in all affairs to the advice of our experienced spiritual fathers and doing nothing without asking them.

The second method of exercising the mind is always to examine things and probe deep for knowledge of them, in order to see clearly which of them are good and which bad. We should judge them not as the world and the senses do, but as they are judged by right season and the Holy Spirit, or by the word of the divinely-inspired Scriptures, or that of the holy fathers and teachers of the Church. For if this examination and deepening of knowledge is right and proper, it will quite certainly enable us to understand clearly that we must with all our heart regard as valueless, vain and false, all that the blind and depraved world loves and seeks.

In particular, we shall then see that the honours, pleasures and riches of this world are nothing but vanity and death to the soul; that the slander and abuse, with which the world persecutes us, bring us true glory, and its afflictions—joy; that to forgive our enemies and to do good to them is true magnanimity—one of the

34

greatest traits of likeness to God; that a man who scorns the world shows greater strength and power than a man who rules over the whole world; that willing obedience is an action, which shows more courage and strength of spirit than subjugating great kings and ruling over them; that humble self-knowledge should be preferred to all other kinds of knowledge, however high; that to overcome and kill one's own evil tendencies and lusts, however insignificant, is more worthy of praise than the capture of many fortresses, or the defeat of powerful and well-equipped armies; more even than the power to perform miracles and to raise the dead.

CHAPTER EIGHT

On reasons for our wrong judgment of things and how to form a right judgment of them

The reason why we have wrong judgment of the things we mentioned earlier is that we do not look deeply into them to see what they are, but conceive a liking for them or a dislike of them from the very first glance, judging by appearances. These likes and dislikes prejudice our mind and darken it; and so it cannot form a right judgment of things as they really are. So, my brother, if you wish to be free of this prelest in your mind, keep strict attention over yourself; and when you see a thing with your eyes, or visualise it in your mind, keep a firm grip on your desires and do not allow yourself at the first glance either to conceive a liking for the thing or a dislike for it, but examine it in a detached way with the mind alone. Unobscured by passion, the mind then remains in a state natural to it, which is free and pure, and has the possibility to know the truth and to penetrate into the depths of a thing, where evil is often concealed under a deceptively attractive exterior and where good is sometimes hidden under a bad appearance.

But if desire comes first and at once either likes a thing or turns away from it, your mind no longer has the possibility to know it rightly as it should. For if this predisposition, or rather this passion precedes every judgment, it enters within, becomes a wall between the mind and the thing and, obscuring the mind, makes it form its judgment from passion. In other words, it sees it not as it really is, which strengthens still more its original predisposition. The further this predisposition runs ahead, or the more it likes or dislikes a thing, the more it obscures the mind in relation to it, until it darkens the mind completely. Then passion in relation to this thing reaches its ultimate limits, so that it appears to a man either as the most desirable or the most hateful of all the things he ever liked or disliked. Thus it happens that when the rule I have indicated is not observed, that is, when desire is not restrained from forming likes and dislikes before a thing is properly examined, then both these powers of the soul—mind and will—always work wrongly, plunging ever deeper and deeper from darkness to darkness, and from sin to sin.

So watch, my beloved, with all attention and protect yourself from liking or disliking a thing out of passion, before you have had time to examine it properly in the light of reason and the just word of the Divine Scriptures, in the light of grace and prayer, and with the help of the judgment of your spiritual father; otherwise you may sin in taking for evil what is truly good, and for good what is truly evil. This mostly happens in the case of certain actions, which are good and holy in themselves, but which according to circumstances, namely that if they are done at a wrong time, or are out of place, or are not done in the right measure, cause considerable harm to those who do them. We know from experience what afflictions are suffered by some through such worthy and holy deeds.

CHAPTER NINE

On protecting the mind from too much useless knowledge and idle curiosity

Just as it is necessary to guard the mind from ignorance, so is it equally necessary to protect it from the opposite, namely from too much knowledge and curiosity. For if we fill it with a quantity of information, ideas and thoughts, not excluding such as are vain, unsuitable and harmful, we deprive it of force, so that it is no longer able to understand clearly what is useful for our true self-correction and perfection. Therefore in relation to the knowledge of earthly things, which is not indispensable, even if it is permissible, your attitude should be as of one already dead. Always collect your mind within yourself, with all the concentration you can, and keep it free of thoughts about all worldy things.

Let tales of the past and news of the present pass you by, and let all the changes in the world and its kingdoms be for you as though they did not exist at all. If anyone brings you such news, disregard it and turn it away from your heart and imagination. Listen to what St. Basil says: 'Let listening to worldly news be bitter food for you, and let the words of saintly men be as combs filled with honey.' Listen also to the words of David: 'The proud have digged pits for me, which are not after thy law' (Ps. cxix. 85). Love to hear only of spiritual and heavenly things and to study them, and wish to know nothing in the world save our Lord 'Jesus Christ, and him crucified' (I Cor. ii. 2), save His life and death and what He demands of you. Acting thus, you will act in a way pleasing to God, Who has for His chosen and beloved those who love Him and try to do His will.

All other enquiry and investigation is the offspring and food of self-love and pride. They are the nets and shackles of the devil; he sees the strength and firmness of will of those who pay attention to spiritual life, and strives to conquer their minds by means of such curiosity, in order to gain possession of their mind and will. For this purpose, he is wont to suggest to them thoughts that are lofty, subtle and wondrous, especially to those who are sharp-witted and quick to make lofty speculations. Attracted by the pleasure of possessing and examining such lofty thoughts, they forget to watch over their purity of heart and to pay attention to a humble opinion of themselves and to true self-mortification; and so they are enmeshed in the bonds of pride and conceit; they make an idol of their own mind and thus, little by little, without realising it, they fall into the thought that they no longer need any advice or admonition from others, since they are accustomed in all cases to hasten to the idol of their own understanding and judgment.

This is a very dangerous thing and not easily cured; pride of mind is much worse than pride of will. For pride of will, being visible to the mind, can sometimes be easily cured by forcing it to submit to the yoke of what is good. But when the mind is firmly grounded in the self-relying thought that its own judgments are better than all others, who can cure it in the end? Can it ever obey anyone, if it feels certain that the judgments of others are not as good as its own? When this eye of the soul—mind—with whose help man could see and correct pride of will, is itself blinded by pride and remains uncured, who will cure the will? Then everything within is so disorganised that there is neither place nor person for applying a healing poultice. This is why you must hasten to oppose this pernicious pride of mind, before it penetrates into the marrow of your bones. Resist it, curb the quickness of your mind and humbly subject your opinion to the opinions of others. Be a fool for the love of God, if you wish to be wiser than Solomon: 'If any man among you seemeth to be wise in this world, let him become a fool, that he may be wise' (I Cor. iii. 18).

CHAPTER TEN

How to train one's will to have but one ultimate aim
in all things, both external and internal—
to please God

In addition to training your mind to learn, you should also control your will, so as not to let it lean towards your own desires, but instead to lead it to be perfectly as one with the will of God. Moreover keep it firmly planted in your mind, that it is not enough for you merely to desire and seek to please God always and in everything; you must desire it as if moved by God Himself, and for one single aim—to please Him with a pure heart. To be firmly grounded in this aim, we have to endure a much greater struggle with our nature than in anything we have mentioned above. For our nature is so accustomed to please itself, that it seeks its own comfort and pleasure in all its doings, even the most righteous and spiritual, and secretly and lustfully feeds on it as though it were food.

And so it happens that when we see the chance of spiritual doing lying before us, we immediately desire it and impetuously rush towards it; yet not as men moved by the will of God, nor for the sole purpose of pleasing Him, but for the sake of the comfort and joy which is born in us, when we desire and seek that which

God wants from us. This prelest is the better concealed and hidden, the higher and more spiritual is the nature of what we desire. This is why I say that we should not be satisfied with desiring what God wills, but must desire it how He wishes it, when He wishes it and for the reason and purpose He wishes it. The Apostle also teaches us to prove what is the will of God, that it is not only good, but also acceptable to Him and perfect in all respects. He says: 'Be not conformed to this world: but be ye transformed by the renewing of your mind, that ye may prove what is that good, and acceptable, and perfect, will of God' (Rom. xii. 2). For if our action is faulty, even in one respect, or if we do something not with our whole will and strength, it is clear that it is, and is called; imperfect. This should lead you to the conclusion that even when we desire God Himself and seek Him, even this desire and search can contain some fault or omission, and may be mixed with some pandering to our self-love or vainglory; since we may have in view more our own good than the will of God, and do something rather for our own sake than for the sake of God. Yet He considers only those actions acceptable, which are done solely for His glory and wishes us to love Him alone, desire Him alone and work for Him alone.

Thus, my brother, if you wish to safeguard yourself from such hidden obstacles on the path to perfection, if you wish to be firmly grounded in such an attitude as to desire and do all things only because God wishes it, desirous only to please and glorify Him and to work for Him alone, since He wishes to be the beginning and the end in every action and every thought of ours— act in the following manner.

When there lies before you some work, which accords with the will of God, or is good in itself, do not immediately incline your will towards it and do not desire it, without previously raising your mind to God, so as to be clear whether it is the direct will of God that you should desire and perform such actions and whether they would be acceptable to God. And when you compose your thoughts in such a way that the inclination of your will is determined by God's will itself, then wish it and do it, but only because God wishes it, only for the sake of pleasing Him and for His glory alone.

In the same way, when you wish to draw back from something not in keeping with God's will, or not good, do not immediately turn away from it, but first fix the eye of your mind on the will of God and make sure that it is God's direct will that you should turn away from it for the sake of pleasing Him. For the self-flattery of our nature is very subtle and few can discern it. Secretly it pursues only its own ends, though meanwhile its outward conduct is such, that it seems to us we have but the single aim of pleasing God, though in actual fact this is not so.

Thus it often happens that in actual fact we want or do not want something for our own sake, for our own gratification, and yet think that we want it solely to please God. The one exclusive means to avoid such self-deception is purity of heart, which consists in rejecting the old Adam and clothing ourselves in the new man. This is the aim and purpose of the whole unseen warfare.

If you wish to learn the art of doing this, then listen. When you start to do anything you must, as far as you can, strip yourself of all wishes of your own and neither desire to do that thing nor turn away from it, until you perceive that the only thing which moves and draws you towards it is the consciousness of God's will. If you cannot always actively perceive God moving you in all your actions, whether external or, what is more important, internal, those of your soul, then be content to make this perception possible; in other words, always sincerely dispose yourself to keep nothing but God's pleasure in view.

We may have real feeling of God moving us to an action either through divine enlightenment or mental illumination, in which God's will is revealed to pure hearts in contemplation,—or through an inner divine inspiration, by some inner word,—or through some other actions of divine grace, acting in a pure heart, such as life-giving warmth, unspeakable joy, leaping of the spirit, being moved to tenderness, heartfelt tears, love for God and other blessed and God-loving feelings, produced not according to our will but coming from God, not by our own action but in our passivity. All such feelings serve as assurances that what we seek to do accords with God's will. But before all things we must address to God the warmest and purest prayer, begging Him with all diligence, once, twice and many times, to illumine our darkness and to teach us. Pray three times, say the great fathers Barsanuphius and John, and then do as your heart inclines. Moreover you must not forget that all the decisions, formed in you as a result of the inner spiritual movements we have mentioned, must be verified by the advice and judgment of the experienced.

As regards activities whose completion takes a more or less long time, or which go on continually, we should establish in our heart a firm resolve to practise them solely to please God, and this not merely in the beginning, when we undertake them, but later too this right resolve should be renewed frequently to the very end. For if you fail to do this, you will be in danger of becoming once more enmeshed in the self-love so natural to us, which, inclining more towards pleasing ourselves than towards pleasing God, in the course of time often succeeds in turning us imperceptibly away from our original good disposition and in changing our first good aims and intentions. Therefore St. Gregory of Sinai wrote: 'Pay heed, also, to the intention of your will, watching which way it inclines: whether it is towards God, whether it is for the sake of good itself and for the benefit of your soul that you sit in silence, psalmodise, recite prayers or perform any other good works, lest you be imperceptibly robbed' (Philokalia).

So if a man does not watch himself well, he may begin some activity with the sole purpose of pleasing the Lord, but later, little by little, introduce into it a self-interest, which makes him find in it also a satisfaction of his own desires, and this to such an extent that the will of God becomes completely forgotten. Then he becomes so tightly bound by enjoyment of the work, that if God Himself were to hinder him in this practice, either through some illness, or through temptations from men or demons, or by some other means, he is filled with indignation, often blames one man or another for having interfered in the course of things he so loves, and sometimes even murmurs against God Himself. This is a sure sign that the disposition of his heart did not come from God, but has sprung from the rotten and corrupted root of self-love.

A man who is moved towards doing one thing or another purely by the consciousness of God's will and the desire to please Him, never prefers one activity to another, even if one is great and lofty, and another petty and insignificant; but he has his will equally disposed towards either, so long as they are pleasing to God. So whether he does something lofty and great or petty and insignificant, he remains equally calm and content; for he has but one intention and one aim, to the exclusion of all else—to please

God always and in all he does, whether in life or in death, as the Apostle says: 'Wherefore we labour, that, whether present or absent, we may be accepted of him' (II Cor. v. 9). Therefore, beloved, be ever watchful over yourself, be collected within and strive by all means in your power to direct all your activities towards this single aim.

If you are moved to do something by an inner urge to escape the torment of hell or to inherit heaven, here too you can mentally direct your activity towards the same ultimate aim—to please God by obeying His will; since it is God's wish that you should go to heaven rather than be cast into hell.

None can fully conceive how great is the strength and power in our spiritual life of this motive and aim—to please God. For even if some activity is in itself quite simple and unimportant, if it is done for the sole purpose of pleasing God and to His glory, it becomes in the eyes of God infinitely more valuable than many other great and glorious deeds, performed without this aim. Thus God is more pleased to see you give a small coin to a beggar, solely with the purpose of pleasing His divine majesty, than if you strip yourself of all your possessions for some other purpose, even if you do so for the sake of receiving heavenly blessings, although such purpose is good and desirable.

This inner task, which you must practise in anything you do— the task of directing your thoughts, feelings and actions only towards pleasing God, will seem difficult at first, but will later become easy and light, if, firstly you constantly exercise yourself in this spiritual effort and, secondly, if you constantly keep warm your yearning for God, sighing for Him with a live longing of the heart, as for the only perfect good, worthy of being sought for Its Own sake, to be served, and to be loved above all things.

The more often this search for limitless good in God is practised in our consciousness and the deeper it penetrates into the feeling of the heart, the more frequent and warm will be the actions of our will I have described, and the more quickly and easily shall we form the habit of doing everything solely through love of the Lord, impelled only by desire to please Him, since He is the most worthy of all love.

CHAPTER ELEVEN

*Some reminders that can impel our will towards
desire to please God in every activity*

In order that you may move your will more easily to this one
desire in everything—to please God and to work for His glory
alone—remind yourself often, that He has granted you many
favours in the past and has shown you His love. He has created
you out of nothing in His own likeness and image, and has made
all other creatures your servants; He has delivered you from your
slavery to the devil, sending down not one of the angels but His
Only-begotten Son to redeem you, not at the price of corruptible
gold and silver, but by His priceless blood and His most painful
and degrading death. Having done all this He protects you, every
hour and every moment, from your enemies; He fights your
battles by His divine grace; in His immaculate Mysteries He prepares the Body and Blood of His beloved Son for your food and
protection.

All this is a sign of God's great favour and love for you; a
favour so great that it is inconceivable how the great Lord of
hosts could grant such favours to our nothingness and worthlessness. Judge from this what honour and devotion we must offer to
the boundless Majesty of Him, Who has done such wonderful
things for us. If we cannot help offering thanks, honour, glory
and obedience to earthly kings for their favours, how much more,
immeasurably more, must we worthless ones offer to the Almighty
Lord of hosts, Who loves us and bestows upon us favours beyond
counting.

But more than all we have just said, keep always in your
memory the realisation that God's greatness is in itself worthy of
all honour, worship and wholehearted service acceptable to Him.

CHAPTER TWELVE

On the many desires and tendencies existing in man and on their struggle with one another

Know, that in this unseen warfare, two wills existing in us fight against one another: one belongs to the intelligent part of our soul and is therefore called the intelligent will, which is the higher; the other belongs to the sensory part and is therefore called the sensory will, which is the lower. The latter is more frequently called the dumb, carnal, passionate will. The higher will is always desiring nothing but good, the lower—nothing but evil. Each equally happens by itself; so that neither is a good desire in itself reckoned as good, nor an evil desire as evil. The reckoning depends upon the inclination of our own free will. Therefore, when our will inclines towards a good desire, it is reckoned in our favour; but when we incline towards an evil desire, it is reckoned against us. These desires follow one upon another: when a good desire comes, an evil desire immediately opposes it; and when an evil desire comes, a good desire at once rises against it. Our will is free to follow the one and the other, and whatever desire our will inclines towards, it becomes victorious on this particular occasion. It is in this that all our unseen spiritual warfare consists. Its aim should be never to let our free will incline towards the desire of the lower, carnal and passionate will, but always to follow only the intelligent, higher will. For it is the will of God, to follow which is the basic law of our being: 'Fear God, and keep his commandments: for this is the whole duty of man' says the Preacher (Ecclesiastes xii. 13). Each of these desires draws our will towards itself and wishes to subjugate it. Stifle the lower desire and incline towards the higher—and victory is yours; but disregard the higher and choose the lower, and you will find yourself vanquished. St. Paul writes of this: 'I find then a law, that, when I would do good, evil is present with me. For I delight in the law of God after the inward man: but I see another law in my members, warring against the law of my mind, and bringing me into captivity to the law of sin which is in my members' (Rom. vii. 21-23). And he gives to all the rule: 'Walk in the Spirit, and

44

ye shall not fulfil the lust of the flesh' (Gal. v. 16). And this cannot be accomplished without struggling with the flesh.

A particularly great effort and laborious toil must be experienced to start with by those who, before deciding to change
their worldly and carnal life to a righteous one and to give themselves up to the practices of love and sincere service of God, had
enmeshed themselves in evil habits through frequent satisfaction
of the desires of their carnal and passionate will. Although the
demands of their intelligent will, which they wish to follow, stand
on one side of their free will and are made active by God, yet on
the other side there stand the desires of the carnal and passionate
will, towards which they still feel a certain sympathy. Opposing
the former, these desires pull it towards their side with the same
force as a beast of burden is pulled by its halter; and only the
grace of God gives them strength to remain firm in the decision
they have taken. Long-drawn resistance and not yielding them
victory saps the strength of carnal desires; yet this does not end
the struggle.

So let no one dream of acquiring a true Christian disposition
and Christian virtue, and of working for God as he should, if he
does not want to compel himself to renounce and overcome all
the passionate impulses of the will of the flesh, whether great or
small, which he was formerly accustomed to satisfy, willingly and
fondly. The chief reason why so few people attain to full Christian
perfection is exactly their reluctance, through self-pity, to force
themselves to deny themselves absolutely everything. But if,
having overcome great passionate tendencies, they do not wish,
thereafter, to compel themselves to overcome small ones, which
seem unimportant, then, since these small tendencies are the
outcome and expression of the great, by indulging in them they
inevitably feed the latter, and so make them continue to live and
act in the heart, in spite of the fact that they no longer manifest
themselves on a large scale. And so the heart remains passionate
and impure, and, above all, in no whit freed from self-indulgence
and self-pity, which always make any practice to please God of
doubtful value.

For example, there are men who refrain from appropriating
other people's possessions, but are excessively attached to their
own, and who, on the one hand, lay too much trust in what they
have, and on the other, are slow to bestow alms. Others do not

seek honours by evil means, yet do not count them as nothing, and often even welcome them, if those honours can be made to appear to come against their will. Others again keep long fasts according to the statutes, yet do not refrain from satisfying their desire to eat their fill, and to eat well, which deprives the fast of all value. Others lead a chaste life, yet continue their connections and acquaintanceship with people they like, and enjoy it, not wishing to understand that, through this, they build a great obstacle to perfection in spiritual life and union with God.

I shall add to this the fact that some people disregard the natural defects of their character, which, although not dependent on self-will, nevertheless make a man guilty if, seeing how much they interfere with spiritual life, he does not trouble not only to destroy them completely, but even to try and keep them within harmless bounds, although this could be achieved with the help of God's grace, due attention to oneself and zeal. Such defects are, for example: aloofness, hot temper, and excessive sensibility, with the consequent thoughtless hastiness in words, movements and actions, harshness and querulousness, obstinacy and argumentativeness, and so on. All these natural imperfections and faults should be corrected, in some by reducing excess, in others by adding what is lacking, and by translating both one and another into corresponding good qualities. For no natural feature, no matter how savage and stubborn it is, can stand up against the will if, armed with the grace of God, it resists it with all attention and diligence.

And so it happens that some perform good deeds, but these deeds remain imperfect, lame, mixed with the lusts, which reign in the world (John ii. 16). And so such people make no progress on the path to salvation, but turn round and round on one spot, and often even turn back and fall again into their former sins. This shows that even from the first their love for true life in Christ was not wholehearted, that they were not sufficiently filled with the feeling of gratitude to God, Who had delivered them from the power of the devil, and not perfect in their decision to work only for Him and to please Him. As a result such people remain for ever untrained in good, are blind and fail to see the danger in which they stand, thinking that their position is secure and that no harm threatens them.

Owing to all this, my beloved brother in Christ, I beseech you to love the hard toil and heavy burdens which inevitably accompany our unseen warfare, if you do not wish always to be overcome. The wise Sirach counsels the same: 'Hate not laborious work' (Ecclesiasticus vii. 15). For this is the very foundation of the whole of inner warfare. The more you love this hard toil, or this pitiless driving of yourself, the more quick and complete will be your victory over yourself and over that in yourself, which resists the higher good. And through this you will be filled with every virtue and good disposition, and God's peace will come to dwell in you.

CHAPTER THIRTEEN

On how to fight against the dumb sensory will, and on the training necessary for the will to acquire experience in virtues

Every time your free will is acted upon and pulled on the one hand by the dumb sensory will and on the other by the will of God, voiced through conscience, each of them seeking to conquer it, you must, if you are sincerely to strive for good, use suitable methods on your part to assist God's will in gaining victory. For this purpose, then:

(a) As soon as you feel impulses of the lower, sensory and passionate will, you must immediately use every effort to resist them and not allow your own will to incline towards them, however slightly. Crush them, cut them off, drive them away from yourself by an intense effort of will.

(b) To achieve this more successfully and with a better result, hasten to kindle in yourself a wholehearted aversion to such impulses, as to your enemies, who seek to steal and destroy your soul—be angered with them.

(c) At the same time do not forget to appeal to our Lord Jesus Christ, our Helper in all endeavour, asking for His assistance and protection, and for the strengthening of your better will; for without Him we can succeed in nothing.

(d) If these three inner actions are sincerely practised in your soul, they will never fail to give you victory over evil impulses. But this would mean only driving the enemies away. If you wish to strike at their very heart, then, if it is feasible, at once do something opposed to the suggestion of the passionate impulse and, if possible, resolve to do so always. This latter practice will finally free you completely from the renewal of the attacks you experience.

I shall illustrate this by an example. Supposing someone has offended you in something whether great or small, and has aroused in you a movement of displeasure and irritation, accompanied by a suggestion of retaliation. Pay attention to yourself and hasten to realise that these movements are bent on enticing you towards evil. Therefore take up the attitude of a warrior on the defensive: (a) Stop these movements, do not let them penetrate any deeper and on no account allow your will to take their part as though they were right. This will mean resisting them. (b) But they still remain in sight, ready for a renewed attack. So rouse aversion against them, as against your enemies, and be angry with them for self-protection, until you are able to say sincerely: 'I hate and abhor lying' (Ps. cxix. 163), or: 'I hate them with perfect hatred: I count them mine enemies' (Ps. cxxxix. 22). This will be a great blow for them, and they will retreat, but not vanish. Then: (c) Call to the Lord: 'Make haste, O God, to deliver me; make haste to help me, O Lord' (Ps. lxx. 1). And do not cease calling thus, until not a trace of the hostile movements remains and peace is restored in your soul. (d) Having thus regained peace, do to your offender something which would show your kind and conciliatory disposition towards him, such as a friendly word, some timely favour, and so on. This would mean following the advice of David: 'Depart from evil, and do good' (Ps. xxxiv. 14). Such actions lead straight to acquiring the habit of the virtue opposed to the passionate movements which had troubled you; and this habit strikes them to the heart and kills them. Try to forestall, or accompany, or conclude these actions with an inner resolve, which would make such passionate impulses for ever impossible in the future. For instance, in the foregoing example, consider yourself worthy of every insult and bring yourself to welcome every kind of insult and calumny; welcome them and be ready to receive and accept them with joy as the most salutary remedies. In other cases, try to incite and establish in yourself other corresponding feelings and dispositions. This would mean driving the passion out of your heart and replacing it by the virtue opposed to it, which is the aim of the unseen warfare.

I will give you a general indication, suitable for all occasions, in accordance with the guidance of the holy fathers. Our soul has three parts or powers—the thinking, the desiring and the excitable. Owing to their corruption, these three powers give birth to three corresponding kinds of wrong thoughts and movements. The thinking power gives birth to thoughts of ingratitude to God and complaints, forgetfulness of God, ignorance of divine things, ill-judgment and all kinds of blasphemous thoughts. The desiring power gives birth to pleasure-loving thoughts, thoughts of vainglory, love of money and all their numerous ramifications, belonging to the domain of self-indulgence. The excitable power gives birth to thoughts of anger, hatred, envy, revenge, gloating, ill-will, and generally to all evil thoughts. You should overcome all such thoughts and impulses by the methods indicated above, trying on every occasion to arouse and establish in your heart good feelings and dispositions opposed to them: in place of unbelief—undoubting faith in God; in place of complaints—a sincere gratitude to God for everything; in place of forgetfulness of God—a constant deep remembrance of the ever-present and all-powerful God; in place of ignorance—a clear contemplation or mental examination of all the soul-saving Christian truths; in place of ill-judgment—faculties trained to discriminate between good and evil; in place of all blasphemous thoughts—praise and glorification of God. In the same way, in place of love of pleasure —every kind of abstinence, fasting and self-mortification; in place of vainglory—humility and desire of obscurity; in place of love of money—contentment with little and love of poverty. Again, in place of anger—meekness; in place of hatred—love; in place of envy—rejoicing with others; in place of revenge—forgiveness and a peaceful disposition; in place of gloating—compassion; in place of ill-will—well-wishing. In short, with St. Maximus, I shall condense all this in the following propositions: adorn your thinking power with a constant attention to God, prayer and knowledge of divine truths; the desiring power—with total self-denial and renunciation of all self -indulgence; the excitable power—with love. If you do this, then, I assure you, the light of your mind will never be dimmed and wrong thoughts will never find place in you. If you are active in setting up such good thoughts and dispositions in yourself morning, evening and at all other hours of the day, invisible foes will never come near you. For then you will be like a general, who constantly reviews his troops and disposes them in battle order; and enemies know that to attack such a general is impracticable.

Pay most attention to the last point, namely, to actions opposed to those dictated by passionate thoughts and to setting up feelings and dispositions contrary to passions. Only by this means can you uproot passions in yourself and achieve a safer position. For so long as the roots of passions remain in you, they will always bring forth their offspring and thus cloud over the face of virtues, and at times completely cover and banish them. In such cases we are in danger of falling once more into our former sins and destroying all the fruits of our labours.

Therefore know that this last means should be practised not merely once, but often, many times, constantly, until you smash, disorganise and destroy the passionate habit against which you fight. Since this habit has acquired power over your heart through frequent repetition of certain actions, which satisfy the passion dwelling in the heart, opposing it in the heart is not enough to weaken and destroy this power; you must use actions which are contrary to your former ones, actions opposed to the passion, smashing and destroying it. Their frequent use will banish the passionate habit, kill the passion which stimulates it and plant in the heart the virtue opposed to it and a habit of corresponding actions. Moreover—and I shall not waste many words on this, since it is self-evident—to acquire good habits it is necessary to perform a greater number of right deeds, than the number of evil deeds required to establish bad habits; for bad habits take root more easily, since they are aided and abetted by the sin living in us, that is, by self-indulgence. Therefore, however hard, however difficult it may seem to you, to perform such actions, opposed to your passions, because your will for good is still weak, and because of the resistance of your passionate self-indulgent will, you must never abandon them, but must compel yourself in every way to practise them always. However imperfect they may be at first, they will still support your steadfastness and courage in battle, and pave the way to victory.

I shall add another thing: stand wakeful and, collecting your attention within yourself, fight with courage. And fight not only the great and strong, but also the small and weak stirrings of your passions. For the small open the way to the great, especially when they have become a habit. Experience has many times confirmed the fact that when a man pays little attention and care to repulsing small passionate desires from the heart, after he has overcome the great, he is subjected to sudden and unexpected attacks of the enemy, so impetuous that he is unable to hold his ground in battle and his downfall is more grievous than those of old.

Moreover I remind you of the fact that you should cut off and kill every passionate attachment to things which, although permissible, are not indispensable, as soon as you notice that they weaken the intensity of your will for good, distract attention away from yourself and disorganise the good order you have established in your life. Such are, for instance, taking walks, evening parties, conversations, new acquaintances, meals, sleep and other such things. You will gain much profit from this, by thus training yourself to self-mastery in all other things as well; you will become stronger and more expert in struggling against temptations and will avoid a great many snares of the devil, who knows how to spread his nets on these inoffensive paths, and, I assure you, your actions will win God's favour.

So, beloved, if you follow my advice and undertake such holy tasks with alertness, be assured that in a short time you will achieve success and will become spiritual in truth and actual deed, instead of deceitfully and only in name. But know that to oppose yourself and to compel yourself is here an immutable law, which excludes all pleasing of yourself even in the spiritual order of life. If you introduce into it, or choose exclusively deeds which please you, even if they belong to the spiritual order of things, you will ruin your work. You will labour, but in place of real fruit, you will get a sterile flower, and you will not be firmly established in anything spiritual. You will seem to have something spiritual, but in actual fact it will not be so. For all truly spiritual things are produced by the grace of the Holy Spirit; and this grace descends only on those, who have crucified themselves in sufferings and voluntary privations, without any self-pity, and have thus become united with our Lord and Saviour, crucified for their sakes.

CHAPTER FOURTEEN

*What to do when the higher, intelligent will
seems to be entirely overcome by the lower
will and by the enemies*

If you feel sometimes such a strong upsurging of sin that resistance to it will seem impossible and the very zeal to oppose it will appear exhausted, take care, brother, not to give up the struggle, but rouse yourself and stand firm. It is a subterfuge of the enemy, who, with the thought that resistance is hopeless, strives to undermine your firm stand and by making you lay down all your arms to force you to surrender to him. Make your mind see this subterfuge of the enemy more clearly and do not give ground. For so long as your will does not incline towards this passionate urge you are still among the victors, the fighters and slayers of the enemy, even if your sympathy is already ranged on the side of the passion. Nothing and nobody can force your will or steal victory from your hands and overthrow you against your will, no matter how obdurate and bitter the war waged in you by the enemies of your salvation. God endowed our free will with such power, that even if all a man's faculties, the whole world and all the demons rose up in arms against him and attacked him, they could not compel it. It is always left free to desire what they offer or demand, if it so wishes, or not to desire it, if it does not wish. On the other hand, for this very reason his will bears the responsibility for everything and is subject to judgment. Remember this well: no matter how weak and exhausted you may feel, you cannot find excuses for inclining towards a passionate suggestion. Your conscience will tell you the same. So the stronger the attacks the stronger the resistance you must prepare, and never abandon this resolve, repeating on all such occasions the words of command of one of our war leaders: 'Watch ye, stand fast . . . , quit you like men, be strong' (I Cor. xvi. 13).

Thus keeping your will inflexible against the uprising of sin and ranged on the side of the demands of the higher will, bring into action your spiritual weapons, one after another. The chief among them is prayer. Make it your inspiration, saying: 'The Lord is my light and my salvation; whom shall I fear? the Lord is the strength of my life; of whom shall I be afraid? . . . Though an host should encamp against me, my heart shall not fear: though war should rise against me, in this will I be confident' (Ps. xxvii. 1, 3). 'I will not trust in my bow, neither shall my sword save me . . . . In God we boast all the day long, and praise thy name for ever' (Ps. xliv. 6, 8). 'Neither fear ye their fear, nor be afraid. Sanctify the Lord of hosts himself; and let him be your fear, and let him be your dread. And he shall be for a sanctuary. . . . Gird yourselves, and ye shall be broken in pieces. . . . Take counsel together, and it shall come to nought; speak the word, and it shall not stand : for God is with us' (Isaiah viii. 12–14, 9, 10).

Thus inspired, do what a warrior in physical warfare does sometimes when he is hard pressed by the enemy; he steps back a little, to find a better point of vantage and see more clearly how best to speed his arrow at the heart of the foe. So you too, collect your thoughts within, and, re-establishing the consciousness and feeling of your nothingness and of your impotence to achieve by yourself what this moment demands, appeal to God to Whom all is possible, calling for His help against the attack of passion with warmth of trust and tears, saying: 'Arise for our help, and redeem us for thy mercies' sake' (Ps. xliv. 26). 'Fight' (my Jesus) 'against them that fight against me. Take hold of shield and buckler, and stand up for mine help. . . . Let them be confounded and put to shame that seek after my soul: let them be turned back and brought to confusion that devise my hurt' (Ps. xxxv. 1, 2, 4). 'Holy Virgin, do not let me yield to the enemies and be vanquished by them. O my guardian Angel, cover me with your wings against enemy arrows, and with your sword strike them down and cut them off from me.'

Persevere in these appeals and help will soon come. At the same time, keep acute attention on yourself. The foe knows the power of such appeals to God and hastens to forestall them, or spoil them by inciting senseless complaints against God for having allowed such enemy attacks and such danger of downfall to assail you. In this way the enemy strives to prevent or stop your appeals to God and make you unworthy of God's help. As soon as you notice such an ungodly impulse, hasten to re-establish the true and sincere conviction that 'God cannot be tempted with evil, neither tempteth he any man: but every man is tempted, when he is drawn away of his own lust, and enticed' (James i. 13, 14). Then, examine carefully your preceding deeds, feelings and thoughts, and you will find that it is they that gave birth to the inner storm, which put you in this dangerous position. The enemy defamed God, and covered up your own shortcomings. By faith you must justify God in yourself and, by reasoning, cast off the flattering veil, with which the enemy has covered you. You must shed the load of inattention and self-indulgence, repent and confess your inner sin to God and return to the appeals we have indicated, which will bring back God's help, since He is ever ready to come to your assistance, especially on such occasions.

After this, when the inner storm has died down, the struggle should proceed in accordance with the general rules of unseen warfare, which have been mentioned in part already.

CHAPTER FIFTEEN

War should be waged ceaselessly and courageously

If you want to gain a speedy and easy victory over your enemies, brother, you must wage ceaseless and courageous war against all passions, especially and pre-eminently against self-love, or a foolish attachment to yourself, manifested in self-indulgence and self-pity. For it is the basis and source of all passions and cannot be tamed except by constant voluntary self-inflicted sufferings and by welcoming afflictions, privations, calumnies, persecutions by the world and by men of the world. Failure to see the need of this pitiless attitude to yourself has always been, is and will be the cause of our failure to achieve spiritual victories, and of their difficulty, rarity, imperfection and insecurity.

So this spiritual warfare of ours must be constant and never ceasing, and should be conducted with alertness and courage in the soul; they can easily be attained, if you seek these gifts from God. So advance into battle without hesitation. Should you be visited by the troubling thought of the hatred and undying malice, which the enemies harbour against you, and of the innumerable hosts of the demons, think on the other hand of the infinitely greater power of God and of His love for you, as well as of the incomparably greater hosts of heavenly angels and the prayers of saints. They all fight secretly for us and with us against our enemies, as it is written: 'The Lord will have war with Amalek from generation to generation' (Ex. xvii. 16). How many weak women and small children were incited to fight by the thought of this powerful and ever ready help! And they got the upper hand and gained victory over all the wisdom of the world, all the wiles of the devil and all the malice of hell.

So you must never be afraid, if you are troubled by a flood of thoughts, that the enemy is too strong against you, that his attacks are never ending, that the war will last for your lifetime, and that you cannot avoid incessant downfalls of all kinds. Know that our enemies, with all their wiles, are in the hands of our divine Commander, our Lord Jesus Christ, for Whose honour and glory you are waging war. Since He Himself leads you into battle, He will certainly not suffer your enemies to use violence against you and overcome you, if you do not yourself cross over to their side with your will. He will Himself fight for you and will deliver your enemies into your hands, when He wills and as He wills, as it is written: 'The Lord thy God walketh in the midst of thy camp, to deliver thee, and to give up thine enemies before thee' (Deut. xxiii. 14).

If the Lord delays granting you full victory over your enemies and puts it off to the last day of your life, you must know that He does this for your own good; so long as you do not retreat or cease to struggle wholeheartedly. Even if you are wounded in battle, do not lay down your arms and turn to flight. Keep only one thing in your mind and intention—to fight with all courage and ardour, since it is unavoidable. No man can escape this warfare, either in life or in death. And he who does not fight to overcome his passions and his enemies will inevitably be taken prisoner, either here or yonder, and delivered to death.

It is not without profit to bear in mind also the purpose for which God is pleased to leave us in this state of war. This purpose is the following. In the days of old, when God led Israel into the promised land, He did not order them to destroy all the peoples dwelling there, but left five tribes alien and hostile to Israel—first, to prove the chosen people and to see how firmly they believed in Him and faithfully kept His commandments, and secondly, to teach His people the art of warfare (Judges ii. 21-23;

iii. 1–2). In the same way, He does not destroy all our passions at once, but leaves them in us, letting them fight against us till our very death, for just the same purpose, namely, to prove our love for Him and our obedience to His will, and to train us in spiritual warfare. The blessed Theodorite speaks of this in greater detail. God, he says, does this for the following ends: (a) to prevent us falling into carelessness and negligence, and to make us watchful, diligent and attentive; (b) to remind us that the enemy is ever ready to attack us, lest we unexpectedly find ourselves surrounded by the enemy and overcome by passions; (c) so that we should always have recourse to God, asking and hoping for His help; (d) so that we should not be proud, but should think humbly of ourselves; (e) so that we should learn to hate with our whole heart the passions and enemies, who so tirelessly attack us; (f) to prove whether we keep to the end God's honour, love and faith; (g) to urge us to a more strict observance of God's commandments, so that we do not overlook the least of them; (h) to learn from experience the great value of virtue and so never to consent to abandon it and fall into sin; (i) in order that constant warfare should give us the possibility to gain greater and greater crowns; (j) that we should glorify God and shame the devil by our patience to the end; (k) that we should get accustomed to warfare during life and so not fear it in the hour of death, when we are to be subjected to the hardest of all attacks.

Thus, since we are always surrounded by so many enemies, whose hatred of us is so bitter, we can expect no peace or respite from them, no cessation or postponement of attacks, but must be ready for an onslaught at any moment and, when it comes, must immediately engage the enemy with courage. Naturally it would have been better, if we had not originally opened the doors of our being and let enemies and passions enter our heart and soul; but since they have already found their way into us, we cannot afford to be negligent, but must arm ourselves against them to drive them out of us. They are shameless and stubborn and will not leave, unless driven out by force.

CHAPTER SIXTEEN

How a warrior of Christ should prepare for battle in the morning

As soon as you wake up in the morning, pray for a while, saying: 'Lord Jesus Christ, Son of God, have mercy upon me.' Then your first work should be to shut yourself in your own heart, as if taking up position in an arena. Having established yourself there, bring yourself to the consciousness and feeling that your enemy and the passionate urge against which you struggle at the moment is already there, on your left, ready for immediate attack; therefore rouse against them a firm resolve to conquer or die, but never to submit. Realise also that on your right there stands, invisibly present, your Commander, our Lord Jesus Christ, with His Holy Mother and a host of holy Angels, with Archangel Michael at their head, ready to come to your aid. So take heart and be of good cheer.

Lo, the prince of the nether world, the devil, rises against you with his host of demons and begins to fan the flame of passionate attraction, trying to persuade you with various promises flattering to your self-indulgence, to cease struggling against that passion and to submit to it, assuring you that this submission would be better and less troublesome. But you must keep attention in yourself—and at the same time you should hear from the right the warning and inspiring voice of your guardian angel who, speaking for all those standing on your right, will assuredly say to you: 'You are now faced with a battle against your passion and your other enemies. Fear not and be not afraid; let not this fear drive you to run from your post on the battlefield. For our Lord Jesus Christ, the Commander, is near you, surrounded by the commanders and centurions of His incorporeal armies and all the hosts of holy Angels, ready to fight with you against your enemies and not let them overcome and conquer you, as is promised: "The Lord shall fight for you" (Exodus xiv. 14).' Therefore stand firm, compel yourself not to give ground and strive by all possible means to stand up to the trial which has assailed you, calling from the bottom of your heart: 'Deliver me not over unto the will of mine enemies' (Ps. xxvii. 12). Appeal to your Lord, to the

Holy Virgin, to all the Angels and saints. Help will come, and you will be victorious, for it is written: 'I write unto you, young men' (emboldened and intrepid warriors), 'because ye have overcome the wicked one' (I John ii. 13). You may be weak and tied by bad habits, while your enemies are strong and numerous; but much more powerful help is ready for you from Him, Who has created and redeemed you. God your Protector is incomparably stronger than all others in this battle. As it is written: 'The Lord strong and mighty, the Lord mighty in battle' (Ps. xxiv. 8). Moreover His desire to save you is greater than that of your enemy to destroy you. So fight and never weary of the labours of this warfare. For victory is won by these labours, by forcing yourself and mercilessly tearing yourself from vicious habits despite the pain; and thus a great treasure is gained, whereby the kingdom of heaven is purchased and the soul for ever united with God.

Thus every morning begin in God's name your struggle with the enemies, armed with distrust of yourself and a daring hope in God, with prayer and a merciless self-compelling to fitting labours and spiritual tasks, and above all, armed with prayer of the mind in the heart:* 'Lord Jesus Christ, have mercy upon me!' Wielded in the heart like a two-edged sword, this terrible name strikes down both demons and passions, and drives them away. This is why John of the Ladder says: 'Flog the foes with the name of our Lord Jesus.' We shall speak further of this prayer in a separate chapter. So, I repeat, with these weapons smite that enemy, that passion and that evil tendency which assails you, in the order indicated in the thirteenth chapter. Namely, first, oppose the passion, then hate it, and finally practise the particular virtue opposed to it, doing all this, if we can so say—in an atmosphere of prayer. If you do this, your activity will be pleasing to your God, Who, together with the Church triumphant in the heavens, stands by invisibly and watches your struggles.

Such struggles are extremely hard and arduous; but grieve not, nor drop your task, bearing in mind that, on the one hand, it is our duty to work and to please our God, and on the other, as has been said already, to fight is unavoidable if we want to live; for once we stop fighting, we shall straightway be stricken to death.

* Literally 'mind-heart' prayer. There is no equivalent composite epithet in English. As will be seen in this book, the joining of mind and heart represents a definite state of attainment; that attainment is wisdom. For further explanation of this term see Ch. XLVII et seq.

Do not let the enemy seduce you by the suggestion: 'Let go just for an hour.' Very well, just for an hour. But what will become of you, if you relinquish your life in God, and abandon yourself to the world and its comforts, and to bodily enjoyments? You will be a renegade from God; which is terrible for a single moment, let alone for an hour. And is it likely to be but an hour? Is it not more probable that hour after hour will pass in this ungodly life, then day after day, and year after year? And beyond this, what? Even if the Lord takes pity on you and gives you time to come to yourself, to get free of this net of the devil and awake from your sinful sleep, you will still have to rejoin the same battle, from which you flee now to seek an easy life, with the only difference that then the fight will be incomparably harder, more acute, more painful and, in addition, less successful.

But if the Lord leaves you in the hands of your enemies and of your own will? What then? I shall not repeat it, I shall say only: remember; for who is there who does not know it? After a life spent in the wearisome bonds of evil passions, at times intoxicated by sensuality, but always deprived of true joys, the hour of death will suddenly come—a terribly painful state of the soul, which even the word of God could not describe, but merely said: then they will cry to the mountains: 'Fall on us' (Rev. vi. 16). This cry, beginning at the hour of death, will go on ceaselessly for all time after death, till the end of the world, and will be heard at the moment when the last judgment comes—and always in vain. Then be not so unmindful as to cast yourself knowingly into the eternal torment of hell, for the sake of avoiding the momentary struggles and labours of spiritual training. If you are intelligent and, I would say, prudent, it is better for you to undertake now the temporary labours and hardships of spiritual struggle so as to overcome your foes, receive a crown and be united with God both here and beyond—in the kingdom of heaven.

CHAPTER SEVENTEEN

In what order should you fight your passions?

It would be very useful for you, my brother, to know well the order in which you should fight your passions, so as to do this work as it should be done, instead of simply haphazardly, as some people do, without great success, and at times even with harm to themselves. The order in which it is necessary to fight your enemies and struggle with your bad desires and passions, is the following: enter with attention into the heart and examine carefully with what thoughts, dispositions and passionate attachments it is specially occupied, and which passion is most predominant and tyranically rules there. Then against this passion first of all take up arms and struggle to overcome it. On this one concentrate all your attention and care, except only at the times when some other passion happens to arise in you. In that case you should deal with this one without delay and drive it away, after which you must once more turn your weapons against your chief passion, which constantly manifests its presence and power. For as in every kind of warfare, so in our unseen battle, we must fight first what is actually attacking us at the present moment.

CHAPTER EIGHTEEN

How to fight sudden impulses of passions

If, my beloved, you are not yet accustomed to overcome sudden impulses and the excitement of passions, roused, for example, by insults or by other clashes, I advise you to do this: make it a rule every morning, while you still sit at home, to review in your mind all the occasions you may meet with in the course of the day, both favourable and unfavourable, and visualise the passionate impulses, lusts and irritations they may provoke; then prepare in yourself beforehand how to stifle them at the very inception, without allowing them to develop. If you do this, you will never be taken unawares by any movements of passions, but will always be ready to resist them, without being troubled with anger or enticed by lust. This review of what may happen should be practised especially when you have to go out and visit places where you are bound to meet people, who can either attract or irritate you. Being prepared, you will easily avoid the one and the other. If a wave of passion arises, it will roll over your head or will break against you as against a rock, instead of carrying you with it like a flimsy boat. Let the holy prophet David convince you of this as regards anger, when he says: 'I made haste, and delayed not to keep thy commandments' (Ps. cxix. 60).*

But this preparation is not yet everything. Passion can still be excited, and excited suddenly. In such a case act as follows: as soon as you feel a passionate impulse, whether of lust or irritation, hasten to curb it by an effort of will, descend into your heart with the attention of your mind, and try in every possible way not to let the passion enter the heart. Watch to prevent the heart being irritated by what irritates, or attracted by what attracts. If, however, either the one or the other happens suddenly to be born in your heart, to begin with try to prevent it from coming out; do not express it either by word, look or gesture.

Further, compel your mind and heart to rise to God on high and, having produced in yourself a clear consciousness and feeling of God's boundless love and of His impartial truth, try through this to thrust out the passionate movement and to replace it by its opposing good. If it is a question of meeting someone, it may be difficult to do all this fully and successfully; still do not abandon your good intention and try to do what you can. Even if for the moment your effort is unsuccessful, you will achieve your end when the meeting, which rouses your passion, is over. But take great care not to show the passion roused within. This effort will prevent its developing. And, as soon as you are free from the inflow of evil impressions, hasten to enter your heart and strive to throw out the reptile which has found its way there.

But the best and most efficient protection against a sudden uprising of passions is getting rid of the causes which are always giving birth to such movements. These causes are twofold: like and dislike. If you, my beloved, are caught and made captive by a liking for some person, or by attachment to some thing, whether great or small, it is natural that if you meet them and see them

---

* The Slavonic text reads: 'I made ready, and so did not succumb.'

insulted or harmed, or someone wishes to entice them away or steal them from you, you immediately become indignant, grieve, become agitated and rise up in arms against those who do it. Therefore if you wish to be free of such sudden disturbances, take care to overcome and uproot from your heart this wrong attraction or wrong attachment. And the further it has gone, the more care you should use to have an equable mind and acquire a sensible attitude to things and people. For the stronger your attraction or passionate attachment, the more tempestuous the sudden uprising of passion in all the cases I have indicated.

In the same way, if you feel dislike towards some person or aversion from some thing, it is equally natural for indignation or disgust to rise up suddenly in you if you meet them, and especially if you hear someone praise them. Therefore if you wish to preserve the peace of your heart in such cases, urge yourself to stifle these bad feelings on this occasion, and later to annihilate them altogether.

You will be helped in this by reasoning as follows (in relation to people)—that they too are God's creatures, fashioned, as you are, in God's image and likeness and by the all-powerful hand of the living God, that they are redeemed and regenerated by the priceless blood of Christ our Lord, that they too are your brothers and co-members, whom it is wrong for you to hate even in thought, as it is written: 'Thou shalt not hate thy brother in thine heart' (Lev. xix. 17). Especially you must remember that, even supposing they are worthy of dislike and hostility, if you conceive friendship and love towards them, you will, in so doing, be likening yourself to God, Who loves all His creatures and despises none of them, as the wise Solomon says in praising the Lord: 'Thou lovest all the things that are, and abhorrest nothing which thou hast made: for never wouldest thou have made any thing, if thou hadst hated it' (Wisdom of Solomon xi. 24). With no regard for human sins He 'maketh his sun to rise on the evil and on the good, and sendeth rain on the just and on the unjust' (Matt. v. 45).

CHAPTER NINETEEN

How to struggle against bodily passions

In struggling against bodily passions, my brother, a different method should be used than in struggling against the others. If you want things to proceed in the right order, know that you should do one thing before you are tempted by these passions, another thing during temptation and yet another when it is over.

Before temptation, attention should be concentrated on the causes, which habitually give birth to temptation or which excite passion. The rule here is to use every means to avoid all occasions, which may upset the calm of your body, especially meeting people of the other sex. If you are forced to converse with such a person, let the conversation be short, and preserve not only modesty but a certain sternness of countenance; let your words be friendly, but reserved rather than forthcoming.

'Never trust thine enemy' (Ecclesiasticus xii. 10) says the wise Sirach. So never trust your body; for as iron produces rust by itself, so the corrupted nature of the body produces evil stirrings of lust. 'For like as iron rusteth, so is his wickedness' (Ecclesiasticus xii. 10). I repeat again, do not trust yourself in this respect, even if you no longer feel and have not felt for some time this sting of your flesh. For this thrice-cursed wickedness sometimes achieves in one hour or one moment what it has not done for many years, and always makes its preparations for attack silently. Know that the more the flesh pretends to be your friend and gives no cause for suspicion, the greater the harm it inflicts later, and often strikes to death.

All must fear people of the other sex, communion with whom is regarded as good in ordinary life, either because they are relatives, or because they are pious and virtuous, or because they have done you a favour and you feel under the obligation to express your gratitude as often as possible. You should fear this because, without fear and attention to yourself, such communion is practically always mixed with the pernicious sensory lust which, gradually and insensibly, steals into the soul to its very depths and so obscures the mind that a man thus infected begins to disregard all the dangerous causes of sin, such as passionate glances, sweet

63

words on both sides, seductive movements and postures of the body and the pressing of hands. Thus he finally succumbs to the sin itself and to other snares of the devil, from which at times he never manages to extricate himself completely.

So, my brother, flee this fire, for you are gunpowder, and never dare to think in your conceit that you are damp gunpowder, moistened with the water of a good and firm will. No, no! Better think that you are as dry as dry and will catch fire as soon as you are touched by that flame. Never rely on the firmness of your resolve and your readiness to die rather than to offend God by sin. For, although it can be assumed that this resolve makes your gunpowder damp, frequent communication and sitting together in private will gradually dry the moisture of your righteous will by bodily fire, and you will never notice how you are set aflame with bodily love to such an extent, that you will cease to be ashamed of men and to fear God, and will disregard honour, life and all the tortures of hell in your longing to commit sin.

So avoid in all possible ways:

(a) Communion with people, who can be a temptation to you, if you sincerely desire to escape the captivity of sin and paying its wages, which is death of the soul. The wise Solomon calls a man wise, who fears and avoids the causes of sin; and he calls foolish a man who, with great self-reliance, confidently neglects to avoid them, saying: 'A wise man feareth, and departeth from evil: but the fool rageth, and is confident' (in his actions) (Prov. xiv. 16). Did not the Apostle point this out when he advised the Corinthians: 'Flee fornication' (I Cor. vi. 18).

(b) Flee idleness and laziness; stand on guard watchfully, in all things peering closely at your thoughts, and wisely arranging and conducting the activities, demanded by your position.

(c) Never disobey your spiritual teachers and fathers, but obey them willingly in everything, executing their orders quickly and readily, and especially those which can teach you humility and go against your own will and inclination.

(d) Never allow yourself boldly to judge your neighbour; judge and condemn no one, especially for the particular bodily sin of which we are speaking. If someone has manifestly fallen into it, rather have compassion and pity for him. Do not be indignant with him or laugh at him, but let his example be a lesson in humility to you; realising that you too are extremely weak and as

64

easily moved to sin as dust on the road, say to yourself: 'He fell
to-day, but to-morrow I shall fall.' Know that, if you are quick to
blame and despise others, God will mete out a painful punishment
to you by letting you fall into the same sin for which you blame
others. 'Judge not, that ye be not judged' (Matt. vii. 1); you will
be condemned to the same punishment, in order to learn from it
the perniciousness of your pride and, thus humbled, to seek a cure
from two evils: pride and fornication. Even if in His mercy God
protects you from downfall and you keep the chastity of your
thought inviolate, stop blaming others if you were blaming them,
and instead of relying on yourself, be still more afraid and do not
trust your own steadfastness.

(e) Pay attention to yourself and watch over yourself. If you
have gained some gift or another from God, or find yourself in a
good spiritual state, do not in your vainglory accept vain illusions
about yourself, thinking that you are something and imagining
that your enemies would not dare to attack you, that you abhor
and despise them so much that you will immediately repulse them,
if they dare to come near you. As soon as you think thus, you will
fall as easily as an autumn leaf from a tree.

That is what you must do before the temptation of bodily
passion assails you.

At a time of actual temptation, do as follows: hasten to discover
the cause which provoked the attack and sweep it away immediately. This cause may be internal or external. External causes may
be: undisciplined eyes, words sweet to the hearing, songs which
delight your ears by their content or melody, fine garments made
of soft materials, perfumes pleasing to the nose, free behaviour
and conversations, physical touch and pressing of hands, dances
and many other things. Remedies against these are: simple and
humble attire, the will not to see, hear, smell, say or touch anything which may produce this shameful impulse, and especially
avoidance of all intercourse with people of the other sex, as has
been already said above. Inner causes are, on the one hand, ease
and comfort of the body, when all bodily desires find full satisfaction; on the other—shameful thoughts, which either come of
themselves brought by memories of things seen, heard and experienced, or which are excited by evil spirits.

As regards a life of physical ease and comfort, it should be
hardened by fasts, vigils, sleeping rough, and especially by a great

number of bowings and prostrations to exhaust the body, and by various other voluntary mortifications of the flesh, as advised and counselled by our wise and experienced holy fathers. The remedy against thoughts, no matter whence they come, is various spiritual exercises, compatible with your present state and dictated by it, such as: reading of holy and salutary books, especially of St. Ephrem the Syrian, St. John of the Ladder, the Philokalia and others of the same kind, devout meditations and prayer.

When shameful thoughts begin to assail you, pray thus: immediately raise your mind to our Lord, crucified for us, and call on Him from the bottom of your heart: 'My Lord Jesus! My sweetest Jesus! Hasten to help me and do not let my enemy ensnare me!' At the same time embrace mentally (and also physically if there is one near you) the life-giving cross upon which your Lord was crucified, kiss often His wounds and say to Him with love: 'Most beautiful wounds, most holy wounds, immaculate wounds! Wound my wretched and impure heart and do not let me offend and shame Thee by my uncleanness.'

During the time when shameful thoughts of bodily lust multiply in you, your reflections must not be directed straight against them, though many advise this. Do not attempt to picture in your mind the uncleanness and shame of the sins of bodily lust, nor the remorse of conscience which follows upon them, nor the corruption of your nature and loss of your pure virginity, nor the besmirching of your honour, and other similar things. Do not attempt, I say, to think of these things, for such reflections are not always a reliable means of overcoming bodily temptations and may only give strength to the attacks and, at times, lead to your downfall. For, although your mind remonstrates with the lust and mentally upbraids it, yet the thought dwells on its objects, to which the heart feels such predilection. So it is not surprising that while the mind is lavishly pouring out severe condemnations of these things, the heart delights in them and consents to them—which means inner downfall. No, you must think of such subjects as would screen off these shameful things and completely distract your attention from them, things which, by their nature, would have a sobering effect on your heart. Such subjects are the life and passion of our Lord Jesus, Who took on flesh for our sakes, the inevitable hour of our death, the terrible day of judgment and the various aspects of torment in hell.

If, as often happens, shameful thoughts should persist in spite of this, and should attack you with special force and impetuosity, fear not, do not stop reflecting as we have said, and do not attempt a direct attack on them to expose their shameful nature. Refrain from this, but continue to direct your whole attention to reflections upon the sobering and awe-inspiring subjects indicated above, without bothering about the shameful thoughts, as though they were not your own. Know that no better means exists of driving them away than disregarding and neglecting them. As often as possible, interrupt your meditation by this or a similar prayer: 'Deliver me, my Creator and Saviour, from my enemies, to the glory of your passion and your infinite mercy.' Conclude your meditation by a similar prayer.

Take care not to cast the eye of your mind upon this bodily uncleanness, since merely visualising it is not without danger; and do not pause to converse with these temptations or about them, in order to find out whether consent to them had occurred in you or not. Although such analysis may appear good, in actual fact it is a trick of the devil, who strives by this means to weigh you down, to cast you into faintheartedness and despair, or to make you dwell on these thoughts as long as possible, in order thus to drive you to sinful action, of this kind, or some other.

Instead of all such investigations of the thoughts which trouble you, go, confess all in detail to your spiritual father, and thereupon remain undisturbed in your heart and thought, untroubled by any questions, but content with the ruling of your father. Only, you must reveal to him everything, which has troubled and is troubling your mind and feeling in this temptation, concealing nothing and not letting your tongue be tied by shame, but humbling yourself in self-abasement. For if, to gain victory, we need profound humility in all struggle with our enemies, how much more so at moments of warfare of the flesh? For in this case the very temptation is mostly either born of pride or is a reproof and punishment for it. Therefore St. John of the Ladder says that he who has fallen into fornication or some other sin of the flesh, had previously fallen into pride; and that his fall into sin was allowed, to humble him. 'Where a downfall has happened, there pride has dwelt before it; for pride comes before a fall.' And again: 'Punishment for the proud is to fall' (Chapter 23).

When shameful thoughts are at last subdued and temptation

67

ceases, you must do the following: however much you are convinced that you are now free from attacks of the flesh, and however sure you are of yourself, take every care to keep your mind and attention away from things and people, who were the cause of this upsurging of temptation. Do not satisfy the impulse to see them, under the pretext that they are your relatives, or that they are devout and your benefactors. Admonish yourself with the thought that this too is a sinful blandishment of our corrupt nature and a net of our cunning enemy the devil, who assumes here the form of an Angel of light, in order to cast us into the darkness of which St. Paul speaks (II Cor. xi. 14).

CHAPTER TWENTY

How to overcome negligence

To avoid falling into the pernicious evil of negligence, which will stop your progress towards perfection and deliver you into the hands of the enemies, you must flee all kinds of inquisitiveness (trying to find out what's here, or what's there, idle wandering, empty chatter, gaping around), any kind of cleaving to something earthly, all arbitrary actions or 'doing what I like', which is totally out of keeping with your position. On the contrary, you must force yourself to follow, willingly and quickly, every good guidance and command of your teachers and spiritual fathers and to do everything at the time and in the manner they wish.

Never delay in undertaking any work you have to do, for the first brief delay will lead to a second, more prolonged one, and the second to a third, still longer, and so on. Thus work begins too late and is not done in its proper time, or else is abandoned altogether, as something too burdensome. Having once tasted the pleasure of inaction, you begin to like and prefer it to action. In satisfying this desire, you will little by little form a habit of inaction and laziness, in which the passion for doing nothing will possess you to such an extent that you will cease even to see how incongruous and criminal it is; except perhaps when you weary of this laziness, and are again eager to take up your work. Then you will see with shame how negligent you have been and how many necessary works you have neglected, for the sake of the empty and useless 'doing what you like'.

Scarcely perceptible at first, this negligence permeates everything and not only poisons the will, planting in it aversion to all kind of effort and all forms of spiritual doing and obedience, but also blinds the mind, and prevents it from seeing all the folly and falsehood of the arguments which support this disposition of will; for it hinders the mind from presenting to the consciousness the sound reasonings, which would have the power of moving the slothful will to perform the necessary work as quickly and diligently as possible, without putting it off till another time. For it is not enough to perform the work quickly; each thing has to be done in its proper time, as required by its nature, and needs to be performed with full attention and care, to make it as perfect as possible. Listen to what is written: 'Cursed be he that doeth the work of the Lord deceitfully'* (Jeremiah xlviii. 10). And you incur this disaster, because you are too lazy to think of the value and worth of the work you have to do; for this thought would impel you to do it in its proper time and with such resolution as to banish all the thoughts of the accompanying difficulties, which laziness suggests in order to turn you away.

Let the conviction never leave your thought that a single raising of your mind to God, and a single humble genuflexion to His glory and in His honour has infinitely more value than all the treasures of the world; that every time we banish negligence and force ourselves to do the work we should with diligence, Angels in heaven prepare for us the crown of a glorious victory; and that, on the contrary, not only has God no crowns for the negligent, but that little by little He takes back from them the gifts He had bestowed upon them for their former diligence in His service, and will finally deprive them of His kingdom if they continue to be negligent, as He said in the parable of guests bidden to supper, who were too lazy to come: 'For I say unto you, That none of those men which were bidden shall taste of my supper' (Luke xiv. 24). Such is the lot of the negligent. For those who are diligent and who force themselves without self-pity to every good work, the Lord multiplies His blessed gifts in this life, and prepares a life of eternal bliss in His heavenly kingdom, as He said: 'The kingdom of

* The Slavonic text reads: 'neglectfully'.

heaven suffereth violence, and the violent take it by force'* (Matt. xi. 12).

If an evil thought comes to try and cast you into negligence, and suggests that the work necessary to acquire the virtue you love and desire is extremely long and hard, that your enemies are strong and numerous, while you are weak and alone, that you must do much, and perform great deeds to attain your aim; if, I say, the thought of negligence suggests all this to you, do not listen to it. On the contrary, look at the matter this way: of course you must work, but not much, you must undertake labours, but they are very small and will not last long; you will meet enemies, but instead of many there will be only one, and, although he is too strong against you alone, yet you are incomparably stronger than he, since you can always rely on God's help in return for your great trust in it. If you have this attitude, negligence will begin to retreat from you and in its place, under the influence of good thoughts and feelings, there will gradually enter into you a diligent zeal in everything, which will finally possess all the powers of your soul and body.

Do the same in relation to prayer. Supposing the performance of some sacred service demands an hour of diligent prayer, which seems burdensome to your laziness; then, in starting this work, do not think that you must stand for an hour, but imagine that it will last only a quarter of an hour. In this way, the quarter of an hour of prayer will pass imperceptibly. Thereupon say to yourself: 'Let us stand for another quarter of an hour—it's not much, as you see.' Do the same for the third and the fourth quarter, and you will complete your task of prayer, without noticing any hardship or difficulty. If, in the course of this, you feel it so onerous that this feeling interferes with the prayer itself, leave off reciting prayers for a while and then, after a short interval, resume it again and finish what you have omitted.

Do the same in relation to manual work and the tasks of your obedience. Sometimes your tasks may seem too many; you become flustered and are ready to give them up. But refrain from thinking of their great number; instead, force yourself, take up the most immediate task and do it with diligence, as though the others did not exist; and you will do it without trouble. Then do the same

* The Slavonic text reads: 'The kingdom of Heaven is taken by force and those who force themselves ravish it.'

in relation to other tasks, and you will finish them all calmly, without fuss and bother.

Behave thus in everything, and know that, if you do not listen to reason and do not thus try to overcome the sense of burden and difficulty, which the enemy presents to you in the tasks which lie before you, then negligence will finally take complete possession of you. Then you will feel as if you were carrying a mountain on your shoulders, not only when you are faced with some immediate task, but even when it is still far ahead; you will be weighed down and tormented by it, like a slave bound in slavery with no hope of release. Then, even at times of rest, you will have no rest, and will feel yourself overburdened with work, even while doing nothing.

Know also, my child, that this disease of laziness and negligence gradually undermines with its poison not only the first small roots out of which virtuous habits may grow, but even those which are already deep rooted and serve as a foundation of the whole order of righteous life. As a worm gradually gnaws at the root of a tree, so negligence, if it persists, insensibly wears away and destroys the very nerves of spiritual life. Through it the devil manages to spread his nets and set the snares of temptations for every man; and exerts particular care and sly cunning in the case of those who are zealous in spiritual life, knowing that a lazy and negligent man easily submits to lusts and falls, as it is written: 'The soul of the sluggard desireth, and hath nothing' (Prov. xiii. 4).

So be for ever watchful, pray and take good care of everything good, as it behoves a courageous warrior: 'The soul of the diligent shall be made fat'* (Prov. xiii. 4). Do not sit with folded hands, putting off the sewing of your wedding garment to the moment when it is time to go out in festive raiments to meet the coming bridegroom, Christ our Lord. Remind yourself every day that *now* is in our hands, but *to-morrow* is in the hands of God, and that He Who gave you this morning has not bound Himself with the promise to give you the evening too. Refuse to listen to the devil when he whispers to you: give me *now*, and you will give *to-morrow* to God. No, no! Spend all the hours of your life in a way pleasing to God; keep in your mind the thought that after the present hour you will not be given another and that you will have to

* The Slavonic text reads: 'The hands of the courageous are ever diligent.'

71

render a strict account for every minute of this present hour. Remember, that the time you have in your hands is priceless and if you waste it uselessly, the hour will come when you will seek and not find it. Consider as lost a day when, although performing good deeds, you have not struggled to overcome your bad tendencies and desires.

To end my lesson on this subject, I shall repeat the Apostle's commandment: 'Fight the good fight' always (I Tim. vi. 12). For one hour of diligent work has often gained heaven and one hour of negligence has lost it. Take great care if you want to prove before God your firm faith in your salvation. 'He that putteth his trust in the Lord shall be made fat'* (Prov. xxviii. 25).

CHAPTER TWENTY-ONE

On the control and right use of the outer senses

Those who are zealous for righteousness, must think deeply and work constantly on a strict control and right direction of our five outer senses—sight, hearing, smell, taste and touch. Our heart constantly craves and seeks comforts and pleasures. It should find them in the inner order of things, by keeping and bearing in itself Him, in Whose image man has been created, Who is the very source of every comfort. But when in our downfall, we fell away from God, preferring ourselves, we lost also our foothold in ourselves, and fell into the flesh; thereby we went outside ourselves and began to seek for joys and comforts there. Our senses became our guides and intermediaries in this. Through them the soul goes outside and tastes the things experienced by each sense. It then delights in the things which delight the senses; and out of all these together it builds the circle of comforts and pleasures, whose enjoyment it considers as its primary good. So the order of things has become inverted: instead of God within, the heart seeks for pleasures without and is content with them.

Those who have listened to the voice of God—'Repent!'—do repent and lay down for themselves the law of re-establishing the

* The Slavonic text reads: 'He that putteth his trust in the Lord, will abide in diligence.'

72

original order of life, that is, of returning from without to within, and from within to God, in order to live in Him and by Him, and to have this as their first good, bearing within themselves the source of every comfort. Although the first step in re-establishing this order is strong desire and firm resolve, it is not achieved at once. A man who has taken this resolve is faced with a long work of struggling with his former habits of pleasing, pampering and pandering to himself, until they fall away and are replaced by others, in keeping with his new order of life. And here is the great importance of the control and use of the outer senses.

Each sense has its own range of subjects, pleasant and unpleasant. The soul delights in pleasant things and, becoming accustomed to them, acquires a lust for them. In this way each sense introduces into the soul several lusts or tendencies and passionate attachments. They all hide in the soul and keep silent, when there are no causes to stimulate them. Sometimes they are stimulated by thoughts about the objects of these lusts, but the main and strongest cause of their excitement is when these objects are directly present and experienced by the senses. In this case, lust for them arises uncontrollably and in a man who has not yet resolved to resist it 'bringeth forth sin: and sin, when it is finished, bringeth forth death' (James i. 15). Then the words of the prophet are fulfilled in this man: 'Death is come up into our windows' (Jer. ix. 21), that is, into the senses which are the windows of the soul for communication with the outer world. In a man, who has let it enter, it rouses a struggle, not without danger of downfall. Therefore a man should make himself an immutable law to control and use his senses in such a way that no sensory lusts become excited, but only those impressions come in, which stifle them and excite opposite feelings.

You see, brother, in what danger your senses can place you. So pay attention to yourself and learn to forestall it. Try in every way to prevent your senses from wandering hither and thither as they choose, and do not turn them only on sensory pleasures, but, on the contrary, direct them towards what is good, or useful, or necessary. If till now your senses sometimes broke out and rushed to sensory pleasures, from now on try to the utmost to curb them and turn them back from these enticements. Control them well, so that, wherever they were previously enslaved by vain and harmful delights, they should now receive profitable impressions from

73

every creature and every thing, and introduce these into the soul. Giving birth to spiritual thoughts in the soul, such impressions will collect the soul within itself and, soaring on wings of mental contemplation, will raise it to the vision and praise of God, as the blessed Augustine says: 'As many creatures as are in the world converse with righteous men, and although their language is dumb and wordless, it is none the less wholly effective and, for such men, easily heard and understood. From this they conceive blessed and pious thoughts and are incited to an ardent love of God.'

You too can do it in the following way. When to your outer senses there is presented some physical object, which they either see, or hear, or smell, or taste, or touch,—separate in your mind what is sensory and material in the object from that part, which comes from the creative divine Spirit; think how impossible it is for its being and all it contains to come from itself, but that all in it is the work of God, Whose invisible power gives it its being, its good qualities, beauty and wise structure, this power to act on others and this capacity to receive influences from them, and everything good there is in it. Then transfer such thoughts to all other visible things, and rejoice in your heart that the one God is the origin and cause of such varied, such great and marvellous perfections, manifested in His creatures—that He contains in Himself all possible perfections, and that these perfections, seen in His creatures, are no other than a weak reflection and shadow of the boundless perfections of God. Exercise your mind in such thoughts at the sight of every creature, and you will get accustomed to looking at visible things, without your attention dwelling solely on their external aspect, but penetrating within them to their divine content, to their unseen and hidden beauty, thus revealed to the mind. If you do this, the external side of things, attractive to your own sensory side, will escape your attention and feeling, leaving no trace, and only their inner content will impress itself on your mind, evoking and feeding its spiritual contemplations and inciting you to praise the Lord.

Thus, looking at the four elements—fire, air, water and earth— and thinking of their essence, power and action, you will be filled with great spiritual delight and will call to the great Creator Who has made them: 'Great God, immeasurable Power and wondrous Action! I rejoice and am glad that Thou alone art the origin and cause of the essence, power and action of every creature!' Looking up at the sky and the heavenly bodies: sun, moon and stars, and reflecting that they received their light and brilliance from God, you will exclaim: 'O Light most brilliant of all lights, from which all light came into being, both material and immaterial! O wonderful Light, the first joy of Angels and delight of the blessed, in which the eyes of the cherubim are immersed in ceaseless contemplation and wonder, to which all physical lights are as the deepest darkness! I praise and glorify Thee, O True Light, which illumines every man coming into the world! Grant me always to see Thee mentally, to make my heart rejoice with fullness of joy!' —In the same way, in looking at trees, grasses and other plants, and seeing in your mind how they live, feed, grow and reproduce their kind, and that their life and all they have comes not from themselves, but from the Creative Spirit, Whom you do not see, but Who alone animates them, you can cry: 'Here is the true Life, in Whom, from Whom and by Whom all live, feed and multiply! O life-giving Delight of my heart!' In the same way, seeing the dumb animals you can soar with your mind to God, Who gave them their senses and the power to move from place to place, say: 'O prime Mover of all things, Who, setting all things in motion, Thyself remains at rest! How I rejoice and am glad in Thy immobility and Thy firm immutability!'

Looking at yourself or at other people and thinking that you alone have been given high rank, that you alone of all living beings on earth have the gift of reason, and serve as the point of union and connection between material and immaterial creatures, rouse yourself to glorify and thank your God and Creator, and say: 'O eternal Trinity, Father, Son and Holy Spirit! Be Thou blessed for ever! How greatly must I give Thee thanks at all times, not only because Thou hast created me out of earth and hast made me King over all earthly creatures, not only because Thou hast honoured my nature with Thy likeness, with reason, speech and a living body, but above all because Thou hast given me the power, of my own free will, through virtues to resemble Thee, that thereby I may possess Thee in me and rejoice in Thee for ever!'

I shall now turn to each of the five senses separately, and I say to you: seeing the beauty and shapeliness of creatures, separate in your mind what you see from its spiritual meaning, which you do not see, and reflect that all this visible beauty is the work of the invisible and most beautiful creative Spirit, in Whom lies

75

the cause of all external beauty. Then, filled with joy, say: 'O rich streams flowing from an uncreated source! O life-giving rain drawn from the boundless sea of all blessings! How I rejoice in my innermost heart, when I think of the ineffable beauty of my Creator—the origin and cause of all created beauty! What spiritual sweetness fills me, when I hold in my mind to the thought of the beauty of my God, which no word can describe nor thought comprehend, and which is the principle of all beauty!'

If you hear a pleasant voice or a harmony of voices and singing, turn your mind to God, and say: 'Harmony of harmonies, O my Lord! How I rejoice in Thy boundless perfections, all blending in Thee in transubstantial harmony; thence are they reflected in the hosts of Angels in the heavens, and in the countless creatures here below; this is the symphony of all, perfect beyond imagining!' And: 'O my Lord, when will my hour come to hear with the ears of my heart Thy most sweet voice, saying: My peace I give unto Thee—peace from passions! "For sweet is thy voice", as the bride sings in the Song of Songs' (Song of Songs ii. 14).

If you happen to smell some perfumed ointment or the scent of flowers, transfer your thought from this physical fragrance to the secret fragrance of the Holy Spirit and say: 'O the fragrance of the all-sweetest Flower, and inexhaustible Ointment, Which was poured out on all God's creatures, as the Song of Songs says: "I am the rose of Sharon, and the lily of the valleys" (Song of Songs ii. 1); and: "Thy name is as ointment poured forth" (Song of Songs i. 3). O all-pervading source of fragrance, richly breathing Thy divine breath upon all things, from the highest and most pure Angels to the basest creatures, bathing all things in Thy fragrance.' Thus Isaac, smelling the smell of his son Jacob said: 'See, the smell of my son is as the smell of a field which the Lord hath blessed' (Gen. xxvii. 27).

Again, when you eat or drink, reflect that it is God, Who gives all food a taste which pleases us. So, delighting in Him alone, say: 'Rejoice, O my soul, for, although you can find no satisfaction, delight or comfort in anything outside God, you can know Him and cleave to Him, and can find every delight in Him alone, as David invites, saying: "O taste and see that the Lord is good" (Ps. xxxiv. 8), the truth of which Solomon testifies, saying: "His fruit was sweet to my taste" (Song of Songs ii. 3).

In the same way, when you move your hands to do something,

bring to your mind the thought that God, Who gave you the power and capacity to act, is the first cause of all movement, and that you are nothing but a living instrument in His hand, and rising to Him in thought, say: 'O God Most High, Lord of all, what joy fills me at the thought that without Thee I can do nothing and that Thou art the prime and principal mover in every action!'

When you see in other people either goodness, or wisdom, or truth, or some other virtue, again separate the visible from the invisible, and say to your God: 'O inexhaustible treasure-house of all virtue! How great is my joy to see and to know that every good thing comes from Thee alone, and that compared with Thy divine perfections all our good is—nothing! I thank Thee, my God, for this and for every other good thing Thou doest to my neighbour. But remember, O our Benefactor, also my own beggarly state and how greatly I fall short in every virtue.'

In general, every time you feel in God's creatures something pleasing and attractive, do not let your attention be arrested by them alone, but, passing them by, transfer your thought to God and say: 'O my God, if Thy creations are so full of beauty, delight and joy, how infinitely more full of beauty, delight and joy art Thou Thyself, Creator of all!'

If you keep to this practice, my beloved, then, through your five senses, you will be able to learn knowledge of God, by always raising your mind from creature to Creator. Then the being and structure of everything created will be for you a book of Theology, and while living in this sensory world, you will share in the knowledge belonging to the world beyond the world. For, indeed, the whole world and all nature is nothing but a certain organ, in which, beneath what is seen, there is invisibly present the Architect and Artist Himself, the Maker of all things, either acting and manifesting His art visibly, or revealing His invisible and immaterial actions and perfections in the visible and the material, discernible to the sight of intelligent creatures. Therefore the wise Solomon says on the one hand: 'By the greatness and beauty of the creatures proportionably the maker of them is seen' (Wisdom of Solomon xiii. 5) and on the other the blessed Paul testifies that: 'The invisible things of him from the creation of the world are clearly seen, being understood by the things that are made, even his eternal power and Godhead' (Rom. i. 20). In

77

the world of God all the creatures of God, wisely fashioned, are ranged on one side, while on the other are ranged men, endowed with the power of reason, to the end that with this power of reason they may contemplate the creatures and, seeing infinite wisdom in their creation and organisation, may rise to the knowledge and contemplation of the hypostatical Word, that is before time, the Word, by Whom 'all things were made' (John i. 3). Thus from actions we naturally see Him Who acts; so we have but to judge rightly and soundly, and finding faith in what He has created (ἐν τῇ κτίσει τὴν πίστιν) we shall see in the creation its Creator, God.

CHAPTER TWENTY-TWO

The same sensory objects we were speaking of can be means and instruments for a right control of our senses, if from them we pass to reflections on the incarnation of God the Word, and the mysteries of His life, passion and death

I have shown you above how from sensory things we can raise our mind to the contemplation of God. Now learn of another method of raising your mind from the sensory to the divine;—namely, through passing from the sensory to reflection on the incarnation of God the Word and on the holy mysteries of His life, passion and death. All the sensory objects of this world can serve as occasion for such reflection and contemplation, if, on looking at them, you traverse in your mind, as we described above, the thought that the Almighty God is the first cause of their existence and of everything in them—powers, perfections, functions, position among other creatures, and if you then think how great and measureless is the goodness of that same God when, being the sole cause of every created being, He desired to stoop to such humility and degradation as to become a man, to suffer and to die for men, allowing the very work of His own hands to rise in arms against Him and crucify Him.

Thus, whenever you see, or hear of, or touch weapons, ropes, lashes, pillars, branches of thorn, nails, hammers or other such things, think in your mind how all these have once served as instruments of torture of your Lord.

When you see poor homes, or live in such, bring to your memory the cave and the manger in which your Lord was born as man. When you see the rain fall, remember the drops of blood and sweat which fell from the divine body of the most sweet Jesus, sprinkling the earth of the garden of Gethsemane. When you see the sea and boats upon it, remember how your God walked on the waters and, standing in a boat, taught the people. When you see rocks, let them remind you of the rocks which were rent asunder at the moment of your Lord's death, and let the earth upon which you walk remind you of the earthquake, which followed upon Christ's passion.

The sun should bring to your mind the darkness which covered it then; water should remind you of the water, mixed with blood, which flowed from the divine side of the Lord, when the soldier pierced it after His death on the cross. When you drink wine or some other drink remind yourself of the vinegar and gall, which they gave to your Lord to drink on the cross.

When you dress, remember that the Immortal Word was clothed in human flesh, that you might be clothed in His Divinity. Seeing yourself clothed, think of Christ our Lord, Who let Himself be stripped, to be scourged and crucified for your sake. If a voice should seem to you sweet and attractive, transfer this feeling of fond attraction to your Saviour, into Whose lips were poured all grace and sweetness, as is sung in the psalms: 'Grace is poured into thy lips' (Ps. xlv. 2); through the sweetness of His tongue, the people were ever following Him, reluctant to cease listening to Him, as St. Luke says: 'All the people were very attentive to hear him' (Luke xix. 48). When you hear the murmur and shouts of a crowd, think of the lawless cry of the Jews: 'Away with him, away with him, crucify him' (John xix. 15), which then assailed the ears of the Lord. When you see a beautiful face, remember that He, Who was 'fairer than the children of men' (Ps. xlv. 2), our Lord Jesus Christ, was crucified out of love for you, 'despised and rejected of men; a man of sorrows, and acquainted with grief' (Is. liii. 3). Every time the clock strikes, let it bring to your mind the exceeding sorrow which filled the heart of our Lord Jesus, when in the garden of Gethsemane He was troubled at the approaching hour of His passion and death; or imagine that you hear the blows of hammers which resounded when our Lord was being nailed to the cross. In general, I would say that every time some sad occasion occurs in your life or another's, bear in mind that every affliction, pain and sorrow of ours is nothing compared with the painful torment and wounds inflicted on the body and soul of our Lord during His passion suffered for our salvation.

CHAPTER TWENTY-THREE

How to translate sensory impressions into profitable lessons

When you see things beautiful to the eye and valued on earth, think that they are all as nothing, as mere dust, compared with the beauties and riches of heaven, which you will certainly receive after death, if you renounce the whole world.

Looking at the sun, think that your soul is still more beautiful and radiant, if it is filled with the grace of its Creator; and if it is not, it is darker and more despicable than outer darkness.

Turning your eyes to the skies, raise the eyes of the soul to the highest heaven beyond and cleave to it with your thought, since it is the heavenly dwelling place prepared for you, if your life here on earth is sinless and holy.

When you hear the songs of birds in the trees in springtime, or other sweet singing, raise your mind to the sweetest songs of paradise and think how the heavens echo for ever with Halleluia and other angelic praises, and pray God to let you sing His praises for ever, in company with those heavenly spirits, of whom Revelation says: 'And after these things I heard a great voice of much people in heaven, saying, Alleluia; Salvation, and glory, and honour, and power, unto the Lord our God' (Rev. xix. 1).

If you feel attracted by someone's beauty, bring to your mind the thought that under this attractive exterior hides the serpent of hell, ready to slay you, or at least to wound you, and say to it: 'Accursed serpent! It is you who stand here like a thief, seeking to devour me! Vain effort, for God is my helper!' Then, turning to God, say: 'Blessed art Thou, my God, Who hath revealed to us our secret enemies and "hath not given us as a prey to their teeth" (Ps. cxxiv. 6).' Thereupon take refuge in the wounds of Him, Who was crucified for us, dedicating yourself to them and thinking how much our Lord suffered in His holy flesh, to free you from sin and instil in you a disgust of carnal lusts.

I remind you of one more weapon to repel the seduction of physical beauty, namely: when you fall into it, hasten to sink your mind deep into the thought of what this creature, so attractive to you now, will become after death? Stinking putrefaction filled with worms.

When you are walking somewhere, think at each step that every stride takes you nearer the grave. Seeing birds flying in the air, or rivers with swiftly flowing waters, reflect that your life flies still faster, hastening towards its end.

When strong winds blow, the sky is overcast with black clouds and you hear shattering thunderclaps and see blinding flashes of lightning, remember the terrible day of judgment and, falling on your knees, bow to your Lord and God and pray Him to grant you time and His grace to prepare yourself to stand then without shame before the face of His terrible majesty.

When various troubles assail you, do not forget to exercise your mind in edifying thoughts about them and connected with them, but above all do this: rise to the contemplation of the all-governing will of God and strive to establish in yourself the assurance that it is for your good and for the sake of your salvation, that the loving wisdom and just will of God has graciously ruled that you should suffer what you now suffer and in the measure that you suffer. So rejoice that God shows you His love in such cases, and provides an occasion to prove how willingly and wholeheartedly you submit to His will in everything He chooses to send you. Say from your heart: 'This is the will of God fulfilled in me, for in His love of me He has ordained before all time that I should suffer this affliction, or sorrow, or loss, or injustice. Blessed be the name of my most merciful Lord.'

When a good thought comes to your mind, turn to God and, realising that it was sent by Him, give thanks.

When you are occupied with reading the word of God, háve in mind that God is secretly present beneath every word, and take these words as issuing from His divine lips.

When while the sun reigns in the heavens, you see darkness

approach and veil its light, as happens in eclipses, grieve and pray to God not to let you fall into outer darkness.

Looking at the cross, remember that it is the emblem of our spiritual warfare and contains unconquerable power; that if you turn away from it, you will be delivered into the hands of our enemies, but that if you remain under it, you will reach heaven and enter it in triumph and glory.

When you see an icon of the Most Holy Mother of God, turn your heart to Her, the Queen of heaven, and give thanks that She showed such readiness to submit to the will of God, to give birth, suckle and bring up the Saviour of the world and to be an unfailing protector and helper in our unseen warfare.

Let the icons of saints bring to your mind how many inter-cessors you have always praying for you before God, and how many allies fighting for you in your unceasing battles. Having themselves courageously fought the enemies throughout their lives and overcome them, they have revealed and shown you the art of waging war. If, with their help, you are alert in fighting your battles, you will, like them, be crowned with victory in the eternal glory of heaven.

When you see a church, among other good thoughts remember also that your soul too is the temple of God, as it is written: 'Ye are the temple of the living God' (II Cor. vi. 16) and therefore you must keep it pure and immaculate.

Every time you hear church bells, bring to mind the greeting of the Archangel to the Mother of God, 'Hail, thou that art highly favoured' and dwell on the following thoughts and feelings: give thanks to God for sending from heaven to earth these good tidings, by which the work of your salvation began; rejoice with the Holy Virgin in the transubstantial greatness to which She was raised for Her deep humility; in company with Her and the Arch-angel Gabriel, adore the divine Fruit which was then forthwith conceived in Her most holy womb. You will do well to repeat this glorification often in the course of the day, accompanied by the feelings I have described; make it a strict rule to repeat it at least three times a day: in the morning, at midday and in the evening.

In brief I give you the following advice: be always awake and attentive in relation to your senses and never allow the im-pressions you get through them to excite and feed your passions. On the contrary, use your senses in such a way as not to deviate even a hair's breadth from your decision to please God always and in everything, or to be guided by His will. To achieve this, in addition to transferring your thoughts from the sensory to the spiritual, as we have indicated, it is very useful to practise the small rule mentioned in the first chapters—not to be spontaneously attracted by anything or spontaneously repelled by anything, but by strict and steadfast reasoning to determine, in each particular case, the attitude to be adopted to the impressions received through the senses, in order that it should conform to the will of God, which we know through His commandments.

I shall also add, that if I have described above methods of turning the use of the senses to spiritual benefit, it does not mean that you should constantly practise them. No, what you must practise constantly is to collect your mind in the heart and remain there with the Lord, thus having Him as a Teacher and Helper in your victory over enemies and passions, either through direct inner resistance, or through the practice of virtues opposed to them. What I described was said only with the intention that you should know these methods and make use of them when necessary. All the same, it is unquestionably very useful, in our warfare, to cover all sensory things with a spiritual veil.

CHAPTER TWENTY-FOUR

General lessons in the use of the senses

It remains for me now to indicate the general rules for the use of the outer senses, to prevent the impressions they transmit from breaking up our moral and spiritual order. So listen!

(a) Above all, my brother, keep a most firm hold on those quick and wicked robbers—*your eyes*—and do not allow curious looks at the faces of women, whether they are beautiful or not, or at those of men, especially the young and beardless. Neither let them look at naked bodies, not only those of others, but also your own. For such curiosity and lustful looking may easily give birth in the heart to passionate lust of adultery, which is not without guilt, as the Lord says: 'Whosoever looketh on a woman to lust after her hath committed adultery with her already in his heart'

83

(Matt. v. 28). And some wise man wrote: 'Looking gives birth to desire.' Solomon too warns us against being enticed by the eyes and wounded by lust for beauty: 'Lust not after her beauty in thine heart; neither let her take thee with her eyelids' (Prov. vi. 25). Here are examples of the evil results of licentious glances: sons of God, descendants of Seth and Enoch were attracted by the daughters of Cain (Gen. ch. vi): Shechem, the son of Hamor the Hivite, saw Dinah, the daughter of Jacob and fell with her; Samson was captivated by the beauty of Delilah (Judges ch. xvi); David fell from looking at Bath-sheba (II Sam. ch. xi); two elders, judges of the people, were intoxicated by the beauty of Susanna (Dan. ch. xiii).

Beware also of looking with too much attention at rich food and drink, remembering our ancestress Eve, who looked with evil eyes at the fruit of the forbidden tree in the garden of Eden, desired it, plucked and ate it and so subjected to death herself and all her descendants. Do not look covetously at beautiful garments, silver and gold and glittering worldly attire, lest the passion of vanity and love of money enter your soul through your eyes; as David prayed: 'Turn away mine eyes from beholding vanity' (Ps. cxix. 37). I will say, in general, beware of looking on dances, banquets, pageants, disputes, quarrels, idle chatter and all other unseemly and shameful things, beloved of the foolish world and forbidden by the law of God. Flee and close your eyes to all this, lest you fill your heart with passionate movements and your imagination with shameful images, and provoke in yourself an insurrection and battle against yourself, thus breaking the continuity of your progress in the struggle you must wage with your passions. But love to visit churches and look at the holy icons, sacred books, tombs, cemeteries and other such good and holy things, the sight of which can have a salutary effect on your soul.

(b) You must guard too your ears. First of all, do not listen to shameful and lustful speech, songs and music, which fill the soul with fancies, render it dissolute, and fan the flame of carnal lust in the heart.

Secondly, do not listen to noisy and laughter-provoking talk, empty and idle tales and inventions; and, if you happen to hear them, do not enjoy or assent to them. It is unseemly for Christians to find pleasure in such talks, which delight only those depraved people of whom St. Paul said: 'And they shall turn away their ears from the truth, and shall be turned unto fables' (II Tim. iv. 4).

Thirdly, do not take pleasure in listening to gossip or criticisms, or the calumnies, which some people spread about their brethren; but either stop them, if you can, or withdraw, so as not to hear them. For St. Basil the Great considers as equally deserving of excommunication defamers and slanderers and those who listen to them without trying to stop them.

Fourthly, do not listen to vain and empty talk, in which the majority of world-loving people spend their time, and do not take pleasure in it. For the law says: 'Thou shalt not raise false reports. (Ex. xxiii. 1). And Solomon says: 'Remove far from me vanity and lies' (Prov. xxx. 8). And the Lord said: 'But I say unto you, That every idle word that men shall speak, they shall give account thereof in the day of judgment' (Matt. xii. 36).

Fifthly, beware in general, of listening to any words and speeches which may harm your soul, not the least of which is flattery and the praise of flatterers, as Isaiah says: 'O my people, they which lead thee cause thee to err, and destroy the way of thy paths'* (Isaiah iii. 12). But love to hear divine words, sacred songs and psalms and all that is good, holy, wise and profitable to the soul. Especially love to hear reproaches and abuse, directed against yourself.

(c) Guard your sense of smell from luxurious perfumes, which may provoke carnal thoughts and impulses. Do not use them on yourself, do not anoint yourself with them and do not breathe them in voluptuously and beyond measure. All this is suitable for bad women, but not for men who love wisdom, for it weakens the virility of the soul and provokes carnal passions and lusts, which may lead to downfalls. So the warnings of the prophet are thus often fulfilled in the case of men, who use such stimulating perfumes: 'Woe to them . . . that anoint themselves with the chief ointments' (Amos vi. 1.6); and: 'It shall come to pass, that instead of sweet smell there shall be stink' (Isaiah iii. 24).

(d) Guard your palate and your belly, lest they are captivated by various sweet and fattening foods and inflaming aromatic drinks. For the effort to obtain all that you need for such pleasures of the table can lead you to lies, deceit, even theft and many other enslaving passions and evil deeds; and when you have acquired

* The Slavonic reads: 'they which indulge you, flatter you . . .'

the wherewithal for them and begin to enjoy them, they can cast you down into the moat of those carnal pleasures and bestial lusts, which are wont to act below the belly. Then you will fall under the strictures of the Prophet Amos: 'Woe to them that . . . eat the lambs out of the flock, and the calves out of the midst of the stall . . . that drink wine in bowls' (Amos vi. 4.6).

(e) Beware of gripping with your hands, squeezing and embracing a body, not only someone else's, whether a woman's or a man's, old as well as young, but also your own; especially, unless there is absolute necessity, do not touch certain parts. The more unlicensed is such touching, the more acute and lively are the carnal impulses of lust, and the more unrestrained their attraction of a man towards sinful action itself. And all the other senses back up the movement of lust and in some way influence indirectly the committing of sin; but when a man reaches the point of touching what should not be touched, then it is already exceedingly hard for him to draw back from sinful action.

To temptations of touch refer also head-dresses, garments and shoes. So beware of adorning your body with soft, multicoloured and brilliant clothes, your head with rich head-dresses and your feet with costly shoes. All this is effeminate and unsuitable for a man. But dress respectfully and humbly, satisfying the need to protect your body from cold in winter and heat in summer; lest you hear the words addressed to the rich man who was clothed in purple and fine linen: 'Remember that thou in thy lifetime receivedst thy good things' (Luke xvi. 25), and lest the threat of the Prophet Ezekiel refer to you: 'Then all the princes of the sea shall come down from their thrones, and lay away their robes, and put off their broidered garments' (Ezek. xxvi. 16).

To the same category belong all other comforts of the flesh, such as: frequent baths, too beautiful houses, soft carpets, costly furniture, soft beds and lounging on them. Beware of all this, since it is dangerous to your chastity and is the near cause of excitement of impure movements and impulses to carnal lusts and actions, lest you inherit the fate of those whom the Prophet Amos threatens: 'Woe to them . . . that lie upon beds of ivory, and stretch themselves upon their couches' (Amos vi. 1.4).

All I have just mentioned is the dust that the serpent—the tempter—was condemned to eat; and all this is food on which our carnal passions feed. So if you do not regard these things as unimportant and unworthy of attention, but if on the contrary, you arm yourself courageously against them and do not let them enter your soul and your heart through the senses, I assure you, you will easily exhaust the strength of the devil and of passions, since you will deprive them of the food on which they can thrive in you, and you will, in a short time, become a valiant victor in the unseen warfare.

It is written in the book of Job that 'the old lion* perisheth for lack of prey' (Job iv. 11). This lion represents the devil, our constant enemy, who runs away from a man who gives him no food since he has cut off and stifled all passionate movements, excited by the impressions of our outer senses. As a certain monk Jobius in the books of the patriarch Photius says, the devil resembles an ant-lion since he always begins a man's ruin by first casting him into small sins, just as an ant is small, and then, when the man becomes accustomed to such small sins, he casts him into greater. So equally the devil at first seems as weak and small as an ant, and later he appears like a powerful giant—a great lion.

CHAPTER TWENTY-FIVE

On control of the tongue

The greatest necessity of all is to control and curb our tongue. The mover of the tongue is the heart: what fills the heart is poured out through the tongue. And conversely, when feeling is poured out of the heart by the tongue, it becomes strengthened and firmly rooted in the heart. Therefore the tongue is one of the chief factors in building up our inner disposition.

Good feelings are silent. The feelings which seek expression in words are mostly egotistical, since they seek to express what flatters our self-love and can show us, as we imagine, in the best light. Loquacity mostly comes from a certain vainglory, which makes us think that we know a great deal and imagine our opinion on the subject of conversation to be the most satisfactory of all. So we experience an irresistible urge to speak out and in a stream of words, with many repetitions, to impress the same opinion in

* The Slavonic text reads: 'ant-lion'.

87

the hearts of others, thus foisting ourselves upon them as unbidden teachers and sometimes even dreaming of making pupils of men, who understand the subject much better than the teacher.

This refers, however, to cases when the subjects of conversation are more or less worthy of attention. But in most cases loquacity is a synonym of empty talk, and then there are no words to express the many evils, which arise from this ugly habit. In general, loquacity opens the doors of the soul, and the devout warmth of the heart at once escapes. Empty talk does the same, but even more so. Loquacity distracts one's attention out of oneself, leaving the heart unprotected. Then the usual passionate interests and desires begin to steal into it, at times with such success that at the end of such empty talk the heart has not only consented, but has decided to commit passionate deeds. Empty talk is the door to criticism and slander, the spreader of false rumours and opinions, the sower of discord and strife. It stifles the taste for mental work and practically always serves as a cover for the absence of sound knowledge. When wordy talk is over, and the fog of self-complacency lifts, it always leaves behind a sense of frustration and indolence. Is it not proof of the fact that, even involuntarily, the soul feels itself robbed?

Wishing to show how difficult it is for a loquacious man to refrain from saying something harmful, sinful and wrong, the Apostle James said that keeping the tongue within its rightful bounds is the property only of the perfect: 'If any man offend not in word, the same is a perfect man, and able also to bridle the whole body' (James iii. 2). As soon as the tongue begins to speak for its own pleasure, it runs on in speech like an unbridled horse, and blurts out not only the good and seemly, but also the bad and harmful. This is why the Apostle calls it 'an unruly evil, full of deadly poison' (James iii. 8). Long before him Solomon too said: 'In the multitude of words there wanteth not sin' (Prov. x. 19). In general, let us say, like Ecclesiastes, that a loquacious man shows his folly, for as a rule only 'a fool . . . is full of words' (Ecclesiastes x. 14).

Do not prolong your conversation with a man, who is not listening to you with a good heart, lest you weary him and make yourself abhorrent, as is written: 'He that useth many words shall be abhorred' (Ecclesiasticus xx. 8). Beware of speaking in a severe or superior manner; for both are highly disagreeable and make people suspect you of great vanity and a high opinion of yourself. Never speak about yourself, about your affairs or your relatives, except when it is necessary, and even then be brief and say as little as possible. When you see that others speak too much of themselves, force yourself not to imitate them, even if their words appear humble and self-reproachful. As regards your neighbour and his affairs, do not refuse to discuss them, but always be as brief as you can, even when you have to speak of such things for his good.

While conversing, remember and try to follow the precept of St. Thalassius who says: 'Of the five attitudes in conversation with others, use three with discrimination and without fear; use the fourth infrequently and refrain from using the fifth altogether' (Philokalia, the first century, 69). One writer understands the first three as follows: 'yes', 'no', 'of course' or 'this is clearly so'; by the fourth, he understands doubtful things and by the fifth, things totally unknown. In other words, about things you know for certain to be true or false, or self-evident, speak with conviction, saying that they are true, or false, or evident. About doubtful things better say nothing, but when necessary, say that they are doubtful and reserve your judgment. Of what you know nothing, say nothing. Someone else says: we have five forms or modes of speech: the vocative, when we invoke someone; the interrogative, when we ask a question; the desiring or soliciting form, when we express a desire or request; the defining, when we express a decisive opinion on something; the commanding, when masterfully and authoritatively we express a command. Of these five, use the first three freely; the fourth, as rarely as possible; the fifth, not at all.

Speak of God with all homage, especially of His love and goodness; at the same time be fearful lest you commit a sin by speaking wrongly, confusing the simple hearts of the listeners. Therefore, listen rather to others on this subject, collecting their words in the inner treasure-house of your heart.

When the conversation is of other things, let only the sound of the voice enter into your ear, but not the thought into your mind, which must remain unwaveringly directed towards God. Even when it is necessary to listen to the speaker, in order to understand what he speaks of and to give a suitable answer, do not forget, in the midst of listening and speaking, to raise the eye of your mind on high where your God is, thinking of His greatness and remembering that He never loses sight of you and looks at you either with approval or disapproval, according to what is in the thoughts of your heart, in your words, movements and actions.

When you have to speak, before expressing what has entered your heart and letting it pass to your tongue, examine it carefully; and you will find many things that are better not let past your lips. Know moreover that many things, which it seems to you good to express, are much better left buried in the tomb of silence. Sometimes you will yourself realise this, immediately the conversation is over.

Silence is a great power in our unseen warfare and a sure hope of gaining victory. Silence is much beloved of him, who does not rely on himself but trusts in God alone. It is the guardian of holy prayer and a miraculous helper in the practice of virtues; it is also a sign of spiritual wisdom. St. Isaac says: 'Guarding your tongue not only makes your mind rise to God, but also gives great hidden power to perform visible actions, done by the body. If silence is practised with knowledge, it also brings enlightenment in hidden doing' (ch. 31 in Russian edition). In another place he praises it thus: 'If you pile up on one side of the scales all the works demanded by ascetic life, and on the other side—silence, you will find that the latter outweighs the former. Many good counsels have been given us, but if a man embraces silence, to follow them will become superfluous' (ch. 41). In yet another place he calls silence 'the mystery of the life to come; whereas words are the instruments of this world' (ch. 42). St. Barsanuphius places it above preaching the word of God, saying: 'If you are just on the very point of preaching, know that silence is more worthy of wonder and glory.' Thus, although one man 'holdeth his tongue because he hath not to answer', another 'keepeth silence, knowing his time' (Ecclesiasticus xx. 6), yet another for some other reasons, 'for the sake of human glory, or out of zeal for this virtue of silence, or because he secretly communes with God in his heart and does not want the attention of his mind to be distracted from it' (St. Isaac, ch. 76). It can be said in general that a man, who keepeth silence, is found wise and of good sense (Ecclesiasticus xx. 5).

I shall indicate to you the most direct and simple method to acquire the habit of silence: undertake this practice, and the practice itself will teach you how to do it, and help you. To keep up your zeal in this work, reflect as often as you can on the pernicious results of indiscriminate babbling and on the salutary results of wise silence. When you come to taste the good fruit of silence, you will no longer need lessons about it.

CHAPTER TWENTY-SIX

How to correct imagination and memory

After speaking of control of the outer senses, we should now speak too of how to control imagination and memory; since, in the opinion of most philosophers, imagination and memory are nothing but imprints left by all the sensory objects we have seen, heard, smelt, tasted and touched. It can be said that imagination and memory are one general inner sense which visualises and remembers everything, that the five outer senses happened to experience before. In a certain way the outer senses and sensory objects resemble a stamp, and imagination the imprint of the stamp.

Imagination and memory are given to us to make use of when the outer senses are at rest and we have not before us the sensory objects, which have passed through our senses and become imprinted in them (in imagination and memory). Since we cannot always have before us the objects we have seen, heard, tasted, smelt and touched, we evoke them to our consciousness by means of imagination and memory, in which they have been imprinted, and in this way we examine and consider them, as though they were concretely before us.

For example: you have once paid a visit to Smyrna, then left it and so no longer see it with your physical eyes. Yet, whenever you wish it, you can visualise Smyrna by your inner sense, that is, imagination and memory, and can see it again as it is, in its actual aspect, dimensions and disposition. It does not mean that your soul leaves you and goes to Smyrna, as some ignoramuses think; it simply means that you see the image of Smyrna that has been imprinted in you.

This visualisation of sensory objects greatly bothers and disturbs people anxious always to remain with God; for it distracts

91

attention from God and carries it off to vain, and even to sinful objects, thus disturbing the good order of our inner state. We suffer this not only when awake, but also from dreams, the impression of which often lasts for several days.

Since imagination is a force devoid of reason and mostly acts mechanically, obeying the laws of association of images, whereas spiritual life is the image of pure freedom, it stands to reason that its activity is incompatible with this latter life. So I am forced to offer you certain guidance on this subject.

(a) Know that God is beyond all senses and sensory things, beyond all shape, colour, measure and place; is wholly without form and image and, while present in all things, is above all things; therefore He is beyond all imagining. 'No imagination can be admitted in relation to God, for He exceeds all mind' (Callistus and Ignatius ch. 65, quoting from St. Maximus). It follows, therefore, that imagination is a power of the soul such that, by its very nature, it has no capacity for entering the realm of union with God.

(b) Know also that Lucifer, first among the angels, was also of old above all foolish imagination and outside all form, colour or sense—an immaterial, unsubstantial, formless and bodiless mind. But he gave rein to his imagination and filled his mind with images of being equal to God, and so fell down from this formless, imageless, passionless and simple immateriality of mind into a multiform, complex and coarse imagination (as many theologians believe), and thus from a formless, immaterial and passionless angel became a devil, in a certain way material, multiform and subject to passion. As he became, so also did his servants—all the demons. St. Gregory of Sinai writes thus about them: 'At one time they too were minds, but having fallen away from immateriality and refinement, each one of them acquired a certain material coarseness, gaining flesh according to the level and nature of the deeds, whose practice qualified him. For since, just like man, they have lost the delights of angels (the angelic taste or the angelic heaven of delight) and have been deprived of divine bliss, so too, like ourselves, they began to find pleasure on earth, when they became material and acquired the habit of material passions' (ch. 123 Philokalia). For this reason the holy fathers call the devil a painter, a serpent with many forms, feeding on the dust of passions, a breeder of fantasies, and other such names. The word of God represents him as incarnated into a dragon, with a tail, ribs, neck, nose, eyes, jaws, lips, skin, flesh and other such members. Read of this in chapters xl and xli of the book of Job. Understand from this, beloved, that since multiform fantasy is an invention and creation of the devil, it is very welcome to him and useful in achieving our ruin. Holy fathers rightly call it a bridge, by which the murderous demons enter our soul, become mixed with it and make it a hive of drones, a dwelling place of horrible, evil and impious thoughts and of all kinds of impurities both of body and of soul.

(c) Know that according to St. Maximus, a great theologian, the first man, Adam, was also created by God without imagination. His mind, pure and free of images, functioned as mind and so itself acquired no form or image under the influence of the senses or from the images of sensory things. Making no use of this lower power of imagination, he did not visualise the outline, shape, dimensions, or colour of things, but with the higher power of the soul, that is thought, he contemplated purely, immaterially and spiritually only the pure ideas of things or their inner significance. But the devil, slayer of mankind, having himself fallen through his dreams of equality to God, instilled in Adam's mind that he too was equal to God and these fantasies led to Adam's fall. For this he was cast down from this immaterial, pure, intelligent and imageless life, akin to the angels, into this sensory complex, multiform life, immersed in images and fantasies—the state of animals devoid of reason. For to be immersed in images or to live in them and under their influence is the quality of reasonless animals, and not of beings possessing reason.

After man fell into this state, who can tell to what passions, what evil disposition and what errors he was led by his imaginative fantasies? He filled moral doctrines with various deceptions, physics with many wrong teachings, theology with unseemly and senseless dogmas and fables. Thinkers not only of old, but also most recently, wishing to speculate and discourse on God and the divine mysteries, which are simple and inaccessible to imagination and fantasy (since it must be the work of the highest part of the soul—the mind) have approached this work without first cleansing their mind from the passionate forms and illusory images of sensory things, and so have found lies instead of truth. And, what is specially grievous, their soul and heart have embraced these lies and they cling to them fast, as to truth which expresses reality. Thus, instead of theologians, they become fable-mongers having, according to the Apostle, given themselves over to a reprobate mind (Rom. i. 28). (Read of this in St. Isaac the Syrian at the end of his epistle to St. Simeon, ch. 55.)

So, my brother, if you wish easily and effectively to become free of such errors and passions, if you seek to escape the varied nets and wiles of the devil, if you long to unite with God and obtain divine light and truth, enter courageously into battle with your imagination and fight it with your whole strength, to strip your mind of all forms, colours and shapes, and in general of all images and memories of sensory things, whether good or bad. For all this is an obscuring and tarnishing of the light and purity of your mind, a coarsening of its immaterial state, rendering the mind passionate. For practically no passion, whether of soul or body, can approach the mind except through visualising corre-sponding sensory things. So try to preserve your mind colourless, imageless, formless and pure, as God created it.

But you can achieve this only by turning your mind back into itself, imprisoning it in the narrow place of your heart and of the whole inner man, and teaching it constantly to stay there within, either in hidden prayer, calling inwardly: 'Lord Jesus Christ, Son of God, have mercy upon me!' or keeping attention in your-self and examining yourself, but, above all, contemplating God and finding rest in Him. When a snake needs to cast off its old skin, it forces its way with difficulty through some narrow passage, as naturalists tell us; so too the mind, pushing its way through the narrow passage of the heart and of mental prayer of the heart, strips off the clothing of imagination of sensory things and of harmful sensory impressions and becomes pure, bright and apt for union with God, through its likeness to Him, which it thus acquires. Again: the narrower the defile through which water flows, the harder it presses forward and the more swiftly it rises. In the same way, the more the mind is compressed by hidden training in the heart and by attention in itself, the finer and strong-er it becomes and, rising on high, is thus more inaccessible to all passions, all suggestions of thoughts and all images of things, not only sensory but also mental, since all these things thus remain outside and cannot enter in. Here is another illustration, still more to the point. When sunrays are dispersed in the air, and

94

unconnected with one another, they are less bright and warm than when they are concentrated on one point by means of certain lenses; then they produce a blinding light and a burning heat; so too when the mind is collected in the centre of the heart by attention to itself and hidden training, it becomes light-bearing and scorching; it disperses the darkness of matter and passion and burns up and destroys all material and passionate images and movements.

This is the *first* and chief method of control over imagination and memory, which you, well beloved, must practise constantly. By this, not only will you rectify these powers of the soul, but will efface in them all traces and remains of formerly received impressions and images of sensory things, which excite and feed passions. But the more effective and fruitful, the more difficult this method is, and the more difficult, the fewer the people nowadays who wish to use it. I would even say, the fewer are the men, who believe in its power, especially among wise men and teachers, not only of the laity but also of the clergy; not wishing to believe the teaching of the Holy Spirit and of a great number of holy fathers, who indicate this method in the sacred book of the Philokalia, which is more precious than any jewel, they are justly deprived of the fruits of the Spirit, which some uneducated and even illiterate men attain. For, according to the word of the Saviour, God hath 'hid these things from the wise and prudent, and' hath 'revealed them unto babes' (Luke x. 21); since those, who do not believe in the power of this inner doing and do not undertake it, can in no wise understand how beneficent it is, as the prophet says: 'If ye will not believe, surely ye shall not be established' (Isaiah vii. 9).

When you notice that your mind is tiring and can no longer remain in the heart in this prayer of mind and heart, then use the *second* method, namely, let it go out and enjoy freedom in divine and spiritual reflections and contemplations, both those suggested by the Holy Scriptures and those which God's creation inspires. Such spiritual reflections are akin to the mind, since they are subtle and immaterial, and so do not coarsen it or imprison it in external things. On the contrary, satisfying within measure its thirst for unhampered movement in their domain, they dispose the mind by their tenor to return quickly into the heart and to unite with God through immersion in inner remembrance of Him alone. This is why St. Maximus says: 'Doing alone cannot make the mind passionless unless, in addition, it is devoted to various spiritual contemplations.' Yet beware of dwelling only on the physical side of God's creation, whether material objects or living beings, while you are still subject to passion. For, according to St. Maximus, in this case the mind is not yet free from looking with passion on sensory objects, and so, instead of passing from them to spiritual and immaterial thoughts concealed in them, it will be attracted solely by their external beauty and aspect and, in enjoying this, can derive false lessons from them and passionate attachments to them—a danger to which very many natural philosophers have succumbed.

Or else use the *third* method to give relaxation and rest to your mind, namely, reflect on the mysteries of the life and passion of the Lord, that is, His birth in a cave, circumcision, His presentation to God in the temple, His baptism in Jordan, the forty days of His fast in the wilderness, His preaching of the Gospels, His manifold miracles, His transfiguration on Mount Tabor, His washing of the disciples' feet and His giving them the Mysteries at the Last Supper, His betrayal, passion, crucifixion and burial, His resurrection and ascension to heaven, the manifold torments of the martyrs and the strict feats of asceticism practised for long years by the holy fathers.

In like manner, to render your heart contrite and incite feelings of repentance, you can think also of the terrible hour of death, the terrifying day of judgment, the various forms of eternal torment—oceans of eternal fire, dark dungeons of hell, the gloom of Tartarus, unsleeping worms, life with the demons. Think also of the peace and unspeakable joys of the just, of the kingdom of heaven, eternal glory and unceasing bliss, of the voice of those who feast, of perfect union with God, of everlasting companionship and communion with the angels and all the saints.

If, my brother, you draw such thoughts and images on the parchment of your imagination, you will not only free yourself of wrong memories and evil thoughts, but will gain great commendation on the day of judgment for your endeavours, as St. Basil the Great foreshadows in his chapter on virginity, saying: 'Every man, while in the flesh, is like a painter who paints an image in a secret place. When, having finished his picture, the painter brings it out and exhibits it, he is praised by the spectators if he has chosen a good subject and painted it well, and is criticised if the subject chosen is bad or badly painted. In the same way each man, when he comes up for judgment by God after death, will be praised and cherished by God, the angels and the saints, if he has adorned his mind and imagination with luminous, divine and spiritual images and representations, but, on the contrary, will be condemned and put to shame if he has filled his imagination with passionate, shameful and base pictures. St. Gregory of Salonika expresses his wonder at the way in which the effect of sensory things affecting the soul through imagination either brings mental light, leading to life of eternal bliss, or mental darkness, leading to hell (Greek Philokalia 969).

Know, however, that I do not mean by this that you should be always occupied with such thoughts alone. I only mean that you should use them sometimes, until your mind, tired of being imprisoned in the heart, is rested. When it is rested, return it again into the heart and force it to remain there without fantasies or images in a heart-felt remembrance of God. For, as all shell-molluscs and crustaceans find rest nowhere except in their shells, in which they find shelter as in a house, so the mind can naturally find peace nowhere but in the chamber of the heart and in the inner man, where he shelters as in a fortress, and thus successfully wages war with thoughts, enemies and passions, also hidden there, within him, although most people do not know it.

That passions and thoughts are hidden within us, in the heart, and come out thence to fight us, is not my own thought. Listen to what the Lord says: 'For out of the heart proceed evil thoughts, murders, adulteries, fornications, thefts, false witness, blasphemies: these are the things which defile a man' (Matt. xv. 19, 20). And the fact that our enemies, the demons, hide themselves near the heart is not my invention. Thus teach the holy fathers. St. Diadoch is the most definite among them, when he says that before holy baptism Divine grace moves a man towards good from without, while Satan is hidden in the depths of the heart and soul. But after a man has been baptised, the demon hovers outside the heart, while grace enters within (Philokalia 4. 76). However, as he says further (82), even after baptism our enemies are permitted to penetrate into the depths of our bodies and to reach as it were the surface of our heart, as a test to our will. From there they befoul the mind with the humours of carnal

97

lusts. St. Gregory the Theologian teaches the same, explaining what the Lord said of the unclean spirit who goes out of a man, and then returns again, rendering that man's last state worse than the first (Matt. xii. 43–45); St. Gregory points out that the same happens with baptised men if they take no care to remain in their heart. 'The unclean spirit', he says, 'banished by baptism, and not caring to be homeless, seeks rest, walking here and there; finding no home, he returns to the house from whence he came out, for he is shameless. If he finds that Christ is held by the attention and the love of the baptised man, and is established and dwelling in the place from whence he had been cast out, that is in the heart, he fails to enter and again turns away. But if he finds his former place empty, occupied by no one, through absence of attention towards God and memory of Him, he enters hastily, with greater malice than before. And the last state of that man is worse than the first' (40). I have purposely spoken at length about this to urge you the more strongly to remain ceaselessly in your heart with the memory of our Lord and Saviour and with prayer to Him, if you wish always to be victorious in troubles caused by thoughts and passionate movements, which assail the heart. When you are there with the Lord the enemy will not dare to come near.

But over and above it all I say to you, keep vigil over yourself and do not let your imagination and memory remember things previously seen, heard, smelt, tasted and touched, especially if there was something shameful and unseemly in them. It is this that pre-eminently constitutes our battle, and is more difficult and persistent than struggling with the senses or their use. Every one who fights knows this from experience. Not to accept some temptation through one sense or another is easily managed; but it is very difficult to control the imagination and memory of it, once it is accepted. For example, to see or not to see some face, or to look at it with passion or without passion, is not very difficult and does not need much effort; but after you have seen it and looked at it with passion, to banish from your memory the image of this face is already not easy, but demands much effort and no small inner struggle. And the enemy can play with your soul as with a ball, tossing your attention from one memory to another, stirring up desires and passions beneath them, and so keeping you always in a passionate state. Therefore I say to you: stay awake and, above all, watch imagination and memory.

CHAPTER TWENTY-SEVEN

*A warrior of Christ should use all means to avoid
worries and agitations of the heart, if he
wishes really to overcome his enemies*

Just as it is a pressing duty of every Christian when he loses his
peace of heart to do all he can to restore it, so is it no less obligatory for him to allow no accidental happenings of life to disturb
this peace; I mean illness, wounds, death of relatives, wars, fires,
sudden joys, fears and sorrows, memories of former sins and errors,
in a word everything which usually troubles and agitates the
heart. It is indispensable in such cases not to allow oneself to feel
worry and agitation, for, having succumbed to them, a man loses
self-possession and the capacity to understand events clearly and
see the right way to act, each of which gives the enemy the possibility to agitate a man still more and push him to take some step,
that is difficult or quite impossible to remedy.

I do not mean to say you must not admit sorrow, for this is not
in our power. What I mean is—do not let sorrow take possession
of your heart and agitate it; keep it outside the bounds of your
heart and hasten to soften and restrain it, so that it may not prevent you from reasoning soundly and acting rightly. With God's
help this is in our power, if religious and moral feelings and
dispositions are strong in us.

Each affliction has its own peculiarities and each requires its
own remedies; but I speak now about them in general, having in
view their common quality—to trouble and agitate the soul, and
having in mind a general remedy against them. This remedy is
faith in the good Providence, which arranges the course of our life
with all its accidental happenings, for the good of each of us, and
a serene compliance with God's will, expressed in our attitude, in
accordance with which we call from the bottom of our heart: Let
God's will be done! As the Lord wills, so let it be, and be for our
good.

This good is realised and felt differently by different people.
One realises: this goodness of God's leads me to repentance;
another feels: it is because of my sins that the Lord has sent me

this trial, to purify me of them; I am bearing God's penance; a *third* thinks: the Lord is testing me, whether I serve Him sincerely. Those who look from outside at a man subjected to afflictions may think the *fourth*: this is sent him, that the works of God may be revealed in him. But such a verdict can be in place only when affliction is ended, and when God's help is evident in the soul of the afflicted man. Only the first three feelings should have place. No matter which of them enters the heart, each has the virtue and strength to still the rising storm of sorrow and establish peace and good cheer in the heart.

And here is a general means for making peace in the heart, when some affliction tries to disturb it: with all your strength make firm your faith in the goodness of God's Providence towards you and revive in your soul a devoted submission to God's will; then introduce into the heart the reflections mentioned above and urge it to feel that the affliction you suffer at this moment is either a means by which the Lord puts you to the test, or a purifying penance He imposes on you, or that He thus presses you to repent, either in general, or particularly in connection with some wrong action of yours, which has remained forgotten. As soon as the heart begins to have one such feeling, the pain immediately abates and these two other feelings also can come in. All these together will very quickly establish such peace and good cheer in you that you cannot but cry out: 'Blessed be the name of the Lord for ever!' These feelings in the troubled heart are as oil on the waves of the sea: the waves are stilled and there is a great calm.

Thus bring peace to the heart, in whatever degree it be troubled. But if by long effort on yourself and by many spiritual endeavours you implant these feelings in your heart, so that it is always filled with them, then no affliction will ever trouble you, for this disposition will most effectively prevent them. I do not mean that feelings of sorrow will never assail you: they will come, but will at once retreat, as waves from a mighty cliff.

CHAPTER TWENTY-EIGHT

What to do when we are wounded in battle

If you happen to be wounded by succumbing to some sin through weakness, or through the faulty nature of your character (I mean here pardonable sins: an unfitting word has slipped out, you lost your temper, a bad thought flashed in your head, an unfitting desire flared up, and so on), do not lose heart and fall into senseless turmoil. Above all do not dwell on yourself, do not say: 'How could I be such as to allow and suffer it?' This is a cry of proud self-opinion. Humble yourself and, raising your eyes to the Lord, say and feel: 'What else could be expected of me, O Lord, weak and faulty as I am.' Thereupon give thanks to Him that the thing has gone no further, saying: 'If it were not for Thy boundless mercy, O Lord, I would not have stopped at that, but would certainly have fallen into something much worse.'

With this feeling and consciousness of yourself you must not, however, admit the self-indulgent and heedless thought that since you are what you are, you have as it were a right to behave wrongly. No, in spite of the fact that you are weak and faulty, you are accounted guilty for all the wrong things you do. For since you possess a will, all that comes forth from you is subject to it, and so everything good is counted in your favour and everything bad—to your detriment. Therefore, conscious of your general wickedness, admit yourself guilty also in the particular wickedness, into which you have fallen at the present moment. Judge and condemn yourself, and only yourself; do not look around, seeking on whom you could put the blame. Neither the people around you nor the circumstances are guilty of your sin. Your bad will alone is to blame. So blame yourself.

Yet do not imitate those who say: 'Yes, I have done it; but what of that?' No, having recognised your fault and reproached yourself, make yourself face the inescapable justice of God and hasten to warm up your feelings of repentance, that is, contrition and remorse, not because of your own degradation through sin, but because by your sin you have offended God, Who has shown you yourself so much mercy in calling you to repentance, in remitting your old sins, in letting you participate in the grace of the

101

Mysteries, in guiding and protecting your progress on the right path.

The deeper the contrition, the better. But however deep the contrition, never admit a shadow of doubt about forgiveness. Forgiveness is already fully prepared and the record of all sins has been torn up on the Cross. Repentance and contrition alone are expected of every man, before he too can participate in the power of the redemption of the sins of the world through the Crucifixion. Trusting in this, prostrate yourself in body and soul and cry: 'Have mercy upon me, O God, according to Thy loving-kindness' (Ps. li. 1) and do not cease to cry thus, until you feel yourself together guilty and forgiven, so that guilt and forgive-ness merge into one feeling.

This grace descends finally on every penitent. But it must be accompanied by a decision, sealed by a vow, not to indulge one-self in the future, but strictly to guard and protect oneself from all downfalls, whether large or small, together with a diligent prayer for the help of grace in this undertaking. After such recent experience of the unreliability of one's own powers and efforts, the heart will naturally appeal to God of its own accord: 'Create in me a clean heart, O God; and renew a right spirit within me . . . Restore unto me the joy of thy salvation; and uphold me with thy free spirit' (Ps. li. 10. 12).

All this—self-condemnation, contrition, hopeful prayer for forgiveness, the inspiring decision to watch oneself in the future, prayer for help and for the gift of grace in this endeavour, all this you must practise inwardly every time you commit sin with eyes, ears, tongue, thought or feeling. Not for a single moment must sin remain in the heart unconfessed to the Lord and un-cleansed by heartfelt repentance before Him. Again you fall, again and again do the same, and however often you sin, cleanse yourself each time before the Lord. If possible, tell all in the even-ing to your spiritual father, and if impossible on the same evening, tell him when a chance comes. Such a confession of everything to one's spiritual father is most beneficial in the work of our spiritual warfare.

Nothing routs the murderous enemy and defeats his wiles more effectively than this method of action. This is why the enemy strives to prevent it by all possible means, both inwardly and out-wardly:—inwardly by thoughts and feelings, and outwardly by contriving various meetings and incidents. What these obstacles are you will see for yourself when you undertake this work. I shall mention only one thing: the enemy strives hard to suggest that you should not start on the work of inner purification immediately the sin is noticed, but should wait just a little—not a day, not an hour, but just a little while. But as soon as you agree to this, he brings along another sin:—after a sin with the tongue—a sin with the eye, and again with some other sense; and so you willy-nilly postpone the purification of this second sin, since it is first necessary to purify yourself of the first. And in this way, putting it off continues for a whole day and sin after sin fills the soul. By evening—a time to which purification by repentance is usually relegated, nothing is clearly seen in the soul, for it is filled with the noise, tumult and darkness of the many trespasses which were condoned. The soul then resembles eyes filled with dust or water much muddied with muck which has fallen into it. Since nothing can be seen, the work of repentance is abandoned altogether, and the soul is left muddy and befouled. This makes the evening prayer imperfect and leads to bad dreams. Thus never delay inner purification for a single moment, as soon as you are conscious of something wrong in you.

Another usual suggestion of the devil is not to tell your spiritual father what has happened. Do not listen to it and oppose it by disclosing everything to him. For just as this confession does good, so, and even more so, does harm come of concealing what takes place in us and with us.

CHAPTER TWENTY-NINE

The order of battle pursued by the devil in spiritual warfare against us all and how he seduces people of different inner states

Know, my beloved, that the devil cares only for compassing the ruin of everyone of us, but that he does not use one and the same method of warfare against us all. To help you to see and understand this more clearly, I shall describe to you five inner states of people and the corresponding wiles, and circuitous approaches and enticements of the enemy. These states are the following: some people remain in the slavery of sin, with no thought of liberation; others, although thinking of this liberation and desiring it, do nothing to achieve it; there are also people who, having been freed from the shackles of sin and having acquired virtues, again fall into sin with still greater moral corruption. In their self-delusion some of these latter think that, in spite of it all, they are still advancing towards perfection; others heedlessly abandon the path of virtue; yet others turn the very virtue they possess into a cause and occasion of harm for themselves.

The enemy influences each of them in accordance with their state and disposition.

CHAPTER THIRTY

How does the devil confirm sinners in their slavery to sin?

When the devil keeps a man in slavery to sin, he takes special care to darken him more and more by spiritual blindness, banishing from him every good thought, which could bring him to realise the perniciousness of his life. Not only does he banish thoughts, which could lead to repentance and turn the man to the path of virtue, but instead of them he implants evil and depraved thoughts, at the same time presenting opportunities for committing the sin, which is most habitual to him, and enticing him to fall into it or into other more grievous sins as often as possible. Thus the poor sinner becomes more and more blind and darkened. This blindness strengthens in him the habit and constant impulse to go on ever sinning and sinning. Led from sinful action to greater blindness, and from blindness to greater sins, the unhappy man whirls in this vortex and will do so right up to death itself, unless special Divine grace is sent to save him.

If a man finds himself in this perilous state and wishes to be freed from it, then, as soon as a good thought, or rather, a suggestion comes to him, calling him from darkness to light and from sin to virtue, he should immediately and without delay accept it with his whole attention and desire, and put it at once into practice with all diligence, calling from the bottom of his heart to the generous Giver of all blessings: 'Help me, O Lord God, help me quickly, and let me no more linger in this sinful darkness.' Let him never weary in appealing to God in these or similar words. At the same time let him also seek help on earth, by turning to those who know for advice and guidance as to how better to free himself from the bonds of sinful slavery that hold him. If he cannot do it immediately, he should do so as soon as the chance presents itself, at the same time never ceasing to appeal to Lord Jesus, crucified for us, and to His Holy Mother, the Immaculate Virgin, imploring them to have mercy on him and not to deprive him of their speedy help. He should know that victory and triumph over the enemy lie in not delaying and in quick readiness to follow a right prompting.

CHAPTER THIRTY-ONE

How the enemy keeps in his nets those who have realised
their perilous position and wish to be free of it,
but make no move.   And the reason why our
good intentions are so often not fulfilled

Those, who have realised how dangerous and evil is the life they lead, the devil succeeds in keeping in his power, mainly by the following simple but all-powerful suggestion: 'Later, later; to-morrow, to-morrow.' And the poor sinner, deluded by the appearance of good intention accompanying this suggestion, decides: 'Indeed, to-morrow; to-day I shall finish what I have to do, and then, free of all care, will put myself in the hands of Divine grace and will follow unswervingly the path of spiritual life. To-day I shall do this and that; to-morrow I shall repent.' This is the net of the devil, my brother, with which he catches a great many, and holds the whole world in his hands. The reason why this net catches us so easily is our negligence and blindness. Nothing but negligence and blindness can explain why, when the whole of our salvation and all the glory of God are at stake, we fail to use immediately the most easy and simple and yet the most effective weapon, namely: to say to ourselves, resolutely and energetically: 'This moment! I shall start spiritual life this moment, and not later; I shall repent now, instead of to-morrow. *Now, this moment* is in my hands, *to-morrow* and *after* is in the hands of God. Even if God will grant me *to-morrow* and *after*, can I be sure that I shall have to-morrow the same good thought urging me to mend my ways?' Moreover, how senseless it is when, for example, a sure remedy is offered for curing one's illness, to say: 'Wait, let me be sick a little longer!' And a man who delays the work of salvation does exactly this.

So, if you wish to be free of the prelest of the enemy and to over come him, take up at once this trusty weapon against him and obey immediately in actual deed the good thoughts and prompt-ings coming from the Lord and calling you to repent. Do not allow the slightest delay, do not permit yourself to say: 'I have made a firm resolve to repent a little later and I shall not abandon this intention.' No, no, do not do this. Such resolutions have always proved deceptive and many many people, who relied on them, have for many reasons remained unrepentant to the end of their lives.

(*a*) The first of these reasons is that our own resolutions are not based on distrust of ourselves and a firm trust in God. Therefore we are not devoid of high opinion of ourselves, the inevitable consequence of which is always withdrawal from us of the blessed Divine help and our consequent inevitable downfall. This is why a man, who decides in himself: 'To-morrow I shall abandon the path of sin without fail', always meets with the opposite effect—that is, instead of rising up he falls down worse than before, which is followed by downfall after downfall. God sometimes allows this to happen deliberately, in order to bring the self-reliant to the realisation of his weakness and urge him to seek Divine help, renouncing and abandoning all trust in himself, since God's help alone can be trusted. Do you want to know, O man, when your own decisions will be firm and reliable? When you abandon all trust in yourself and when all your hopes are based on humility and a steadfast trust in God alone.

(*b*) The second reason is that in making such resolutions we mostly have in view the beauty and radiance of virtue, which attract our will, however weak and impotent it may be; and so naturally the difficult side of virtue escapes our attention. To-day this side escapes notice, because the beauty of virtue strongly attracts our will; but to-morrow, when the usual works and cares present themselves, this attraction will not be so strong, although the intention is still remembered. When desire weakens, the will also becomes weaker or relapses into its natural impotence, and at the same time the difficult side of virtue stands out and strikes the eye; for the path of virtue is by its nature hard, and is hardest of all at the first step. Now let us suppose that the man, who decided yesterday to enter upon this path, to-day does so: he no longer feels any support for carrying out his decision. The desire has lost its intensity, the will has weakened, nothing but obstacles are in sight—in himself, in the habitual course of his life, in the usual relationships with others. And so he decides: 'I shall wait a while and gather my strength.' Thus he goes on waiting from day to day, and it is no wonder if he waits all his life. And yet had he started work yesterday, when the inspiring desire to mend his ways came upon him, had he done one thing or another in obedience to this desire, had he introduced into his life something in this spirit—to-day his desire and will would not be so weak as to retreat in the face of obstacles. There must be obstacles, but if the man had something to lean on in himself, he would have overcome them, be it with difficulty. Had he been occupied all day with overcoming them, the next day he would have felt them far less; and on the third day still less. Thus going further and further he would have become established on the right path.

(c) The third reason is that if the good of awakening from sinful sleep is not translated into practice, such awakenings do not easily come again; and even if they do come, their effect on the will is less strong than the first time. The will is no longer as quick in inclining towards following them and so, even if the resolve to do so is there, it is weak and lacks energy. Consequently, if a man was able to put off till to-morrow obedience to a stronger impulse and then lost it altogether, how much more easily will he do this a second time, and still more easily the third. And so it goes on: the more often obedience to good impulses is put off, the weaker their effect. After a time they lose their effect altogether, come and go without leaving a trace, and finally cease to come at all. The man surrenders himself to his downfall: his heart hardens and he

107

begins to feel an aversion from good impulses. Thus delay becomes a straight road to final perdition.

I shall add also that delays occur not only when an inner impulse is felt to exchange one's bad life for a better, but also when a man already leads a good life. For instance, when an opportunity presents itself to do good and a man puts it off till to-morrow or till some other indefinite time. All that was said about the first form of delay applies to this second one, and it may lead to the same consequences. Know that if someone misses a chance to do good, he not only deprives himself of the fruit of the good he might have done, but also offends God. God sends him a man in need, and he says: 'Go away, later!' Although he says this to a man, it is the same as saying it to God, Who has sent him. God will find him another benefactor; but the man who refused will have to answer.

CHAPTER THIRTY-TWO

On the wiles of the enemy against those who have entered the right path

But suppose a man has overcome the first two obstacles, is filled with desire to be free of the bondage of sin and has begun to work for it without delay. Even here the enemy does not leave him alone. He changes only his tactics, but not his evil desire and hope to make the man stumble against some stone of temptation and so ruin him. The holy fathers describe such a man as being under fire from all sides:—from above and below, from left and right, from front and rear, from everywhere arrows speed towards him. Arrows from above are suggestions for excessive spiritual works, above his powers; arrows from below are suggestions to reduce or even completely abandon such works through self-pity, negligence and heedlessness; arrows from the right are when, in connection with some right undertakings and works, the enemies lead a man into temptation and the danger of downfall; arrows from the left are when the enemies present concrete temptations and draw a man towards sin; arrows from the front are when the enemies tempt and disturb a man by thoughts of what is to come; arrows from the rear are when they tempt him with memories of past

108

deeds and events. And all these tempting thoughts attack the soul, either inwardly or outwardly: inwardly, through images and pictures of fantasy, mentally imprinted in the consciousness, or through direct evil suggestions planted in the heart, accompanied by habitual impulses of passion; outwardly—through the impressions received by the external senses in a ceaseless flow, as we have said already. Moreover our enemies have allies in our former sinful habits and our nature corrupted by the fall of man. Having so many means to harm us, the enemy is never daunted by the first failures and constantly puts into use now one, now another means of tripping or leading astray the servant of Christ, who eludes his power.

After a man has decided to abandon his wrong ways and actually does abandon them, the first task of the enemy is to clear a space for an unhampered field of action against him. He succeeds in this by suggesting to a man, who has entered the right path, that he should act on his own, and not go for advice and guidance to the teachers of righteous life, who are always attached to the Church. A man who follows their guidance and verifies all his actions, both inner and outer, by the good judgment of his teachers—priests in their parishes in the case of laymen, experienced startzi* in monasteries— cannot be approached by the enemy. Whatever he may suggest, the experienced eye will at once see where he is driving and will warn his pupil. In this way all his wiles are defeated. But if a man turns away from his teachers, the enemy will at once confuse him and lead him astray. There are many possibilities, which do not look evil; and those he suggests. The inexperienced novice follows them and falls into an ambush, where he is exposed to great dangers or is destroyed altogether.

The second method of the enemy is to leave a novice not only without guidance, but also without help. A man who has decided to dispense with advice and guidance in his life, when left to himself soon comes to the idea that extraneous help is unnecessary in the conduct of his righteous life and actions. But the enemy hastens his coming to this idea by concealing himself and refraining from attacking the novice, who, feeling thus free and unhampered, begins to imagine that this good state is the fruit of his own efforts, and so rests on them, and, while reciting his

* 'Staretz' is literally 'elder'; in these texts it sometimes means head of a monastic community, sometimes 'spiritual teacher'. [Translators' Note.]

prayers about help from above, mutters them through his teeth, merely as a meaningless formula. Help is not sought and does not come; so the novice is left to his own devices and powers. And such a man is an easy prey to the enemy.

The results of this self-delusion are, in some cases, that people undertake excessive tasks which are both untimely and beyond their powers. The strong excitation of energy produced by self-reliance gives them at first the strength to sustain such works for a while. But after a time their strength becomes exhausted and they barely find enough energy to make the most moderate efforts, and often abandon them altogether. Others, firing their self-willed energy more and more, reach such a degree of self-reliance that they end by imagining that everything is possible for them. In this excited state they take disastrous steps: throw themselves into dry wells, jump down from the high rocks where their cave is, stop taking food altogether, and so on. All this is arranged by the enemy, unperceived by the tempted.

Another result of self-delusion and of ascribing one's successes to oneself is to assume the right to give oneself special dispensations and indulgences. There is a form of prelest which, when something new is introduced into life, as for instance in the case of a man who has repented, makes days seem like months, and weeks like years. Thus if a man has made a few efforts in the new order of life, the enemy easily hammers into his head the illusion: 'I have worked so hard, have fasted so long, spent so many nights without sleep and so on. It is time to have a rest.' 'Rest a while,' suggests the enemy, 'give respite to the flesh; a little distraction is indicated.' As soon as the inexperienced novice consents to this, indulgence follows indulgence, until the whole order of his righteous life is upset, and he drops back into the life he has abandoned and begins to live again in negligence and heedlessness, and never rolls up his sleeves.

These temptations—to avoid the advice and guidance of others, to ascribe successes to oneself, to undertake excessive works or to give oneself dispensations—are used by the devil not only at the beginning of righteous life; he attempts to use these suggestions during its whole course. So you can see for yourself how important it is for you to do everything with advice, never to ascribe any successes, however small, to yourself, to your own powers and your own zeal, to avoid all excesses and indulgences and to lead a life which, though even, is energetic and alive, always following the order and rule once established by the example of the saints, who lived before you, and by the good judgment of experienced men, who are your contemporaries.

CHAPTER THIRTY-THREE

How the enemy diverts a man from righteous deeds and spoils them

The wiles of the enemy, indicated above, disorganise the whole righteous life of a man. If a man resists them and follows the right path unswervingly, the enemy devises other wiles and other stumbling blocks. In this case, he does not work against the man's life as a whole, but acts sporadically against every particular undertaking a good Christian sets out to do in accordance with God's will.

From the moment we open our eyes in the morning after sleep to the moment we close them again for the night we are surrounded by a succession of activities, which follow one another and leave no moment empty, provided always we keep attention in ourselves and are not sick with laziness and negligence. Moreover not only the practice of lifting the heart to God in prayer, not only the obligations of dealings with others in truth and love, not only the efforts to achieve a right equilibrium between body and soul in works and self-mortification, but even everyday affairs with laymen must all be directed towards achieving salvation, and practised with strict attention, watchfulness and diligence. God helps those, who show their zeal to do all things rightly, by sending them His grace and by granting them the protection of angels and the prayers of saints. But the enemy never sleeps. In everything we do he strives to disrupt the smooth course of our efforts and to lead us astray from right to wrong actions. He either hastens to stop us undertaking them, or, when they are begun, attempts to interfere with their progress; if he has failed in this, he strives to make their results worthless; or, having once more suffered defeat, plots to deprive them of all value in the eyes of God, by inciting vanity and conceit.

111

St. John of the Ladder speaks thus about it: 'In all the efforts by which we try to please God, the demons dig three pits for us—first, they try to obstruct our good undertaking; second, if they have suffered defeat in this first attempt, they try to make our work not according to God; when these thieves are unsuccessful in this scheme too, then they steal noiselessly to the soul and flatter us by suggesting that we please God in everything we do. The first temptation is opposed by fervent zeal and memory of death; the second—by obedience and belittling oneself; the third—by always reproaching oneself. "It was too painful for me; until I went into the sanctuary of God" (Ps. lxxiii. 16. 17). When Divine fire enters our sanctuary, evil habits no longer have power over us for "our God is a consuming fire" (Heb. xii. 29), consuming every uprising and movement of lust, every evil habit, and all hardness and darkness, whether inner or outer, seen or thought' (ch. 26. 8).

No pen can describe all that this means. Keep attention in yourself and keep only one standard in your mind—to please God in everything, both great and small. Then life itself will teach you to discern clearly and see through the wiles of the enemy. However, I shall give you two or three examples of the confusion, which the enemy brings to our soul to spoil our work, if this work must last a certain time.

For example, if a sick man is disposed to bear his illness with a good heart and does so, the enemy, knowing that he will thus become well grounded in the virtue of patience, attempts to disrupt this good disposition. For this purpose, he begins to remind him of the many good deeds he could have performed had his position been different, and tries to convince him that, had he been in good health, he would have achieved much in the service of God, bringing much profit to himself and others. He would have been able to go to church, to talk to people, to read and to write for the instruction of his brethren, and so on. If he notices that such thoughts are accepted, the enemy introduces them into the man's mind more and more often, multiplies and embellishes them, makes them enter the feelings and incites desires and impulses to such actions by depicting how successful these or other works would have been, and by evoking regret that the man is tied hand and foot by his illness. Little by little, after frequent repetition of such thoughts and inner movements in the soul, regret is gradually transformed into discontent and vexation. Thus the former good-hearted patience is upset and, instead of a medicine sent by God and a field for practising the virtue of patience, the illness presents itself as something hostile to the work of salvation. Thus the desire to be free of it becomes ungovernable, though still with a view to freedom to perform good deeds and to please God in every way. Having led a man thus far, the enemy robs his heart and mind of the good purpose, for which he desires to get well, and leaves only the desire of health for the sake of health, forcing him to look irritably at his illness, not as an obstacle to good but as an evil in itself. As a result impatience, not tempered by good thoughts, takes the upper hand and passes to complainings, thus depriving the sick man of the peace he enjoyed through good-hearted patience. But the enemy rejoices that he has managed to upset him. In exactly the same way, the enemy upsets a poor man who bears his lot with patience, depicting to him the good deeds he could do if he had a fortune.

In a similar way, the enemy often upsets those who practise obedience, either in a monastery or living with some staretz, convincing them that while they continue to lead this kind of life, they will be slow in attaining the desired perfection, and exciting in them a wish to go into seclusion, or the wilderness. And his suggestions are often obeyed, but, having obtained their wish to live in solitude, men give themselves to negligence and so lose what they had acquired with great labour in their former life of obedience.

The reverse also happens, when the enemy succeeds in driving a man away from solitude and seclusion, convincing him that he sits there alone with no profit to himself or others, whereas in a monastery useful works would flow day and night in an abundant stream. But when a man listens to this suggestion and enters a monastery, he does not manage to do the useful things he hoped to perform, and soon loses what he had gained in the wilderness and is left with nothing.

A great many similar cases exist, when the enemy succeeds in drawing a man away from one kind of occupation, tempting him with another, under the pretext that it is more useful, and thus disorganises one and another alike.

A man who has experienced teachers and advisers to talk with and who obeys their instructions with humble submission, is easily delivered from all such temptations. But if for some reason a man is deprived of this blessing, let him keep attention in himself and learn to discriminate strictly between good and evil according to Christian principles, on which the lives of us all should be based. If circumstances, which seem to us to impede our freedom in doing good, are not the result of our will, but are sent by God, accept them submissively and listen to no suggestions, which make you depart from this submissiveness. When God sends such circumstances, He expects nothing more from you than that you should conduct yourself and act as the occasion demands, within the possibilities it offers. Whether you are sick or poor, endure it. God demands of you nothing but to endure. Enduring with a good heart, you will be constantly occupied in good. If you endure with a good heart, then, whenever God may look at you, He will find you either acting or existing rightly, whereas if a man enjoys good health his good actions are intermittent. So if you wish for a change in your position, you wish to exchange better for worse.

But if you should find yourself in a position, which seems to restrict the scope of good deeds possible for you, and this position is the result of your own will, then, since you have probably chosen it for some purpose, keep to this purpose, do not let your thoughts wander off to various other possibilities, but direct your whole attention to what you have to do in your position and keep it held there, thus calmly performing the actions connected with it, fully convinced that if you dedicate them all to God instead of to self-indulgence, the time spent on them will not be wasted and they will be accepted by God as the fullest offering. And remain at peace.

CHAPTER THIRTY-FOUR

How the enemy turns the virtues themselves against those who practise them

But let us suppose that you faithfully and steadfastly follow the path of virtue, turning neither to right nor to left; do not imagine that the enemy will leave you alone. No! In the extract I quoted from St. John of the Ladder, you have already heard that when the enemy sees that all his attempts to lead you into evil have

114

failed, he follows you stealthily and flatters you, suggesting that your life is wholly pleasing to God. This is his last temptation. Our response to his flattery is self-opinion, self-importance and self-complacency, which give birth to vanity and pride; vanity robs our doings of all value, even if they are good, and pride makes us abhorrent to God. So watch and repel all such flattery of the enemy, nor let it reach the heart, but repulse it from the first moment it touches the ears of your soul.

To avoid falling into this evil which threatens you, always keep your mind collected in the heart and be for ever ready to repulse these arrows of the enemy. Standing there within, like a general on the battlefield, choose a place of advantage for battle, fortify it thoroughly and never leave it, but make it your shelter from which to give battle. This place, its fortification and armament, is a profound and sincere realisation of your nothingness, of the fact that you are poor, blind, naked and rich only in weaknesses, faults and deeds that are blameworthy, foolish, vain and sinful. Having taken up this position, never let your mind wander outside your fortress and particularly refrain from going over your apparently fruitful fields and gardens, that is, your good deeds. If you keep to this practice, the arrows of the enemy's pernicious flattery will not touch you, and even if one of them happens to reach you, you will immediately see and repulse it, and throw it away.

But just as warriors entrenched in a fortress do not sit idle, but either go through military training, or repair and strengthen the fortifications, so must you, sheltering in the consciousness of your nothingness, do the same. To be more precise, act as follows. However firmly you hold your mind, it will continue to run away, and it is not surprising if in its wanderings it comes upon works of yours which look good. As soon as it comes upon them, the enemy will immediately seize it and afflict it with self-opinion, in such a way that, on returning home, it will willingly range itself on the side of the enemy and will try to drag you with it. As soon as you notice this, call your mind back to you and say to it: 'Listen, mind: you keep on telling me that this is good and that is not bad. May be so; but what's that to do with me? You were about to praise me. Very well, sing my praises, I am listening. But know that justice demands that you should praise me only for what is my own in me and in my actions; but for those things that come from God and His grace, praise and thanks are due to their

115

source. So let us examine what you and I have of our own and what belongs to God, and let us refer to God what comes from God, and keep what is our own. Then by what we still have—if we still have anything—let us determine our weight and value, and let us praise ourselves for it.

'So, let us begin. Let us glance at the time before we existed: what were we then? Nothing, and we could do nothing, for which the Source of all life could reward us by granting us existence. Thus our existence is a spontaneous gift of God, a divine favour; this is the start, and through this we receive all the subsequent favours granted to us in His measureless mercy. So let us refer this to God.—Then we began to live. How? We do not ourselves know. For many years you and I were not aware of our existence, yet we did exist; then when we did become aware of it, we could do nothing to sustain our life. Other hands cared for us, not of themselves, but moved by the providence of the Provider of all life and being. We were brought up, educated, put on our feet. There was nothing of our own in all this—so let us put it aside.

'Then we began to live on our own. What is there of our own? Take our vital energy and our means of existence: they are not ours, they are a gift of God.

'Direct knowledge of God is a gift of God, conscience is a gift of God, thirst for heavenly life is a gift of God. These three constitute the spirit of our life, urging us heavenwards. You, my mind, are not mine: you were given me by God. Neither are the powers active within me—will, with its energy—mine. Nor does my feeling, the ability to enjoy life and all my surroundings belong to me. My body, with all its functions and requirements, which determine our physical well-being, is not mine either. All this was given by God. And I myself belong not to me, but to God. When he gave me being, God invested me with a calculated complexity of vital energies and gave me consciousness and freedom. He ordained that I should rule over all existing in me, in accordance with the function and value of each part of my being. All this offers no grounds for self-praise, but only for realising the great and heavy duty imposed on us, and for fear of the answer we are to give to the question: What have we done with ourselves and of ourselves?

'Let us now turn to the means of life. There is in us the life of the body, the life of the soul and the life of the spirit. Each of them needs its own means of existence; they are all ready to hand, but they are all a gift of God, and not our own acquisition. Air, fire, water, the earth with all its treasures: the elements, stones, metals, plants and animals, which provide all we need as food, garments and houses, are not made by us but are given. All the concepts we need about our surroundings, the forms of our daily life, of society and government, the arts and crafts and the rules of action in all these domains, we find ready-made and need only to assimilate them, instead of bothering our heads to invent them. Each man coming into the world inherits them from his ancestors. And where did our ancestors get it all? God sends down men endowed with special gifts and special strength of will, and they make new discoveries and improve human life. But if you were to ask any one of these inventors how he has arrived at one thing or another, he would answer: 'I do not know; it just came into my mind, developed, took shape and matured.' So it has always been, and so it will always be to the end of the world: the means of livelihood for the soul are not ours—they are given. Even more is it so in our spiritual—moral—religious life. In the mind of our soul God has placed knowledge of Himself, and in our conscience—knowledge of His will, endowing each alike with the hope of eternal bliss. This is the seed of life of the spirit. It is sown in us and received by us at the moment when God breathes into us His divine spark of life. Each man, when born, brings this seed with him and in him; later the development of this seed is determined by the kind of people who surround him. What an indescribably great blessing it is to be born among people who lead a truly spiritual life! But look around you. We possess knowledge of the one true God, worshipped as the Trinity; we confess the Son of God, Who assumed flesh for our sake and provided all things for our salvation; and we believe in the Holy Spirit, whose grace animates us and who is active in building spiritual life in us; we are planted in the Church of God and receive in it all that is needful for preserving and raising up our spiritual life, and we are inspired by the expectation of the resurrection of the dead and of life in the world to come. All this we have in the most pure and unadulterated form, and none of it is our own—it is a gift of God. So you see how rich are the means which surround you for leading a life, which should be natural to you in all its fullness; not one of them is the fruit of your own efforts, all is

117

given you. You are called to the banquet of life, already prepared. If you and I can boast of anything in this respect, it is perhaps only of how we have used it all. To possess all this in full force represents our wedding garment. Should we glory in it? Should we not rather be afraid, lest the bountiful Host of the banquet should come and say to us: "See what a banquet it is! But what of your garment?"

'Now let us look more closely at this garment. The garment of the soul is chiefly composed of the moral and religious dispositions and feelings rooted in it, rather than of actions alone. But since they are hidden, they are but rarely the occasion of vanity and pride. Actions, however, are visible, and so jump to the eye, and as it were involuntarily, provoke in the doer a feeling of self-importance and self-approbation, and their outer effect is to move the witnesses of a man's deeds to praise, which makes this feeling of self-importance and trumpeting still deeper and more firmly rooted. So let us examine our actions to see whether they contain anything we can incontestably boast about.

'Let us remember that we can boast only of something which is a direct result of our own will and is done by us independently of anything else. But look how our actions proceed. How do they begin? Certain circumstances come together and lead to one action or another; or a thought comes to our mind to do something, and we do it. But the concurrence of circumstances does not come from us; nor, obviously, is the thought to do something our own; somebody suggests it. Thus, in such cases, the origin or birth of the thought to do something cannot or should not be an object of self-praise. Yet how many of our actions are of this kind? If we examine them conscientiously, we shall find that they almost all start in this way. So we have nothing to boast of.

'If we can praise ourselves for anything, it is for doing something we need not have done; for, however strong the external and internal impulses to action, the decision to act always depends on our will. But here again the decision to do a good deed is not always right. A decision is right, if it comes from the realisation that God wills such and such an action, and from obedience to His will. But as soon as something foreign comes in, to please oneself or other people, the quality of the decision becomes tarnished and darkened. Sometimes we take a decision for fear of what people may say if we do not; sometimes, because we expect

118

some profit or satisfaction from the action, either now or in the future, and sometimes simply because we cannot do otherwise; we don't want to but we must. No such acts can be counted as purely good acts, and, although they appear praiseworthy, are not so in their inner quality before God and conscience. Let us examine how many of our deeds are of this kind? Once more we are forced to admit—almost all of them. So again we have nothing to boast of.'

Thus, on strict examination, our good acts do not allow us to open our lips in boasting before others or in trumpeting inwardly to ourselves. But if we bring to memory all our blameworthy deeds—empty, vain, useless, harmful, lawless, abhorrent to God, of which there are sure to be many, what must we feel then? Perhaps someone will say: 'Weigh one side against the other and judge yourself by whichever is heavier.' But here such a method is unsuitable. Actions proceed from within. If wrong actions occur, it means that our inner state is wrong; and it is this inner state which determines our worth before God—our essential worth. If this cannot be approved, then the whole man is unworthy of approval.

I shall add one more thing: all our actions done visibly, in the household, in society, at work, constitute our behaviour. If we look round, we cannot but say that on the whole our behaviour is correct. But we cannot assert that our inner state is equally correct. The eyes of the people around us exert a great pressure on our designs. These witnesses force us not to give expression to the evil which arises in the heart; we refrain from evil—and our behaviour appears correct. Were it not for them our behaviour would look quite different; and it often becomes such as long as we are sure that no other eyes can see us. It happens with some people, that as soon as their outer conditions change and they can live more freely, all that was previously concealed, for fear of being seen by others, bursts out and a formerly well-behaved man becomes a drunkard, a debauchee, or even a robber. All these bad impulses were not born at this moment, they existed before, but were denied expression, whereas now they are given free rein and so become manifest. But even if all this was merely inside, then the whole man was such—a drunkard, a debauchee, a robber —although outwardly he seemed different. Look carefully, maybe you too belong to this category. If it *is* so, to however small a degree, you have no right to boast or to accept praise.

To conclude: if, following all the indications set out above, you begin to make a frequent survey of your life, then, when the enemy begins to blow your trumpet into your ears, saying how good you are, this trumpeting will not find response within you by engendering self-esteem or self-approval, but, on the contrary, will be repulsed on every occasion by the most humble and disparaging thoughts and feelings about yourself.

CHAPTER THIRTY-FIVE

Some indications useful in the work of overcoming passions and acquiring virtue

Although I have already told you a great deal about the means to use in overcoming passions and acquiring virtue, there remains something else to be said about it.

First of all I say to you: brother, in acquiring virtue do not follow the example of those who, in the course of the seven days of the week, arrange their spiritual works in such a way that one should serve one virtue, another—another virtue, and so on, without taking into consideration whether they stand in need of this or that at the actual moment. No, do not act thus, but take up arms pre-eminently against the passion which troubles you most, which has often conquered you and which is ready to attack you again now. Fight it with your whole strength and strive to establish yourself in the virtue opposed to that passion, using for this purpose all suitable practices and tasks. For as soon as you succeed in this, you will, by this very fact, bring to life all other virtues in yourself and will be clothed in them as in armour, which will then protect you from all the arrows of passions. By nature our heart is full of good dispositions; but passions come and stifle them. These passions are not of equal strength in every man, but in one man one passion predominates, in another another passion rules over the rest. As soon as you banish the chief passion, all the others grow weaker and recede by themselves. When this comes to pass, the good dispositions, freed from their yoke, acquire in you the strength natural to them and, standing at the door of your heart, are always ready to serve you, whenever it is required.

120

Secondly: do not allot any definite time for the acquisition of virtues, neither days, nor weeks, months nor years, saying to yourself: 'I shall work, and then rest, and then, having rested, I will start the same work again.' No, no rest is allowed here. Prepare yourself for continual labour, struggle and effort, allowing no thought of alleviation, in imitation of St. Paul, who says of himself: 'I therefore so run,—I follow after, if that I may apprehend, —I press toward the mark' (I Cor. ix. 26; Phil. iii. 12, 14). To stop for rest on the path of virtue means not to gain new strength, but to dissipate the strength one has acquired and to become weakened; and this is the same as turning back, or as destroying what was so laboriously built. By *stopping* I mean—imagining that the virtue is already gained in its perfection, and so paying no attention to its deficiencies and neglecting chances of good actions. Be not like that, but be always watchful and zealous. Do not shut your eyes, do not turn away when you meet with such chances, but, on the contrary, look out for them and strive towards them. Look upon them with love—all, but especially those, which present some difficulties to achieving what is right in them. The straining of our powers to overcome obstacles in right actions brings the habit of virtue more quickly and sends its roots deeper into the heart. Only avoid, all you can, those occasions which, while they offer a chance to manifest the virtue of chastity, at the same time threaten to set unclean lust on fire in you. It is better not to let this fire come near your members, lest you be scorched and burnt by it.

Thirdly: be wise and sensible in undertaking tasks for the body: fasts, vigils, physical work and so on. They are necessary and essential, and do not imagine you can progress in spiritual life without them, but you must be wise in knowing your measure and keeping to it. This measure is the mean between self-pandering indulgence to the flesh and its merciless chastisement, exhausting it utterly without urgent need. Find this mean by experience and in actual deed, instead of by theory, and make gradual progress your rule, moving from below upwards. Seek, and you shall find. As regards the inner virtues of the soul, such as: love of God, renunciation of the world, belittling yourself, turning away from passions and sin, patience and meekness, being at peace with all men, even those who hate and persecute you, and so on, here no definite measure is required, and their gradual progress towards perfection determines itself within you. Your business is constantly and zealously to urge yourself to every action demanded by them, and to do it always without delay or dallying. In this lies all your wisdom and strength.

Fourthly : acting thus think with all the power of your thought, wish with all the strength of your desire and seek with your whole heart one thing only—to overcome the passion you are battling with at that particular moment and which is attacking you now, and to re-establish in its full strength the virtue opposed to it, which is at present stifled. This one thing should be for you the whole world, all heaven and all earth, all your treasure and your final aim, in the conviction that by this alone can you worthily serve God. Whether you eat or fast, work or rest, sleep or wake, are at home or away, are occupied with prayer or with the affairs of daily life, let all of it be directed to this one aim, to overcome the passion which has arisen in you and to re-establish the virtue it has banished. I have already spoken about overcoming your chief passion; here I speak of the passion which has arisen at the given moment, whether it be the chief one or not. As in visible war, it is sometimes necessary to come to grips with a detachment commanded by the commander-in-chief himself, and at other times with one commanded by an ordinary officer; so it happens in spiritual warfare. The chief passion is not always there; sometimes, it sends its assistants in its place, and frequently one has to deal with them more often than with the chief passion itself. But in such cases it is no less needful for you to gain victory.

Fifthly : be an implacable enemy of all earthly comforts and sensory pleasures, which are born of self-indulgence and feed it. Through this you will be less often subject to attack not only by carnal, but generally by all passions, for they are all rooted in self-indulgence. When self-indulgence is subdued and cut off, they lose their power, stability and firmness, since they have no foothold. Do not give way to the thought: 'I will indulge in one pleasure, taste one enjoyment.' Even if it is not sinful in itself, the fact remains that it was admitted only through pandering to oneself; and during this moment of self-indulgence all passions will raise their heads and begin to wriggle like squashed worms when water is poured on them. And it is not surprising if one of them flares up with such force that struggle with it is hard and victory doubtful. So never forget the following words of the Scrip-

122

tures: 'He that loveth his life (that is, the self-indulgent man) shall lose it; and he that hateth his life in this world (a man who does not give way to self-indulgence) shall keep it unto life eternal' (John xii. 25). 'Therefore, brethren, we are debtors, not to the flesh, to live after the flesh. For if ye live after the flesh, ye shall die: but if ye through the Spirit do mortify the deeds of the body, ye shall live' (Rom. viii. 12–13).

Sixthly: finally, I give you this last advice: it is very useful, or rather, absolutely necessary for you first of all to begin with a general confession, with all due attention and all the required practices, examinations and decisions, so that, through this, your soul should be filled with the firm conviction that you stand in the grace of God, the sole Giver of all spiritual gifts, virtues and victories.

CHAPTER THIRTY-SIX

On the order of acquiring virtues

A true warrior of Christ, filled with a whole-hearted desire to achieve the fullness of perfection, must set no limits to his efforts to gain success in all things. Yet he must moderate and direct excessive transports of his spiritual zeal by good judgment. Particularly in the beginning, such transports surge up suddenly with great vigour and carry us away with irresistible force; but later they gradually grow weaker and weaker, until they die down altogether, leaving us stranded in the middle of our journey. For not only should external, bodily virtues be acquired little by little, by gradually ascending, as by the rungs of a ladder, but in the acquisition of the inner virtues of the soul one should also observe a definite order and sequence, since only then does our little become much and remain with us for ever. For example, in the process of acquiring the inner virtue of patience, it is impossible at once to welcome injustice, injuries and all other forms of unpleasantness, to seek them and rejoice in them, although it is possible to endure them with patience when they come. For welcoming them and rejoicing in them are the highest degrees of patience, and before you reach them you should traverse the lower degrees, which are: humble self-depreciation, in which you consider yourself worthy of every insult, overcoming in yourself impulses of revenge, hatred of the least thought of revenge, and so on.

I advise you, besides: do not at once undertake the practice of all virtues, or even of a number of them, but become first grounded in one and thereupon pass to another. In this way every habit of virtue will take root in your soul with greater ease and firmness. For when you are constantly exercising yourself in one virtue above all others, your memory will be almost entirely occupied by this alone, and your mind, thus welded to the thought of it, will acquire more quickly the skill of finding means and occasions for its practice, while your will will cleave to it with greater readiness and desire. All these things help greatly in the work of acquiring habits of virtue, which you will expect in vain, if you undertake many virtues at once.

On the other hand, since the practice itself of any given virtue remains always the same, it follows from the similarity of this mode of action that it gradually becomes less and less difficult and leads more quickly to another virtue. For one virtue usually stimulates another, akin to it, and helps it by the fact that, once it is established in the heart, it predisposes the heart to receive its like by preparing as it were a seat for it.

This calculation of mine is true and reliable, and we know from experience that if a man exercises himself in one virtue well and wholeheartedly, he not only learns in advance by this very fact how to exercise himself in another, but, as his experience in the first virtue increases, he stimulates too all other virtues and makes them grow and strengthen in himself; for they cannot be divided from one another, as all are rays issuing from the same Divine light.

CHAPTER THIRTY-SEVEN

What dispositions are needed to acquire virtues in general and how to undertake training for any one of them

In order to acquire virtues a man's soul should be great and courageous; his will, not weak and indolent, but resolute and strong; he must have a sure foresight of the numerous obstacles and hard struggles and must be ready to undertake and endure them all. At the basis of such disposition should lie a strong love for each virtue and for all virtuous life and a burning zeal for them. This constitutes the force which moves a man on the laborious path of virtue, and it should therefore be constantly kept warm lest it be so weakened and exhausted, that all movement will inevitably stop. So do not neglect to keep warm your zeal for virtue. Make your heart share in reflections about how pleasing to God virtuous life is, and how high and beautiful is virtue in itself and how necessary and beneficial it is for us: for it is the beginning and end of our true perfection, as well as of our progress in it.

So, each morning, try with all your attention to examine and foresee all the occasions you are likely to meet with in the course of the day, which may give a chance to do one or another good action, and accompany this with a firm desire and resolve to make use of them without fail. In the evening examine yourself as to whether your good thoughts and desires of the morning were put into practice and how they were fulfilled. On the following morning renew the same intentions and desires, with the most active zeal and desire to fufil them exactly.

Try to direct all this towards exercising the particular virtue, the habit of which you have decided to acquire at present. Equally, examples of the saints, prayers, meditations on the life and passion of Christ our Lord, and all other things considered necessary and suitable to gain success in virtues and in spiritual life should be directed mainly towards the virtue on which you are working. At the same time, try also to use all the accidental happenings of the day, however varied, not only to prevent them from upsetting your training in the particular virtue you are aiming to attain at the moment, but even to strengthen and deepen your habit of it.

The ultimate limit of such a habit should be to reach a state when your virtuous actions, whether external or internal, should be performed with the same ease and readiness as your former actions, which opposed it, or rather, with the ease with which we satisfy the natural requirements of our being; this means to make the habit or virtue as it were part of our nature. And I would remind you of what I said earlier, that the more obstacles, whether outer or inner, that we meet in our effort to acquire a virtue, the sooner and more deeply it will take root in our soul, if we strive to overcome them resolutely and without self-pity.

Suitable sayings from the Divine Scriptures, if said aloud or merely repeated mentally, have a wonderful power for impressing in our mind the image of the virtue we seek and for arousing a longing for it in the heart. And how great is the help received from both these by a man who strives to attain virtue! So find in the Scriptures appropriate texts concerning the virtue you seek and learn them by heart, so as always to have them ready at hand. Repeat them mentally as often as possible, especially when the opposite passion begins to move in you.

For instance, when you work on attaining the virtue of patience, you may choose, learn by heart and repeat the following texts from the Scriptures: 'He that is slow to wrath is of great understanding' (Prov. xiv. 29). 'The expectation of the poor shall not perish for ever' (Ps. ix. 18). 'Woe unto you that have lost patience!' (Ecclesiasticus ii. 14). 'He that is slow to anger is better than the mighty; and he that ruleth his spirit than he that taketh a city' (Prov. xvi. 32). 'In your patience possess ye your souls' (Luke xxi. 19). 'Let us run with patience the race that is set before us' (Heb. xii. 1). 'Behold, we count them happy which endure' (James v. 11). 'Blessed is the man that endureth temptation' (James i. 12). 'Let patience have her perfect work' (James i. 4). 'Ye have need of patience' (Heb. x. 36).

To these you may add your own short prayers: the following or some others like them—'My God! when shall my heart at last be armed with patience!'—'When shall I, at last, endure every affliction with an untroubled heart, that my God may rejoice over me!' 'O how welcome are the afflictions, which make me more like my Lord Jesus, Who has suffered for my sake!' 'O my Jesus! Grant me at least sometimes to live untroubled among a thousand afflictions, to the glory of Thy name!'—'Blessed shall I be if in the fire of tribulations I shall be set aflame with the desire to endure still greater sufferings!'

In order to make progress in virtues, such prayers should be used as the spirit of faith and piety directs, in accordance with the virtue in which you are particularly training yourself. Such short prayers should be rightly called, in the words of the Prophet, 'ways' to the altars of the Lord in the heart (Ps. lxxxiv. 5), which, starting from a heart filled with faith and hope, ascend to heaven and reach the ears of God. These are the 'pantings' (Ps. xxxviii. 10) which the merciful Lord never fails to see. These are the cries which are always heard and understood by the most bountiful God (Ps. v. 2). But one must not forget to add to them two convictions, which are like a pair of wings: the first, that God rejoices when He sees us working to attain virtue; and that, while filled with an ardent desire to gain perfection in them, we seek nothing but to please God.

CHAPTER THIRTY-EIGHT

Virtue should be practised constantly and with all diligence

In the work of acquiring virtues, it is necessary to act so as always to be 'reaching forth unto those things which are before' (Phil. iii. 13), if we wish to attain our aim quickly and successfully. For as soon as we stop, if only for a short time, we at once fall back. For when negligence and self-indulgence interrupt our good efforts, the passions, which were subdued by diligent work to acquire virtue, immediately raise their heads and come to life, through our propensity to sensuousness and self-indulgence, and they evoke disorderly inner movements and tendencies, especially where our external surroundings favour it. These inner movements always disorganise and weaken our good habits, and, what is especially harmful, deprive us of the gift of grace, without which nothing truly good and spiritual can be achieved.

You must know that progress on the path of spiritual life differs greatly from an ordinary journey on earth. If a traveller stops on his ordinary journey, he loses nothing of the way already covered; but if a traveller on the path of virtue stops in his spiritual progress, he loses much of the virtues previously acquired, as I have already said. In an ordinary journey, the further the traveller proceeds, the more tired he becomes; but on the way of spiritual life the longer a man travels, 'reaching forth unto those things which are before', the greater the strength and power he acquires for his further progress.

The reason for this is that efforts made on the path of virtue gradually weaken the resistance of our lower part, i.e. the flesh.

127

which renders the path of virtue so hard and strenuous by its opposition to the spirit; whereas the higher part where virtue dwells, that is, the spirit, gains ever more and more strength and power. Therefore the more we succeed in virtue and good, the smaller grow the grievous difficulties we meet when we enter this path. Moreover a certain secret sweetness, sent by God, flows into our heart and increases from hour to hour. Through this, as we press forward with ever greater strength and will, we ascend easily from virtue to virtue, and finally reach the very summit of spiritual perfection, where the soul begins to practise every kind of good, no longer urged with effort, lacking all taste for it, but with ready inclination and joy. For, having subdued and conquered passions and renounced all that belongs to the creature, it now lives in God, and there, amid welcome spiritual works, ceaselessly savours the sweetness of peace.

CHAPTER THIRTY-NINE

A man should not avoid opportunities he meets for good actions

If you wish always to press forward on the path of virtue without stopping, you should pay great attention to things, which may serve as chances for acquiring virtue, and never let them slip out of your hands. Therefore those are ill-advised, who do everything in their power to avoid any kind of obstacles on the path of virtue, in spite of the fact that these might have helped towards success in their progress. For example, if you wish to gain the habit of patience, you should not avoid the people, things and circumstances, which particularly try your patience. Meet them with a good will and the resolve to submit to their unpleasant effect on you, but at the same time prepare yourself to suffer them with unshakeable calmness of spirit. If you do not act thus, you will never learn patience.

You should adopt the same attitude towards any work which displeases you, either in itself or because it is imposed on you by a man you dislike, or because it interferes with the work you do like. In other words, you must not avoid it but, on the contrary, must undertake it without digging in your toes, and must do and finish it through, as though it were the most welcome work, never letting your heart be troubled by it, especially by the thought that, were it not for this business, you would be completely at peace. Otherwise you will never learn to bear the afflictions you will meet; nor will you find the true peace you seek by running away from such things, obviously through self-indulgence; for peace does not dwell in self-indulgent hearts.

I advise you to do the same in relation to the thoughts, which at times invade you and trouble your mind with memories of human injustices and other inappropriate things. Do not stifle them or drive them away, but let them leave you of their own accord, not through your opposition, but through the patience with which you endure them. Let them trouble and painfully worry you, for at the same time they will teach you to bear patiently all afflictions in general. He who tells you rather to flee from such accidental disturbances, is advising you to break off from your striving for the virtue you wish to attain.

True, in the case of a beginner inexperienced in battle, it is better to flee from accidental troubles and disregard them, rather than subject himself to their effect and come to grips with them. Yet even in his case it is not always advisable to turn his back and retreat; sometimes it is better to fight the invaders with all attention and circumspection, at other times—to pay no attention to them, according to a man's progress in virtue and the moral strength this progress gives. But in relation to carnal lust alone it is not advisable to do this: here one should flee from all occasions, which may inflame this passion, owing to its unruliness and the deceptive wiles of the enemy, with which he knows how to cover the movements of carnal lust, in order to incline a man to their satisfaction.

CHAPTER FORTY

One should love those opportunities of practising virtue which are particularly difficult

On no account, beloved, must you flee from what may be a chance for acquiring virtue. On the contrary, whenever such a chance offers itself, you should accept it with joy, regarding as best and most welcome such things as are unpleasant to your heart and evoke no sympathy in you. I predict that, with God's help, you will actually do so, if you engrave deeply in your mind the following thoughts.

First, you should realise that the opportunities for virtue you meet with are the best means you can have for acquiring it, given you by God in answer to your prayer. Having formed a desire to gain virtue, you have, of course, prayed God to grant it to you; and in praying for it, you could not avoid praying also for the methods and means of acquiring this gift. But God does not give, for instance, the virtue of patience without afflictions, nor the virtue of humility without humbling occasions of degradation and dishonour. So, after your prayer about these virtues, He sends you corresponding opportunities. What are you doing, then, in running away and avoiding them? You reject God's help for which you prayed, and mock the gift of God.

So decide to welcome gladly the chances you meet for virtue, and the more gladly, the more difficulties they offer. For in such cases our virtuous actions evoke great courage and reveal great moral strength; and through this we make each time a considerable step forward on the path of virtue, which alone should be our constant aim.

I should explain here that, in advising you to use the most important occasions to gain virtue, I do not mean to advise you to disregard the less important chances, or to miss them through neglecting them. No, you should never miss any of them, whether important or unimportant, in order to be working always for virtue. For instance, you should bear patiently not only blatant abuse and reviling, or, if so happens, blows, but even a scowling look and a scornful expression, or a sharp word. Since such un-important cases are more frequent, our right reactions have more chances of showing themselves and so keep our moral strength in a constant state of tension, thus giving us enough force to behave as we should also on important occasions. If we disregard these opportunities, we weaken our moral strength and render it less capable of dealing with important occasions.

Secondly, make firm in yourself the conviction and faith, that all things happening to us happen according to God's will and for our profit, so that we may gain thereby a certain spiritual fruit. Although we cannot suppose that some things, such as our sins and those of other people, are a direct result of a willed action of God's, yet even they do not happen without God's leave, as means of admonishing and humbling us. As regards sufferings and afflic-tions, which are our own fault or due to the malice of others—God Himself sends them, desiring us to suffer and be tormented by them, in order to gain the blessing of virtue, which we are bound to earn if we endure as we should the trial He has sent us. The same applies to other judgments of His, hidden from us, but doubtless right and blessed.

Thus, convinced that God Himself wishes you to endure the hardship and grief, which assails you, either arising from the evil nature of other people, or invited by your own wrong actions, you will cease to think and say as some others do: no, this does not come from God, it is unjust and criminal, and God does not want crime and turns away with loathing from it and from those who commit it. By this they want to justify their lack of patience and the gusts of anger and feelings of revenge they feel at the sight of injustice; but in actual fact the only thing they achieve is to rebel against God's ordinance and to attempt to cast off the life-saving cross, imposed on them by God for their own good, instead of shouldering it with a good heart, which would undoubtedly be pleasing to Him. And what do they get? They cannot cast off their cross, they offend God, and still they gain no peace. On the con-trary, to grief they add contention and useless irritation and render their state unbearable; whereas had they borne what happened with a good heart, they would have been at peace and would have attracted God's benevolence, and would have eaten richly of the fruit of the spirit. So make it a rule for yourself:— when you meet with injustices, injuries and attacks, pay no

131

attention to them, however wrong your offenders may be, but keep your attention firmly on one thing alone—that God let this happen for your good and that you will deprive yourself of this good if you admit impatience, irritation or contention in connection with it. And do not try to analyse the exact reason why God has allowed this. Do you believe that God is always right and merciful? Then believe that on this occasion too He shows you justice and mercy, although you do not see how. And remember how the Lord blesses those who behave thus: 'Blessed are they that have not seen, and yet have believed' (John xx. 29).

Do you believe that the words of your Lord: 'Take up thy cross' refer also to you personally? If you believe this, then take it up. The Lord has laid it on your shoulders in the present grievous case. Do not say, it is too heavy; God knows better the measure of your strength. To some God sends trials and sorrows, brought about by circumstances and in no way dependent on people; these are more easily borne. To others He sends those causes by people, and they are harder, especially when we cannot take the grief caused to us as unintentional, and still harder when we have done some good to those people. The last case is the hardest to bear. If God sends you this, know that it is precisely what is most useful for you, and to this realisation add the inspiring thought: God sees that you are strong enough to bear it and expects you actually to bear it with a good heart, without complaining. So do not disappoint God's expectation.

I must add that God prefers us to endure afflictions coming from the evil nature of people, especially from those to whom we have done some good, rather than those which are the accidental result of unfavourable circumstances. Why? Because our native pride is more easily subdued and exterminated by the former than by the latter. And also because, if obedience to God's will is the chief thing in our spiritual doing, there is no better way of provoking and manifesting it to a greater degree than in such cases, if we bear them with a good heart, giving warm thanks to God for sending them, since they are truly a great blessing, thus testifying to our complete obedience to the Divine will, and to an ardent zeal in conforming ourselves in everything to this will.

This disposition precedes the visitation of rigorous trials. Seeing the birth of such a disposition and wishing to make it stronger and more deeply rooted, God sends us a cup of the strongest temptations, which, when borne with willingness, good heart and gladness, always brings this blessed spiritual fruit. Therefore, knowing this, wishing and seeking it, we must accept this cup from the hands of God, shutting the eyes of inquisitiveness, and, with complete faith, clearly see in it the great love of God for us and the assurance of our spiritual progress. Thus we must drain it with joy, the more willingly the more bitter is its taste.

CHAPTER FORTY-ONE

How to progress in one and the same virtue in different circumstances

In one of the earlier chapters, we said that it is more useful and advantageous to spend some time exercising oneself in one virtue than in many virtues at once, and that therefore one should turn to the profit of this one virtue all the events we meet, however different they may be. Now listen, and I will show you how this can be done without difficulty.

If, for example, it should happen that on the same day, or even in the course of the same hour, you are blamed unjustly for an action blameless in itself or you are refused some request, or if something happens and you are unfairly suspected of something bad, or if some bodily illness afflicts you, or one of your superiors compels you to do something you do not like, or you meet some other unpleasant and unbearable thing, of which our poor human life is so full; then, because of the varied nature of these or similar occurrences differing virtuous actions are demanded of you. But, following the rule you have established, it is better for you to direct them all towards exercising yourself in the particular virtue you are working on at the time.

Thus, if at the moment you meet the occurrences mentioned, you are chiefly exercising yourself in patience, then take care to endure them with patience and joy. If you are chiefly occupied with progress in humility, strive to realise that you deserve every kind of evil and have earned the adversities you have met with. If your work is to acquire the virtue of obedience, force yourself to bend your neck submissively to the mighty hand of God and, for the sake of pleasing Him, submit willingly to His creatures, whether or not they have reason or life, through whom He sends you these adversities and afflictions. If you are striving to succeed in poverty, incite in yourself contentment, joy and thankfulness that you are deprived of all earthly and worldly comfort. If you labour at making your love both higher and more deeply rooted, try to provoke in yourself feelings of love for your neighbour, since at that moment he is an instrument of the good you may extract from these incidents; and urge yourself to love of God since, now as always, He is the first cause of love and sends such afflictions or allows them for your spiritual progress.

From what I have said you can see for yourself how to use, for the exercise of one and the same virtue, adversities which are not brief, but last for a long time, such as illness, for instance, or similar things.

CHAPTER FORTY-TWO

How long should one exercise oneself in each virtue and what are the signs of progress in it?

It is impossible to determine theoretically how long one should exercise oneself in a virtue before becoming established in it. Everyone must determine this for himself, considering his state, circumstances and achievements in spiritual life, and especially according to the judgment of his staretz or the spiritual father who directs him. Still, if a man's zeal for success is alive, and he does not stop at any difficulties or means, considerable progress will soon be shown.

The sign of progress is when, having entered the path of virtue, a man follows it diligently, with a firm resolve never to leave it, however hard it may be and whatever sacrifices it may entail, despite moments of cooling off and darkening of the soul, of spiritual impoverishment and of lack of the blessed joys, all which God in His providence for us allows to happen for your good.

The second and no less sure sign of progress is the degree of intensity of the war, which the flesh wages against good resolutions and actions. The more this battle loses its intensity, the more evident becomes the progress in virtue. So, when you do not

134

feel any struggle or attacks on the part of your lower sensory nature, especially at times when occasions for exciting it are before your eyes, you may believe that your virtue has acquired sufficient strength. But if you begin to do your work on the path of virtue with greater readiness and spiritual joy than before, you may consider this a sign of progress in virtue, even more sure than subjugation of the flesh.

And on St. Isaac's advice, once one has determined the aim, towards which one must direct all the actions of one's life, one should question those who are experienced about the signs and tokens, which show whether one is on the right road or has deviated from it and is following some side track, and keep these signs constantly in mind. He considers these signs and tokens to be the following: 'If you see that your mind is not being forced, but acts freely and presses forward in good thoughts, this is a sign of progress; in the same way when, standing in prayer, your mind does not wander hither and thither, and your tongue suddenly stops in the middle of a verse, and the shackles of silence are laid on your soul, without participation of your will; also, when you notice that with each good thought and memory arising in your soul, and with every spiritual contemplation your eyes are filled with tears, and they run freely down your cheeks, or when sometimes you see that your thought, of its own accord and independently of you, sinks into the depths of your heart and remains in this state for may be an hour, while peace reigns in your thoughts —all these are signs of good progress on the path of the spiritual life you have undertaken' (ch. 44).

Yet it is wrong to be too sure that we are completely established in the desired virtue, or have finally overcome some passion, even if its impacts and impulses have not been experienced for a long time. For this may conceal the evil wiles of the man-hater—the devil—and the craftiness of the sin which lives in us; for these things, which are of a quite different nature, are often seen by us in a good light and we accept them as good through the pride concealed in us. Moreover, if we think of the perfection to which God calls us, then, even if we have followed for a long time the path of virtue, we shall be the more ready to think that we have hardly made a start in the life we ought to lead, let alone being established in it. This is why the holy fathers call even the life of the most perfect men imperfect,—that is, not free from faults.

135

'Even the perfection of the perfect is not perfect', says St. John of the Ladder. And St. Paul sees perfection in constantly pressing on and on, with no looking back or thinking that we have already attained what we seek. Thus he calls himself imperfect, not having yet attained what he seeks. 'Not as though I had already attained' he says, 'either were already perfect: but I follow after, if that I may apprehend . . . Brethren, I count not myself to have apprehended: but this one thing I do, forgetting those things which are behind, and reaching forth unto those things which are before, I press toward the mark for the prize of the high calling of God in Christ Jesus' (Phil. iii. 12–14). And wishing to show that this alone constitutes our perfection, he adds: 'Let us therefore, as many as be perfect, be thus minded' (Phil. iii. 15). In other words: perfection is not to think that we have reached perfection; the virtuous state is not to stand still but constantly to press forward towards virtue.

Moreover, there sometimes lurk in the depth of our heart such subtle and hidden passions, that we do not know them as passions at all. So how can we be so presumptuous as to think that we are completely cleansed of passions? If even the sharp and prophetic eyes of David could not discern them in himself, how can we attribute such capacity of seeing to ourselves? Therefore, if even he never ceased to pray God: 'Cleanse thou me from secret faults' (Ps. xix. 12), how much more do we need to implore Him to cleanse us from our hidden passions? For we sense only the effects and ramifications of passions, and can learn to know their strength and their roots only through enlightenment by the Holy Spirit. Therefore we are aware of passions in ourselves only when they are in action; but as soon as they quieten down, we imagine that we have attained passionlessness.

How can we make sure that passions are not dead in our heart, but merely quiescent? By the fact that, when reassured on that score, we chance to meet objects, which feed the passions lying hidden in us, especially if this happens suddenly, and they immediately come to life and make their presence felt, sometimes with quite violent movements, so that, cast into turmoil, we wonder where they were hiding and whence they suddenly arose. St. Isaac of Syria explains this by the following beautiful illustration: in winter herbs and flowers vanish from the face of the earth, yet their roots remain safe, hidden in its depth. But as soon as they

136

feel the rains and warmth of spring, they immediately begin to sprout and so cover the face of the earth. So too with passions . . . And again: as it is natural for blighted land to produce thorns and thistles, so it is in a certain sense natural for human nature, corrupted by downfall and now conceived in sin and open to its stimulus, to produce passions, which give birth to sins; hence our nature can never be trusted or relied upon.

So, since you are still a beginner in spiritual warfare, exercise yourself diligently in virtue, as though you had not yet laid a foundation for it; and remember that it is better always to care for pressing forward in virtue than to find and define the signs of perfection in it.

God our Lord alone knows our hearts; He enlightens some and lets them see their progress in virtue, but to others He does not grant this knowledge and enlightenment. For He sees that in the first case this knowledge will lead to humility, whereas in the second men will be unable to refrain from vainglory. So, as a loving Father, He removes from the latter the danger of falling into the sin particularly abhorrent to Him, and gives the former an opportunity to increase the virtue of humility, which is especially pleasing to Him. Yet even a man, who is not given knowledge of his progress, can learn of it in due course, if he does not cease to exercise himself in virtue and if it pleases God to reveal this to him for his good.

CHAPTER FORTY-THREE

One should not desire too strongly to be free from the attack of afflictions, but should wholly abandon oneself to God's will

If you are enduring some affliction with thankfulness, pay good heed, lest your enemy succeeds in tempting you, or your self-love conceives a desire to be rid of it. For then you will suffer a double loss. The first is that, although the appearance of such a desire and your consenting to it does not immediately rob you of the virtue of patience, it does greatly undermine it. Therefore, when desire to be free of the affliction sent to you is not fulfilled, your patience gradually weakens and finally brings you to a state of impatience. The second is that from that moment your patience becomes forced, whereas God loves and rewards what is given freely . . . Therefore, from that moment, although you will still have to endure, for the mere desire to be rid of afflictions does not rid one of them, your endurance will be unrewarded. God will reward you for enduring your affliction for the time you have endured it with a good heart, not seeking deliverance. But from the moment this desire came to you, God will grant you no reward for your unwilling endurance. But if you stifle and repel the desire to be free from your affliction, as soon as it presents itself, and abandon yourself entirely to the benevolent will of God, proclaiming your readiness to suffer even a hundred times greater sorrows, should God wish to send them to you, then, even if your present suffering lasts only an hour or less, God will accept it as of the longest duration and will reward you correspondingly.

Do the same in all other cases—do not give way to your desires, but keep a tight rein on them, directing them exclusively to one chief aim—to remain within God's will and to proceed in accordance with God's will. For then your desires will all be good and righteous, and you will remain calm in every trial, finding peace in God's will. If you believe with all sincerity that nothing can happen to you except by God's will, and if you have no other desire but to be actively doing God's will, it is self-evident that no matter what happens to you, you will always have only what you desire.

When I say that nothing can happen to you except by God's will, I mean the afflictions and privations, which God sends to admonish and teach us or to punish us for our sins, but I do not mean your own or other people's sins themselves, since God does not wish sins. These trials are salutary for us and are rightly called a saving cross, which He often imposes on His best beloved and on those who strive to please Him, and the bearing of which is especially welcome to Him.

And when I said: do not wish to be rid of afflictions, it must be rightly understood in the sense of submission to God's will. We cannot help wishing to be free of sorrows, for God Himself placed in our nature the desire for well-being, and so included in the prayer He Himself gave us the request: 'Lead us not into temptation', which we repeat several times a day. If after this prayer, which God is sure to hear, He sends us sorrow, it is clearly His special will, to which we, His creatures, conscious of our duty to obey Him in everything, should submit with a good heart and endure our trial as something essential to your and my salvation. Also, in repeating the prayer: 'Lead us not into temptation', mean by it: 'Not as I will, but as thou wilt' (Matt. xxvi. 39), imitating our Saviour. In other words, say this prayer, not because you abhor temptations and want to avoid them at all costs, but only because the Lord commanded us to pray thus, keeping in the soul a complete readiness to accept with a good heart all that God pleases to send us, and refusing to pander to the self-loving desire for uninterrupted well-being, which is impossible on earth, since it belongs to the future eternal life.

CHAPTER FORTY-FOUR

Warning against evil counsels of the devil in relation to good actions

When the deceitful devil sees that we are advancing rightly on the path of virtue, with lively eagerness, and in good order, in spite of his attempts to lead us astray by his obvious enticements to evil, then he transforms himself into an angel of light and, now by seemingly good thoughts, now by texts from the Holy Scriptures, now by examples of the Saints, he urges us to undertake excessive and untimely efforts for spiritual perfection, in order to cast us down into the abyss at the moment when we imagine we stand on the summit. Thus he teaches some cruelly to mortify their flesh by fast, flagellation, sleeping on bare earth and other similar bodily hardships, in order to make them fall into pride and imagine that they are achieving great things; or to make them fall ill from extreme exhaustion and become incapable of performing even the smallest righteous deeds, or to make them so wearied by the burden of their efforts, that they become indifferent to all spiritual endeavour, and even to salvation itself, and thus, with their ardour for good gradually getting cooler and cooler, should throw themselves into carnal lusts and worldly comforts with even more zest than before.

What numbers of souls have perished in this snare of the enemy, for, carried away by the ardour of foolish zeal and in their self-mortification exceeding the measure of their own strength, they perished in ascetic feats of their own invention and became the laughing stock of evil demons! Of course, this would never have happened, if they had followed good judgment and advice, and had not forgotten that these feats of self-mortification, though praiseworthy and fruitful where there is sufficient strength of the body and humility of the soul, must always be controlled by good sense and used only as a means to spiritual progress, instead of becoming an aim in themselves, and must sometimes be reduced, sometimes increased, sometimes changed and sometimes stopped altogether for a time.

Those who cannot be as strict with themselves as the saints, nor rise to such efforts, can imitate their life in another way; namely, they can provoke and establish good dispositions in their hearts, acquire the habit of warm prayer, wage an unrelenting war against passionate thoughts and desires, protect the purity of their hearts, love silence and solitude, be humble and meek with all men, do good to those who have caused them suffering, guard themselves against all evil, however insignificant. All these righteous activities of the heart are more pleasing to God than excessive feats of mortification of the flesh, when the latter are not demanded by our moral condition.

Moreover, I advise you to use good judgment in undertaking feats of physical asceticism, when there is a need for them. Do not launch out with lofty standards, but begin at the bottom; for it is better to climb upwards gradually, than suddenly to undertake something lofty and be forced to climb down, to your shame. At the same time I advise you also to avoid the other extreme, into which even such men fall as are considered spiritual. Ruled by self-pity and self-indulgence, they exhibit too great a concern for the preservation of their physical health, and take such great care of themselves that they tremble at the slightest effort, afraid to impair their health. Nothing is more in their thoughts, nothing a more favourite subject of their talk than preserving their life Yet, by inventing delicate dishes, which pander more to their refined tastes than healthy food, they weaken and often impair their health and deprive themselves of the blessing they prize so highly, because they cannot do what is necessary to attain it.

Although they justify their actions by the desire to work better for the Lord, in actual fact it is nothing but an effort to reconcile two irreconcilable enemies—flesh and spirit, not only with no profit for either, but on the contrary with obvious harm to them both alike; since by this they deprive the body of health, and the spirit of its salutary state. Therefore a moderate and orderly mode of life, controlled by reason, which takes into account the requirements of the soul and the particular constitution of the body, together with its state of health, are less dangerous and more useful both for the soul and for the body. For in this respect the standard is not the same for every man, although one law applies to all —to keep the body subservient to the spirit. Remember also what was said earlier, that the acquisition of virtues, whether of body or soul, should be gradual, proceeding upwards little by little.

CHAPTER FORTY-FIVE

Our severe judgment of others comes from a high opinion of ourselves and the instigation of the devil. How to overcome this tendency

Self-love and high opinion of ourselves give birth in us to yet another evil which does us grievous harm; namely, severe judgment and condemnation of our neighbours, when we regard them as nothing, despise them and, if an occasion offers, humiliate them. This evil habit or vice, being born of pride, feeds and grows on pride; and in turn feeds pride and makes it grow. For every time we pass judgment our pride takes a step forward, through the accompanying effect of self-importance and self-gratification.

Since we value and think of ourselves so highly, we naturally look at others from on high, judge and despise them, for we seem to ourselves far removed from such faults as we think others possess. And here, seeing our evil disposition, our ever-wicked enemy stands by watchfully and, opening our eyes, teaches us to keep a sharp watch for what others say and do. From these observations he makes us draw conclusions as to their thoughts and feelings; and, on these suppositions, form an opinion of them, generally not good, exaggerating this supposed defect into a deep-rooted feature. These judges do not see and realise that the very

141

origin of their judgment, the suspicion of wrong in others, is impressed on the mind by the action of the enemy, and then fanned by him into a conviction that they are actually such, although it is not so at all.

So, brother, since the enemy watches you constantly, waiting for an opportunity to sow evil in you, be doubly watchful over yourself, lest you fall into the nets spread for you. As soon as he shows you some fault in your neighbour, hasten to repel this thought, lest it take root in you and grow. Cast it out, so that no trace is left in you, and replace it by the thought of the good qualities you know your neighbour to possess, or of those people generally should have. If you still feel the impulse to pass judgment, add to this the truth, that you are given no authority for this and that the moment you assume this authority you thereby make yourself worthy of judgment and condemnation, not before powerless men, but before God, the all-powerful Judge of all.

This reversal of thoughts is the strongest means, not only for repelling accidental critical thoughts, but also for completely freeing yourself of this vice. The second method, equally very strong, is never to let go from your mind the memory of your own wickedness, your unclean and evil passions and actions, and correspondingly to hold on to the constant realisation of your own unworthiness. You will certainly find in yourself no small number of such passions and passionate actions. If you have not given up and shrugged your shoulders, saying: 'Come what may', you cannot help caring about finding a cure for these ills, which are killing you. But if you act sincerely in this, you should have no time free to concern yourself in the affairs of others and to pass sentence on them. For then, if you let yourself do this, the sayings will keep ringing in your ears: 'Physician, heal thyself' (Luke iv. 23). 'First cast out the beam out of thine own eye' (Matt. vii. 5).

Moreover, when you judge severely some wrong action of your neighbour, you must know that a small root of the same wickedness is also in your own heart, which, by its passionate nature, teaches you to make suppositions about others and to judge them. 'An evil man out of the evil treasure' (of the heart) 'bringeth forth evil things' (Matt. xii. 35). But an eye, that is pure and without passion, looks too without passion on the actions of others, and not with evil. 'Thou art of purer eyes than to behold evil' (Habakkuk i. 13). Therefore when the thought comes to condemn

142

another man for some fault, be indignant with yourself as a perpetrator of the same actions and guilty of the same fault; and say in your heart: 'Unworthy as I am, how can I raise my head to see the faults of others and accuse them, when I am submerged in the same sin and my trespasses are even greater?' By doing this you will turn against yourself the weapon, which evil thought urges you to use against another; and instead of wounding your brother you will put plasters on your own wounds.

If the sin of your brother is not hidden but obvious to everyone, try to see its cause, not in what the wicked passion for judging suggests, but in what a brotherly feeling towards him may indicate, and say to yourself: since this brother has many hidden virtues, so, to protect them from being harmed by vainglory, God has allowed him to fall into the present sin, or to stay a short time in this unbecoming guise, so that he should appear unworthy in his own eyes and, being despised for it by others, should gather the fruits of humility and become even more pleasing to God; in this way the present instance will do him more good than harm. Even if a person's sin is not only obvious, but very grievous and comes from a hardened and unrepentant heart, do not condemn him, but raise your eyes to the wondrous and incomprehensible judgments of God; then you will see that many people, formerly full of iniquity, later repented and reached a high degree of sanctity, and that, on the other hand, others, who were on a high level of perfection, fell into a deep abyss. Take care, lest you also suffer this calamity through judging others.

So stand always on guard in fear and trembling, fearing more for yourself than for others. And be assured that every good word you may utter for your neighbour, and every rejoicing for his sake is the action and fruit of the Holy Spirit in you, whereas every bad word and scornful condemnation comes from your evil nature and suggestions of the devil. Therefore, when you are tempted by some wrong action of your brother, do not let your eyes sleep until you have driven this temptation from your heart and wholly made peace with your brother.

CHAPTER FORTY-SIX

On prayer

Although lack of reliance on yourself, trust in God and constant efforts are quite essential in our spiritual warfare, as has been shown already, yet the most important of all is prayer, the fourth weapon in this war, as we have said in the beginning (end of first chapter). For it is through prayer that the first three weapons are acquired and gain full force, and that all other blessings are obtained. Prayer is the means of attracting and the hand for receiving all the blessings, so richly poured on us from the inexhaustible source of God's infinite love and goodness towards us. In spiritual warfare, by prayer you put your battle-axe into God's hand, that He should fight your enemies and overcome them. But in order that prayer should manifest its full power in you, it is needful that it stay constantly in you, as a natural function of your spirit; and you should protect and inspire it by cultivating the following attitudes.

(1) You should keep always a lively striving to serve only God in all things you do, and serve Him in such way as is acceptable to Him. In order to make and keep this tendency alive, you must have the conviction, and always hold it in mind, that every reasoning creature should render the Lord worship, praise and service, if only because of His wondrous qualities: His goodness, greatness, wisdom and His numberless and immeasurable other perfections. When you add to this a constant remembrance of the fact that in an indescribable way He Himself served and profited you by the dispensation of His incarnation, redeemed you, freed you of the great curse, ministered to the wounds caused by the poison of sin and healed them, not with wine or oil, not with any kind of poultices, but with the priceless blood which flowed from His most holy side, and with His holy flesh tortured by scourgings, thorns, and nails; if you remember all this, how can you fail zealously to dedicate to His service alone every moment of your life by word, thought and deed? Moreover, you must not forget the profit we ourselves gain from such a service, since it makes us masters of ourselves, conquerors of the devil and sons of God.

(2) You must possess a warm and living faith that, in His great

144

mercy and loving kindness, God Himself wishes and is ready to give you all that is needed for you to serve Him rightly, and to bestow upon you every blessing you need. Such faith and such trust will become for you a vessel, which God in His infinite mercy will fill with the treasures of His blessings. And the bigger and more capacious your vessel, the richer the gifts with which your prayer will each time come back to what is deepest within you. How can one think that the Almighty and Unchanging God, Who commanded us to pray to Him and promised to give us the blessings we ask, should refuse them to us, and should not send us His Spirit, if with diligent and patient prayer we beg them from Him? Has He not said: 'How much more shall your heavenly Father give the Holy Spirit to them that ask him?' (Luke xi. 13). And has He not promised: 'And all things, whatsoever ye shall ask in prayer, believing, ye shall receive' (Matt. xxi. 22).

(3) You must approach prayer with an attitude such that you desire only the Divine Will, and not your own, alike in asking and in receiving what you have asked for. In other words, you should be moved to prayer because God wishes it, and you should wish to be heard, again as He desires it. In a word, let it be in your mind and heart completely to unite your will with the will of God, to obey it in everything, and in no way to desire to incline God's will towards your own.

Why should this be so? Because your will is always mixed with self-love, is very often mistaken and does not know what it should wish for. But the will of God is always good, wise, just, beneficent and can never err. Since God's will is an immutable law for all that is and will be, to obey its rule must be the will of all reasoning creatures and the queen of their desires, whom they must submissively follow in all things.

Thus you must always desire, ask for and seek only what is acceptable to God. If ever you are in doubt as to whether one thing or another is acceptable to Him, seek it and ask for it with the thought that you wish to do or have this, if God too desires it. As to things, which you are sure are acceptable to God, such as virtues, you should seek them and ask for them only in order to please God more and to serve Him better, and for no other purpose, be it even spiritual.

(4) Further, you should come to prayer bringing deeds corresponding to your petition, and after prayer work still harder to

145

become worthy to receive the grace and virtue you ask for. Thus the work of prayer should be accompanied by the effort of self-compulsion and of exerting all your strength towards what we ask, for here, in the order of spiritual life, asking for something and seeking it by your own efforts follow one another in alternation. But if a man prays God for some virtue, and at the same time gives himself up to negligence, acquiring no definite means to gain this virtue, and making no efforts towards it, truly this man tempts God, rather than prays. Thus the divine James says: 'The effectual fervent prayer of a righteous man availeth much' (James v. 16). What avails to make prayer effective, according to St. Maximus, is when, besides begging a saint to pray for him about something, the man also prays about it himself and with all diligence does everything necessary for obtaining his request.

(5) You should combine in your prayer the four actions of which St. Basil the Great writes: first, glorify God, then give thanks to Him for the mercies He has shown you, then confess to Him your sins and trespasses of His commandments, and finally ask Him to grant you what you need, particularly in relation to your salvation. In accordance with this you may, for example, pray thus:

'O Lord my God! I sing and praise Thy ineffable glory and Thy infinite greatness.—I thank Thee that, by Thy goodness alone, Thou hast given me to exist and to share in the life-saving blessings of Thy dispensation by incarnation, that Thou hast often saved me, even without my knowledge, from calamities which threatened me, and delivered me from the hands of my unseen foes,—I confess to Thee that countless times have I stifled my conscience and fearlessly transgressed Thy holy commandments, and so shown myself ungrateful for Thy many and varied bounties. O my most merciful Lord, let not my ingratitude be too great for Thy mercy, but overlook my sins and trespasses, look with kindness on the tears of my contrition, and, according to the multitude of Thy tender mercies, help me even now, grant me what is needful for my salvation, and guide my life towards pleasing Thee, so that, unworthy as I am, I too may glorify Thy holy name.'

At the end of this prayer you can enumerate all your present needs, those of the spirit, those of the soul and those of the body: and if at that time you are exercising yourself in some special virtue, mention it too and pray for God's help to make progress towards perfection in it. If you are troubled by the impulses of some passion, pray for help in resisting and vanquishing it. If you suffer some injustice or injury, some loss or affliction, do not forget to give thanks for it to God, since, being sent in accordance with God's will, which is always good, it is visiting you for your own benefit.

(6) In order that your prayer should be effective before God and should attract His benevolence, adorn it and give it wings by a firm faith not only in God's measureless bounty and in the immutable truth of His promise to hear us when we call to Him, even before our prayer is ended (Isaiah lviii, 9), but most of all in the power of the special dispensation of our Lord Jesus Christ, Who assumed flesh for our sakes, suffered death on the cross, was resurrected, ascended to heaven and sits on the right hand of God the Father, where He ceaselessly intercedes for us; since 'He that spared not his own Son, but delivered him up for us all, how shall he not with him also freely give us all things?' (Rom. viii. 32).

In order to be heard, offer also the intercession of the Holy Mother of God, the Virgin Mary, who prays for us day and night, and of all the saints, of archangels and angels, apostles and prophets, shepherds and teachers, together with the martyrs, holy fathers and mothers and those who have pleased God in every possible way, of your guardian angel and your patron saint whose name you bear, and the saint to whom is dedicated the Churches in which you were baptised, and always pray. By prefacing your prayer with these intercessions, you preface it with your humility, which of all things is most pleasing to God, since He looks upon no man with more lovingkindness than a man who is meek and humble. 'A broken and a contrite heart, O God, thou wilt not despise' (Ps. li. 17).

(7) You should always say your prayers with tireless diligence, as the Apostle directs, saying: 'Continue in prayer, and watch in the same' (Col. iv. 2). For humble patience, tirelessness and persistence in prayer conquer the unconquerable God and incline Him to mercy. According to the Lord's parable, the importunity of the widow inclined a wicked and unjust judge to grant her petition. The Lord gave this parable for a special purpose—to teach us not to faint, but to pray patiently, as we read in the Gospels: 'And he spake a parable unto them to this end, that men ought always to pray, and not to faint' (Luke xviii. 1). If, as I say,

an unjust judge was persuaded to grant the petition of the widow because she importuned him, how can God fail to incline His ear to our prayers, if we persist in imploring Him since He is the essence of lovingkindness? Therefore, when you beg God to grant you something, and He is slow in hearing you, continue to pray, keeping firm trust in His help alive in your heart. For diligent prayer is never left by Him unrewarded and He is always ready to pour out rich blessings in return, much exceeding the expectations of those who pray, if they have no inner obstacles and are not in a state when it is better for them that their petition should remain unfulfilled. In this case, instead of what they ask, God sends them some other good, more profitable to them, whether they are aware of it or not. In this sense the conviction that prayer never remains unheard is quite justified; all that happens is that, when we ask and are not aware that what we ask is unprofitable to us, God does not send what we ask, and what He does send remains unseen, because to see it is not without danger to him who receives. So always be patient in prayer, and convinced that prayer never remains without fruit. If you do not receive what you ask, believe that you are receiving or will receive another good in its place. If you do not see it or come to see it, do not try to find out why this is so, but turn to your unworthiness and fill your soul with humble thoughts and feelings. If you provoke and make firm such thoughts in yourself, as a consequence of prayer, then, even if you receive absolutely nothing, whether visibly or invisibly, accept these feelings themselves as the fruit of prayer, both salutary for yourself and most pleasing to God.

Hear what St. John Chrysostom says: 'Prayer is a great blessing if practised in a right inner state and if we teach ourselves to give thanks to God, both when we receive what we ask and when we do not receive it. For when He gives, and when He does not give, He does it for your good. Thus when you receive what you ask, it is quite clear that you have received it; but when you do not receive it, you also receive, because you thus do not receive what is undoubtedly harmful for you; and not to receive what is harmful means to be granted what is useful. So, whether you receive what you ask or not, give thanks to God in the belief that God would have always given us what we ask were it not often better for us not to receive it (ch. 1. εις τως Ανδριαν).

So always pray to God with patience and render thanks to Him

148

for all things, believing and professing your belief that He is good to you, and wisely good, and is your loving Benefactor, both when He gives and does not give what you ask. Firm in this faith, remain humbly obedient to divine Providence, meeting gratefully and gladly everything that happens, whether pleasant or unpleasant.

CHAPTER FORTY-SEVEN

What is mental or inner prayer, and of what kinds can it be?

Mental or inner prayer is when a man at prayer collects his mind in the heart, and from there sends out his prayer to God, not aloud but in silent words, praising and thanking Him, confessing to Him his sins with contrition and begging for his needs in spiritual and bodily blessings. One should pray not only in words but also in mind, and not only in mind but also in the heart, so that the mind sees and understands clearly what is said in words, and the heart feels what the mind thinks. All this yoked together is real prayer, and if something of this is lacking in prayer, it is either imperfect prayer or not prayer at all.

You are sure to have heard these expressions: prayer with words, prayer with the mind, prayer with the heart, and maybe you have heard explanations of each of them separately. What is the reason for this division of prayer into its component parts? The reason is that owing to our negligence it sometimes happens that the tongue says the holy words of prayer, while the mind wanders away somewhere: or the mind understands the words of prayer, but the heart does not respond to them with feeling. In the first case prayer is merely words, and is not prayer at all; in the second—prayer with words is connected with mental prayer, and this is imperfect, incomplete prayer. Full and real prayer is when praying words and praying thoughts are combined with praying feelings.

There also exists, through the grace of God, prayer of the heart only, and this is spiritual prayer, which the Holy Spirit moves in the heart: the man who prays is conscious of it, but does not do it; it acts by itself. This prayer belongs to the perfect. The form of prayer accessible to all and demanded of all is the form where mind and feeling are always combined with the words of prayer.

There is yet another form of prayer, which is called standing in the presence of God, when the man who prays is wholly concentrated in his heart and inwardly contemplates God as being present to him and within him, with corresponding feelings—either of fear of God and the feeling of wonder and awe before His greatness, or of faith and hope, or of love and submission to His will, or of contrition and readiness for any sacrifice. Such a state comes when a man becomes deeply immersed in prayer by word, mind and heart. If a man prays in the right way and for a long time, these states come to him more and more often, and finally this state can become permanent; then it is called walking before God and is constant prayer. This was the state of David, who says of himself: 'I have set the Lord always before me: because he is at my right hand, I shall not be moved' (Ps. xvi. 8).

Thus, my brother, if you wish your prayer to bring much fruit, never be content by oral prayer alone, but pray also with your mind and heart—using your mind to understand and be conscious of all that is said in words, and your heart to feel it all. Above all, pray with your heart. Prayer bursting from the heart is like a streak of lightning, which takes but a moment to cross the heavens and appear before the throne of the all-merciful God. God hears it and inclines towards this most of all. This was the prayer with which Moses prayed standing before the Red Sea; and immediately he heard God's voice: 'Wherefore criest thou unto me?' (Ex. xiv. 15): and God gave him the power to free his people from the danger which threatened them.

CHAPTER FORTY-EIGHT

How to learn to pray in this way

I presume that, having read thus far, you will ask: how to learn this prayer? The answer is: train yourself always to pray precisely in the way I have indicated, that is, not only in words, but also in mind and heart—and you will learn. How did you learn to read?

You began to work at it and learnt. How did you learn to write? You began to write, and you learnt. In the same way you will learn to pray as I have indicated, if you begin to pray in precisely this way.

You know of course the words of prayer—you were taught them from childhood. They are to be found in our prayer-books and the book of church services. They are prayers that poured out of the hearts of saintly men and women when, moved by the Holy Spirit, they expressed before God the desires of their heart. The spirit of prayer is contained in them; so, if you read them as you should, you too will be filled with this spirit, just as the spirit of a writer is communicated to one who reads with full attention. Everyone has experienced this, and I am sure you have had the same experience.

These words of prayer are collected in our prayer-books, so you have no need to work at collecting them. So get yourself a prayer-book and, at the times fixed for prayer, usually in the morning and evening, read the prayers set out there, paying attention to every word, thinking the thoughts expressed there and trying to reproduce in your heart the same feelings as stir in the prayer you read. This is all there is to it; and this is what all people usually do.

You will say: true, all people do this; but if so, why does not everyone have proper prayer? Because, although they do it, that is, open the prayer-book, stand before the icons and read, they do not bring their mind and heart into it: the mind wanders they know not where, and the heart follows its own pleasures, instead of praying. But when you pray you should confine your mind in the words of prayer and make your heart absorb what they say—and you will at once taste the fruit of such recital of prayer.

Thus, since you have the words of prayer and know what it means to understand and feel them, the rest depends on you: prayer and success in it is in your hands. Strive diligently and you will succeed. Yet I shall add some words of guidance to facilitate this success.

(1) Try to ponder over and feel the prayers you have to read, not at the hour of prayer, but at some other free time. If you do this, then, at the time set for prayer, you will have no difficulty in reproducing in yourself the whole content of the prayer you read. As soon as you begin some prayer, the thoughts and feelings

151

contained in it will at once present themselves to your conscious-ness, and you will utter the words as though they were your own, born in your own heart and pouring out of it, instead of having been brought into it.

(2) Having thought about and felt the prayers, take care to learn them by heart. When you have done this, you will carry the prayers in you. While they are in the prayer-book they are outside you; but when you have learnt them by heart, they become within you, so that, whatever the circumstances, you will always have your prayer-book with you. Besides, by memorising the prayers, you engrave the praying thoughts and feelings more deeply in yourself, than if you have merely pondered over and felt their meaning. This study of prayers, when you not only learn the words by heart but also preserve in yourself the thoughts and feelings they contain, will build in you a structure of prayer. This is the best method of forming the habit of proper prayer.

(3) When the time comes for recital of prayers, do not begin to say them as soon as you have torn yourself from your ordinary occupations, but first prepare yourself: 'stand for a while in silence, until your feelings calm down' as the prayer-book teaches, and remember what you are about to approach and to perform, who you are, who are about to pray, and who is He before Whom you are about to recite your prayers, what exactly you are to say and how. This preparation is made necessary—in the morning, because the soul is heavy from immersion in sleep and because the cares of the coming day flood you immediately upon awakening—and in the evening by the varied impressions of the day, and especially things that stand out as striking, whether pleasant or unpleasant. Try to sweep all this out of your consciousness, so that the work of prayer occupies your whole attention and you can consecrate the time before you exclusively to prayer. If some matters have struck you, and you have not succeeded in dealing with them, turn them into a subject for prayer, or thanksgiving, or ask for help and liberation, or commit them, yourself and all that you have to God's will.

(4) Just before you begin to recite prayers, bring yourself to the consciousness and feeling of standing in the presence of God with reverent awe, and bring to life in your heart the faith that God sees and hears you, that He does not turn away from those who pray to Him, but looks with benevolence on them and on you in

this hour of prayer. Let your prayer be winged with hope that He is ready to grant, and will actually grant your request, if it is for the good of your soul.

(5) Having brought yourself to this state, say your prayers, with the deepest attention, taking every care to make them come from the heart, as though they were your own, although they were learned by heart. Do not let your attention wander off, nor your thoughts slip away. As soon as you notice this happening, bring your thoughts back within, and resume your prayers from the point, at which your attention strayed to something else. Remember that attention does not stray when the heart is filled with feelings of prayer. So your first care should be for these feelings. Do not let yourself hurry in reciting prayers, but continue to the end reverently and with patience, as befits a sacred doing.

(6) If, while saying prayers, observing this method and attitude, some subject of prayer especially touches your heart, captures your attention as something very akin to your own circumstances, and incites you to pray in your own words, do not let this occasion slip by, but pause and pray in your own words, until the need or feeling for prayer that had arisen is satisfied.

(7) If you strive to practise the recital of prayer in this way, you will gain the spirit of prayer, which you must try to preserve in force as much as you can. For this reason, do not at once throw yourself into daily affairs and never think that, having performed your rule of prayer, you have finished with your duty to God and can now give rein to your thoughts and feelings. No, for the rest of the day you must also try to keep yourself as during your prayer rule. To succeed in this never forget that you are walking before God and that His hand alone keeps you above the abyss of nothingness. Keeping this in mind, do everything, both great and small, as God wishes it, asking His blessing and turning everything to the glory of His name. Acting thus you will retain the right state for prayer up to the hour of your evening rule. Having performed the evening rule in the same way, you will sleep rightly at night. Thus you will have lived a day and a night in a good prayerful state. In this way pass day after day, and in a few months, or perhaps even weeks, you will see your prayer gain in strength and, like a lamp that never goes out, prayer will constantly burn in your heart.

(8) I will add another small rule, namely, the necessity for this

work of prayer to go on without interruption from the moment it is begun until some success is attained . . . But if to-day you pray well and keep the state of prayer in you, but to-morrow become slack and spend the day dispersed, then, acting thus you will never achieve any success in prayer. It will be the same as building and pulling down. In the end, prayer may dry up altogether and the soul become incapable of it. Having once begun, one must patiently remain in prayer, never weakening and pandering to oneself by special dispensations and indulgences.

CHAPTER FORTY-NINE

On praying in one's own words

Everything said so far was said of prayer or psalmody in already set words which, although said with attention and feeling, are not one's own. Should one for always restrict oneself to these? Prayer itself will answer this question for him who prays. Begin praying rightly with prayers learnt by heart,—and from the start prayer will begin to graft itself to the soul; and the more firmly it becomes grafted, the more it urges a man also to send forth such personal prayer as is fashioned in his heart, according to his needs. So, with his regular prayers, he will also address such prayers to God. Thus one's own prayer has its recognised place and part in the work of prayer.

I have already mentioned in the preceding chapter (par. 6) that when, during recital of prayer, the words of some prayer you utter especially touch your soul and fill it, you must not leave them without attention, but must pause and pray from yourself about the thing that is filling your soul. So do this. The same happens when you read the word of God or the profitable writings of the holy fathers, or when you reflect on divine things—on the greatness and perfection of God, His wonderful works of creation, His omnipotence and providence, and the most wonderful work of dispensation through His incarnation to save us; it is also produced by specially striking and impressive occurrences of daily life. In other words, something particularly strikes the soul, captures its attention and urges it to ascend in prayer to God on

154

high. In all such cases, do not neglect to give attention to the impulse born in you, but respond to its urge, and interrupt for a while whatever you happen to be doing.

These sudden impulses mean that prayer has begun to inhabit your heart and to fill it. For these impulses do not come as soon as you have undertaken training in prayer, but only after a certain time, more or less long. These inner impulses are a proof of progress in the work of prayer; and the more frequent they are, the more the spirit of prayer fills the heart in which they are born. It should all end in praying always in one's own words alone. Though in actual fact it does not happen so, but one's own prayer always enters into the set prayers. For they are of the same nature and the same degree of virtue, and if they are replaced it is by standing in the presence of God, in wordless contemplation.

You must know, moreover, that sometimes in such cases it is the impulse alone for some prayer that is born, but at other times prayer itself accompanies the impulse, forming itself in the heart, without effort on the part of the man who prays. In the first instance, you must yourself fashion a suitable prayer, but in the second you must only listen and not interfere with the prayer pouring from the heart. Moreover, I remind you: do not be tempted by the desire to formulate your own prayers without such inner impulse and necessity. You can compose a very clever speech to God, but it will not be prayer:—it will be merely a combination of words and thoughts, but without the spirit of prayer. Do not do this. You will not avoid vanity and a high opinion of yourself, and these products stifle and stamp out real prayer.

As regards prayer, that forms itself in the heart, when the urge arises in it to pray about something which affects you personally and which you specially need, very often it is actually your own creation from the elements of prayer, collected in the heart from learning and assimilating existing prayers; but sometimes it is produced by the action of Divine grace. In such cases, it is the seed and the germ of the spiritual prayer I mentioned in chapter forty-seven. When you begin to be granted this, it will mean that you are approaching the boundaries of the perfection accessible to you. Give thanks then to God and walk on the path of life with still greater fear and trembling. The more precious the treasure, the more covetous the eyes of the enemies.

CHAPTER FIFTY

On short prayers, or short prayerful sighings to God

It has been said many times already that real prayer is inner prayer, performed not only in words but also with mind and heart. Prayer of this kind captures the whole attention and keeps it within, in the heart. This is why to remain within is an inalienable feature of real prayer and its chief condition. The thought of God, as being present and listening to prayer, and the repulsion of every other thought is inseparable from remaining within in prayer. This is called sobriety or guarding of the heart. Therefore all the care of a man striving to make progress in prayer must be pre-eminently directed and must in fact turn towards this end: that is, never to leave the heart, soberly protecting it from every thought, except the thought of God alone; and to do whatever one has to do with one's attention never turning away from God, conscious of His presence, as though before His Face. This is the highest doing in the work of prayer. Recital of prayer, practised in the manner shown above, is the way to this, and even to realising the need and necessity for it. It is the first to teach the mind to concentrate on the heart and to pay attention exclusively to God. Having learned the value of this concentration, it is natural for a man, who practises prayer, to wish for it to become a permanent condition of his spirit; for then constant prayer would dwell in him; and desire naturally leads to efforts to satisfy it. All those who have felt this need have sought and seek this. All instructions of the holy fathers concerning sobriety and guarding of the heart lead in this direction and have no other source but achievements in this work.

If you too feel this need, then you will ask: how to achieve this constant abiding within, before God's face, with sober guarding of the heart? Recital of prayer opens the way and produces the rudiments, but does not reach the end itself, or does not bring it to the required force and perfection. Recital of prayers is complex. It contains and offers to the attention many subjects which, although holy, may remind one of others, belonging to daily life

156

or social life, and lead through these to worldly, irrelevant subjects, in accordance with the usual laws of association of thoughts and visualisations. And so it happens; the most assiduous recital of prayer can never be practised without the thought darting away and wandering outside. Since this disturbs the prayer and makes it impure, there is no man who practises prayer, who is not chagrined by it and does not wish to be delivered from this incapacity. Attention was drawn to this from the very earliest days of the life of spiritual endeavour. Then what method, following recital of prayer, was invented to cure it? The method was invented of saying short prayers, which would keep the thought always within, before God's face, and would thus give it no chance of straying, nor of going outside. St. Cassian speaks of this, saying that in his time this practice was general in Egypt (Discourses x. 10). From the teachings of other fathers we see that it was used on Mount Sinai, in Palestine, in Syria, and in all other places throughout the Christian world. What other meaning have the invocation: 'Lord have mercy!' and other short prayers, which fill our divine services and our psalmody? Thus, here is my advice: choose for yourself a short prayer or several such prayers, and by their frequent repetition arrive at the stage when they go on repeating by themselves on your tongue, and keep your thought focused on one point only—remembrance of God.

Everyone is free to choose his own short prayers. Read the Psalms. There you can find in every Psalm inspiring appeals to God. Choose from them those which are most closely related to your state and most appeal to you. Learn them by heart and repeat now one, now another, now a third. Intersperse your recital of prayers with these, and let them be on your tongue at all times, whatever you may be doing, from one set time of prayer to another. You may also formulate your own prayers, should they better express your need, on the model of the 24 short prayers of St. Chrysostom, which you have in your prayer book.

But do not have too many, lest you overburden your memory and lest your attention runs from one to the other, which will be totally contrary to the purpose for which they were designed—to keep attention collected. The 24 prayers of St. Chrysostom is the maximum; one can use less. To have more than one is good for variety and to enliven spiritual taste; but in using them one should not pass from one to another too quickly. Taking one

157

which corresponds best to your spiritual need, appeal to God with it until your taste for it becomes blunted. You can replace all your psalmody, or part of it, by these short prayers; make it a rule to repeat them several times—ten, fifty and a hundred times, with lesser bows. But always keep one thing in mind—to hold your attention constantly directed towards God.

We will call this practice short prayerful sighings to God, continued at all moments of the day and of the night, when we are not sleeping.

CHAPTER FIFTY-ONE

On the Jesus Prayer

There have been and still are men of prayer who preferred one short prayer and repeated it constantly. St. Cassian says that the prayer usually repeated in his time by everyone in Egypt was the first verse of Psalm lxx: 'Make haste, O God, to deliver me; make haste to help me, O Lord.' It is written in the life of St. Joanniky that he repeated the following prayer: 'The Father is my hope, the Son is my refuge, the Holy Spirit is my protection.' He also added it to each verse of the thirty psalms he learnt by heart, which constituted his rule of prayer. Another constantly used as prayer the following words: 'Being a man I have sinned; but Thou, being God the Compassionate, have mercy on me.' Others, of course, preferred other prayers. From the most ancient times the prayer chosen by a great many was: 'Lord Jesus Christ, Son of God, have mercy on me, a sinner.' We find indications of it in St. Ephrem, St. Chrysostom, St. Isaac of Syria, St. Hesychius, St. Barsanuphius and John, and St. John of the Ladder. Later it became more and more general, began to be on everyone's lips and became part of the Church's statutes, where it is offered in place of all prayers said at home and of all church services. This is why it is now used with us more than any other short prayer. I advise you too to acquire the habit of it.

This prayer was called the Jesus Prayer because it is addressed to our Lord Jesus. Like any other short prayer, it is verbal; but it becomes and should be called mental, when it is said not only in

158

words, but also in mind and heart, with both consciousness and feeling of its content, and especially if, through long and attentive practice, it becomes so merged with the movements of the spirit, that the words disappear and only these movements are seen within.—Every short prayer can reach this degree. Pre-eminence belongs to the Jesus prayer because it unites the soul with our Lord Jesus, and the Lord Jesus is the only door to union with God, which is the aim of prayer. For He Himself said: 'No man cometh unto the Father, but by me' (John xiv. 6). Thus a man, who acquires it, acquires also the whole force of dispensation by incarnation: and in this lies our salvation. Hearing this, you will not be surprised that those who strove after salvation neglected no effort in trying to form the habit of this prayer and to become possessed of its power. You too should imitate their example.

Externally, acquiring the habit of this prayer consists in reaching the point where it turns on your tongue constantly by itself; internally, it consists in concentrating the attention of the mind in the heart and in constantly standing there in the presence of the Lord, with varying degrees of heartfelt warmth, repulsing all other thoughts, and above all falling at the feet of our Lord and Saviour with contrition and humility. The first step towards this habit is to repeat this prayer as often as possible with attention in the heart. Frequent repetition, becoming established, collects the mind into one, standing in the presence of the Lord. Establishing this order within is accompanied by warmth of heart and by repelling of all thoughts, even simple and not only passionate ones. When the flame of cleaving to the Lord begins to be constantly alight in the heart, then, together with this, a peaceful ordering of the heart will be established within, with contrite and humble inner prostration before the Lord. We are brought thus far by our own efforts with the help of Divine grace. Anything beyond this which may be attained in the work of prayer will be a gift of grace alone. The holy fathers mention this only lest, having reached this limit, a man thinks that he has nothing further to wish for and imagines that he has attained the summit of perfection in prayer, or in spiritual achievement.

Thus, your first task is to repeat the Jesus prayer as often as you can, until you acquire the habit of repeating it unceasingly. Do it in this way:

(1) Reserve in your rule of prayer a place for the Jesus prayer.

159

Repeat this prayer several times at the beginning of your recital of prayers, and several times at the end. If you have the zeal, do the same after every prayer which enters into your recital, imitating St. Joanniky the Great, who, after every verse of the psalms, included in his rule of prayer, repeated his short prayer: 'The Father is my hope, the Son is my refuge, the Holy Spirit is my protection.'

(2) As to the number of times you should repeat this prayer and on what occasions, you should decide this yourself, or ask the advice of your spiritual Father. Only do not undertake too much at first, but increase the number of repetitions gradually, as your enjoyment of this prayer grows. If the desire comes to double the set number, do not deny it to yourself, but take it not as a set rule, but only for this occasion. And whatever the number of such repetitions your heart demands, do not refuse it.

(3) Do not hurry to pass from one prayer to another, but recite them with measured deliberation, as you are wont to address a request to some exalted personage. Yet take care not only of the words, but rather that your mind should abide in the heart, standing there before the Lord, as though He were present, with full consciousness of His greatness, grace and truth.

(4) If you have free time, then, between one time of set prayer and another, give yourself the task of stopping, as you do when you stand up to pray, and send to the Lord this prayer, repeating it several times. If you have no free time, insert this prayer inwardly everywhere in the intervals of your occupations, and even of your talking.

(5) Doing this prayer during your rule, or standing in the posture of prayer between rules, after each repetition make a bow—ten times from the waist, and then a full prostration, and so on till the end. You have, of course, heard or read that in their instructions on prayer the holy fathers ordain a great many bows. One of them said: 'Prayer is not sufficient unless in praying a man wearies his body with bows.' If you decide to follow this advice, as much as you can, you will soon see the fruit of your labour in acquiring the habit of the Jesus prayer.

(6) As regards further instructions, indications and warnings about the Jesus prayer, read in the Philokalia Simeon the New Theologian, Gregory of Sinai, Nicephore the monk, Callistus and Ignatius. The teachings of all other fathers about inner prayer can

also be applied to the prayer of Jesus. Take note that in the instructions of the aforementioned fathers you will find directions as to how to sit, how to hold one's head, how to breathe. As Callistus and Ignatius said, these methods are not essentially necessary, but are merely external aids, not suitable for everyone. For you it is sufficient to keep your attention in the heart, before the face of the Lord and to send Him this short prayer with reverence and humility, with bows if you are standing for your rule, or with only mental prostration, when you do it during your usual tasks.

(7) Note also, that attention should be in the heart, or inside the breast, as some fathers say, namely, a little above the left nipple, —and there the Jesus prayer should be repeated. When the heart begins to ache with tension, follow the advice of Nicephore the monk, namely, leave that place and establish yourself with your attention and with the words of the prayer where we usually converse with ourselves, namely under the Adam's apple in the upper part of the chest. Later again descend over the left nipple. —Do not disdain this remark, however simple and unspiritual it may seem to you.

(8) Reading the holy fathers, you will find many warnings. All of them are the results of experience in wrong practices. To avoid these faults, you should have a counsellor—your spiritual Father, or a colleague of the same mind, with whom you can talk, and verify with him all that occurs while you perform this task. As to yourself, act always in a state of complete simplicity and great humility, never attributing success to yourself. You must know that true success comes within, unnoticeably, without ostentation, as is the case with the growth of a body. Thus, if a voice cries inside you: 'Here it is!'—know that it is the voice of the enemy, presenting to you something imaginary instead of the real. Here lies the origin of self-delusion. Stifle this voice immediately, lest it goes on in you like a trumpet, feeding vainglory.

(9) Do not set a time for achievement in this prayer. Decide only one thing: to work, and to work. Months and years will go by before the first feeble indications of success begin to show. One of the Mount Athos fathers said of himself that two years of work passed before his heart grew warm. With another father this warmth came after eight months. With each man it comes in accordance with his powers and his diligence in this work.

CHAPTER FIFTY-TWO

Aids to success in gaining the habit of prayer

If you desire to seek success in the work of prayer, adapt all else to this, lest you destroy with one hand what the other builds.

(1) Keep your body strictly disciplined in food, sleep and rest. Do not give it anything simply because it wants it; as the Apostle says: 'Make not provision for the flesh, to fulfil the lusts thereof' (Rom. xiii. 14). Give no respite to the flesh.

(2) Reduce your external contacts to the most inevitable. This is for the period of your training in prayer. Later, when prayer begins to act in you, it will itself indicate what can be added without harming it. Especially guard your senses, above all, eyes and ears; also tie your tongue. Without this guarding, you will not make a single step forward in the work of prayer. As a candle cannot burn in wind and rain, so the flame of prayer cannot be lit in a flood of impressions from outside.

(3) Use all the time left from prayer in reading and meditation. For reading, choose mainly such books as deal with prayer and generally with inner spiritual life. Meditate exclusively on God and on divine matters, and above all on the incarnated dispensation for our salvation, chiefly on the passion and death of our Lord and Saviour. Doing this you will always be immersed in the sea of divine light. In addition, go to church, whenever you have the possibility to do so. Merely to be present in church will envelop you in a cloud of prayer. What then will you receive if you stand throughout the service in a true state of prayer?

(4) Know that it is impossible to make progress in prayer without general progress in Christian life. It is absolutely necessary that no sin, not purified by repentance, should burden the soul. If during your work on prayer you do something, which troubles your conscience, hasten to purify yourself by repentance, so that you can look up to the Lord boldly. Keep humble contrition constantly in your heart. Moreover, neglect no opportunity for doing some good, or for manifesting some good disposition, above all humility, obedience and cutting off your own will. It goes without saying that zeal for salvation must always be burning and fill the whole soul; in all things, great or small, it must be the

main impelling force, together with fear of God and unshaken trust.

(5) Thus established, labour in the work of prayer, praying now with set prayers, now with your own, now with short appeals to the Lord, now with the Jesus prayer, omitting nothing which can be of help in this work. And you will receive what you seek. I remind you of the words of St. Macarius of Egypt: God will see your work of prayer and that you sincerely wish to succeed in prayer—and He will give you prayer. For you must know that, although prayer done and achieved with one's own efforts is pleasing to God, yet that real prayer, which comes to dwell in the heart and becomes constant, is the gift of God, an act of Divine grace. Therefore, in your prayer for all other things, do not forget to pray too about prayer.

(6) I shall repeat to you what I heard from a God-loving man. 'I was not leading a very good life,' he said, 'but God had mercy on me and sent me the spirit of repentance. This was during preparation for communion. I was trying hard to plant in myself a firm resolve to mend my ways, and especially before confession I prayed for a long time before the Icon of the Mother of God, begging Her to obtain this resolve for me. Then, during confession, I candidly related everything. My spiritual Father said nothing: but while he was reciting the prayer of absolution over my head, a small sweet flame was lit in my heart. The sensation was like swallowing some delectable food. This little flame remained in the heart, and I felt as though someone was gripping my heart. From that time I prayed continuously, and kept my attention there, where this sensation was, my only care being to preserve it. And God helped me. I had not heard about the Jesus prayer, and when I did hear of it, I saw that what was within me was precisely that which is sought by this prayer.' I mention this story to make you understand what the work of prayer seeks and what are the signs that it is received.

(7) I shall also add the following words of St. Gregory of Sinai (Philokalia, Part I, p. 112 etc.).

'Grace abides in us from the time of our holy baptism; but, through our inattention, vanity and the wrong life we lead it is stifled, or buried. When a man resolves to lead a righteous life and is zealous for salvation, the fruit of his whole labour is, therefore, the restoration in force of this gift of grace. It comes to pass

in a two-fold manner: first, this gift becomes revealed through many labours in following the commandments; in so far as a man succeeds in following the commandments, this gift becomes more radiant and brilliant. Secondly, it manifests and reveals itself through constant invocation of the Lord Jesus in prayer. The first method is powerful, but the second is more so, so that even the first method gains power through it. Thus, if we sincerely wish to open the seed of grace concealed in us, let us hasten to train ourselves in this latter exercise of the heart, and let us have only this work of prayer in our heart, without forms, without images, till it warms our heart and makes it burn with ineffable love of the Lord.'
—This extract contains all of which I reminded you earlier in the fourth paragraph.

CHAPTER FIFTY-THREE

The role of prayer in unseen warfare

In speaking of prayer I drew your attention above all to the means of raising prayer to the level to which it belongs. It might seem strange to you that, since we are speaking of unseen warfare, and you wish to know in what way prayer can help in it, all you have heard of was how to make prayer real prayer. Do not be surprised, for prayer can become a victorious weapon in unseen warfare only when it becomes real, that is, when it takes root in the heart and begins to act there unceasingly. From that moment it becomes an impenetrable, unconquerable and insuperable barrier, protecting the soul from the arrows of the enemy, the passionate assaults of the flesh, and the enticements of the world with its prelest. Its very presence in the heart cuts off the unseen warfare. This is why you were advised to make haste and graft the action of prayer on to your heart, and to see that it should remain in ceaseless movement. For this is the same as to say: do this and you will conquer, even without struggle.

And indeed this is how it actually happens. But until your prayer reaches such power, enemies will give you no peace and you will have no moment of respite from war, or threat of war. Does prayer help at this stage? Assuredly: and more so than any other weapon of spiritual warfare. It always attracts Divine help, and

God's power repulses the enemies, so long as it is practised with zeal and with surrender to God's will. Its place is at the very forefront of resistance to enemy attacks. This is how matters go. When, like a watchful sentry, attention sounds the alarm about the approaching enemy, and enemy arrows begin to be felt, that is, either a passionate thought or stirrings of passion appear within, the spirit, aflame with zeal for salvation, recognises it to be the evil doing of the enemy and, by straining its powers to the utmost, mercilessly repulses it from the heart, not letting it penetrate within. At the same moment, almost as one and the same inner action, it ascends to God in prayer, calling for His help. Help comes, enemies are dispersed, and the battle subsides.

St. John Kolov describes this exactly, saying of himself: 'I am like a man sitting under a large tree, who sees a multitude of beasts and snakes advancing towards him. He cannot stand up to them, so he hastily climbs the tree and is safe. It is the same with me: I sit in my cell and see evil thoughts rise up against me; since I am not strong enough to resist them, I run to God by means of prayer, and so save myself from the enemy' (True Sayings, par. 11).

St. Hesychius writes on the same lines in his chapters on prayer and sobriety: 'You should look within with a keen and intense look of the mind, so as to perceive those who enter; and when you perceive them, you should at once crush the head of the snake by resistance; and along with this call on Christ with groaning. And then you will gain the experience of unseen Divine intercession' (par. 22).

And: 'Every time it happens that wicked thoughts multiply in us, let us throw among them the invocation of our Lord Jesus Christ; and we shall at once see them dispersed like smoke in the air, as experience teaches' (par. 98).

Again: 'Let us conduct this mental war in the following order. The first thing is attention; then, when we notice a wicked thought draw near, let us wrathfully hurl a heartfelt curse at it. The third thing is to turn the heart to the invocation of Jesus Christ and pray Him to disperse forthwith this phantom of the demons, lest the mind runs after this fantasy like a child attracted by a skilful juggler' (par. 105).

And: 'Opposition usually bars the further progress of thoughts, and invocation of the name of Jesus Christ banishes them from the heart. As soon as suggestion is formed in the soul by an image

165

of some physical object, such as a man who has wronged us, or a beautiful woman, or silver and gold, or when thoughts of all these things come to us, it immediately becomes clear that these fantasies were brought to our heart by the spirits of ill-will, lust and avarice. If our mind is experienced, trained and accustomed to protect itself from suggestions and to see clearly, as by the light of day, the seductive fantasies and beguilements of the demons, then, by resistance, contradiction and prayer to Jesus Christ, it immediately and easily repels the red-hot arrows of the devil. It does not allow passionate fantasies to entice away our thoughts, and forbids our thoughts to attach themselves to the suggested image or to fraternise and allow it to multiply or to identify with it, for evil deeds follow upon all this as inevitably as night follows day' (par. 143).

You will find in St. Hesychius many similar passages, and you will see that he gives a complete outline of all our unseen warfare. So I advise you to read as often as possible his chapters on sobriety and prayer.

PART TWO

CHAPTER ONE

The most holy sacrament of the Eucharist

So far, dear reader, I have spoken to you of the four weapons required to overcome the enemies in unseen warfare, namely non-reliance on oneself, an unshakeable hope in God, resisting and struggling with sin, and prayer. Now I want to indicate to you another powerful weapon in this warfare, namely, the most holy sacrament of the Eucharist. This sacrament is the highest among sacraments, and is the most powerful and effective of all spiritual weapons. The four weapons of which we have spoken receive their power from the forces and gifts of grace, obtained for us by the blood of Christ. But this sacrament is Christ's blood itself, and His flesh itself, in which Christ is Himself present as God. When we use those four weapons, we fight the enemy with the power of Christ; in the latter case our Lord Christ Himself strikes down our enemies through us, or in company with us. For he who eats Christ's flesh and drinks His blood abides with Christ, and He in him, as He said: 'He that eateth my flesh, and drinketh my blood, dwelleth in me, and I in him' (John vi. 56). Therefore, when we overcome the enemies, it is the blood of Christ which overcomes, as it is written in Revelation: 'and they overcame him' (the slanderous devil) 'by the blood of the Lamb' (Rev. xii. 11).

This most holy sacrament, this all-conquering weapon, or rather Christ present in this sacrament, can be actively received in a twofold manner: *first*, sacramentally, in the sacrament of Christ's flesh and blood, with the necessary preparation, that is, contrition, confession, purification by penance and the required fast; *secondly*—inwardly and spiritually in mind and heart. The *first* may take place as often as outer circumstances, inner state and the discretion of one's spiritual Father allow; the *second* can take place every moment; so you may always have this all-powerful weapon in your hand and constantly wield it against your enemies. So harken to this and partake of the Holy Mysteries of Christ as often as possible, so long as you have the permission of your spiritual Father. But strive to partake of Christ our Lord inwardly and spiritually without ceasing; I have offered you guidance to this in the preceding chapters on prayer.

CHAPTER TWO

How one should partake of the holy sacrament of the Eucharist, or partake of Christ our Lord sacramentally—in the sacraments

To achieve the aim with which we approach this divine sacrament, we must have certain special dispositions, perform certain special practices and undertake certain special measures before communion, during communion and after communion. Before communion, we must purify ourselves of all the filth of sins, both mortal and not mortal, through the sacrament of repentance and confession, and fulfil whatever our spiritual Father imposes on us during confession, combining it with a firm resolve to serve only our Lord Jesus Christ with our whole heart, whole soul, whole strength and whole mind, and to do only what is acceptable to Him. Since in this sacrament He gives us His flesh and His blood, and with it His soul, His Divinity, and the full force of His incarnated dispensation, when we think how insignificant is what we give Him, compared with His gift, let us at least resolve in our heart to be diligent in doing all we can to His glory; and even if we should gain possession of the greatest gift ever offered to Him by earthly or heavenly intelligent beings, let us profess our readiness to offer it without hesitation to His Divine Majesty.

If you wish to partake of this sacrament, in order to overcome and destroy by its power the Lord's enemies and your own, begin to meditate the evening before, or even earlier, on how much our Saviour, the Son of God and God, desires that by partaking of this sacrament you should give Him a place in your heart, so that He should be united with you, and help you to drive out from it all your passions and overcome all your enemies.

This desire of the Lord is so great and ardent that no created mind can contain it in its perfection. Yet, in order to move even a little towards this understanding, you must try to impress deeply

170

in your mind the following two thoughts: *first*, what unutterable delight it is for the all-merciful God to be in most sincere communion with us, as the holy Wisdom Itself testifies, saying: 'And my delights were with the sons of men' (Prov. viii. 31); and *second*, how strongly God hates sin, both because it prevents his union with us, so desirable to Him, and because it is directly opposed to His divine perfections. Since His nature is infinitely blessed, pure light and ineffable beauty, He cannot but totally abhor sin, which is nothing but the extreme of evil, darkness, corruption, abomination and shame in our souls. God's abhorrence of sin is so great that from the very beginning all the acts of divine Providence for us and all the ordinances of the Old and New Testaments were directed towards exterminating sin and wiping out its traces. Most of all is this true of the most wondrous passion of our Saviour Jesus Christ, Son of God and God. Some theologians and teachers say even that if it were necessary, our Lord Jesus would be ready to take upon Himself endless other deaths to destroy the power of sin (recall the saying of St. Dionysius the Areopagite about the vision of Titus). This is how the wrath of God pursues it.

Having understood from such thoughts and contemplations how great is God's desire to enter your heart, to gain there a final victory over your enemies, who are His enemies also, you cannot help feeling an ardent desire to receive Him into yourself, in order that He should accomplish in you such a deed in actual fact. Thus fully inspired by courage and filled with daring by the sure hope that the heavenly Commander, your Jesus, can enter you, frequently challenge to a fight the passion which troubles you most and which you wish to overcome, and strike it down with hatred, contempt and disgust, at the same time rousing in yourself the prayerful desire for the opposite virtue, and the readiness to do corresponding deeds, precisely such and such.

This is what you should do on the eve of communion.

In the morning, a little before the Holy Communion, make a mental survey of all the times when you were carried away, did wrong, or sinned, from the time of your last communion till now. Remember also the blindness and foolhardiness with which all this was done, as though for you there were no God, Who judges and rewards, Who has seen it all and Who has borne terrible tortures and a shameful death on the cross to deliver you from such things.

171

Realise that you scorned all this every time you inclined towards sin and put your own shameful lusts above the will of your God and Saviour. Let the face of your soul be covered with shame when you realise such ingratitude and foolhardiness. Yet do not let yourself be overwhelmed by the disturbance of all this, and cast out any hopelessness. In His infinite long-suffering the Lord sees your repentance and your profession of readiness to serve henceforth Him alone, He inclines towards mercy and hastens towards you and into you, in order to engulf and drown in the immensity of His loving kindness the immensity of your ingratitude, your foolhardiness and lack of faith. So approach Him with the humble feeling of unworthiness, but with full hope, love and devotion, preparing a spacious tabernacle for Him in your heart, to let the whole of Him enter you. How and in what way? By banishing from the heart not only passionate attachment to and sympathy for any created thing, but even all thought of such, and by closing its door, to prevent anyone or anything entering it, except the Lord alone.

After communion of the holy Mysteries, enter immediately the secret depths of your heart and there worship the Lord with devoted humility, inwardly addressing Him in such wise: 'Thou seest, O my all-merciful Lord, how easily I fall into sin, to my ruin, what power the passion that attacks me has over me, and how powerless I am to free myself from it. Help me, give power to my powerless struggles, or rather take up Thyself my weapons and fight for me, finally to overthrow my cruel enemy.'

Then turn to the heavenly Father of our Lord Jesus Christ and of ourselves, Who together with His Son has in His benevolence entered into you in these mysteries, and to the Holy Spirit, Whose grace has inspired and prepared you for partaking of the blood and flesh of the Lord, and Who now, after communion, richly sheds His grace upon you; and adore the one God, worshipped as the Holy Trinity, Who bestows His favours upon us. Having given Him reverent thanks for the great mercy shown you at this moment, present to Him, as an offering, your firm resolution, readiness and ardent desire to fight your sin, in the hope of overcoming it by the power of the one God in Three Hypostasies. For you should know that if you do not use all the efforts you can to conquer your passion, you will receive no help from God; and if, in striving with all zeal and diligence, you rely only on your own powers, you will have no success. Strive with all diligence, but expect success only from God's help. Help will surely come and, rendering your powerless efforts all-powerful, will give you an easy victory over that against which you struggle.

CHAPTER THREE

*How to kindle the love of God in oneself by
entering deeply into the sacrament
of the Eucharist*

In order to kindle a great love of God in yourself by entering deeply into the heavenly sacrament of the blood and flesh of Christ, turn your thought to the contemplation of the love, which God has shown you personally in this sacrament. For this great and almighty God was not content with creating you in His likeness and image, and when you sinned and offended Him and so fell from your high rank, He was not satisfied with sending His Only-begotten Son to live thirty-three years on earth to deliver you, and, by terrible torment and painful death on the cross, to redeem and snatch you out of the hands of the devil, to whom you became enslaved through sin, and again to restore you to your former rank; no, He also deigned to establish the sacrament of His flesh and blood as food for you, so that the whole power of His incarnated dispensation might imbue your nature most essentially. Make this last token of God's strong love for you the object of your constant contemplation and deep pondering, so that, seeing its manifold fullness and richness, you should thereby feed and inflame your heart with undivided love and longing for God.

(1) Think of the time when God began to love you, and you will see that His love for you has no beginning. For since He himself is eternal in His divine nature, eternal also is His love for you, whereby before all ages He took counsel with Himself and resolved to give you His Son in a miraculous and ineffable manner. Realising this, rejoice in ecstasy of spirit and cry: 'So even in the abyss of eternity my nothingness was watched over and loved by the infinite God; even then did He make provision for my good, and

His love, which is beyond all words, resolved to give me for food His Only-begotten Son. After this, can I permit myself for a single moment not to cleave to Him with all my thought, all my desire and all my heart?'

(2) Think also that all mutual affections between creatures, however great they may be, have their measure and their limit, beyond which they cannot go. Only the love of God for us is limitless. So, when it became necessary to satisfy it in a certain special way, He sacrificed to it His Son, Who is His equal in greatness and infinitude, for His nature is one and the same. Thus His love is as great as His gift, and conversely His gift as great as His love. Both the one and the other are so great, that no created mind can conceive anything greater. So requite this boundless love at least with all the love of which you are capable.

(3) Reflect further that God conceived this love for us not through any necessity, but solely through His natural loving-kindness. He loved us from Himself spontaneously, with love as much beyond measure as beyond understanding.

(4) Reflect also that on our side we could never have forestalled this love by any deed so worthy of praise or reward, that the infinite God would requite our utter poverty with the wealth of His love; that He loved us only because in His loving-kindness He wished it; and not only loved us, but gave Himself to us, His unworthy creatures.

(5) Look at the purity of this love and see that, unlike the love of creatures, it is unmixed with any expectation of future gain from us. For God has no need of gain from outside, being Himself all-sufficing and all-blessed in Himself. Thus, if He wished to pour His ineffable love and loving-kindness upon us, He did so not for the sake of any profit for Himself from us, but for our own good.

Thinking of all this, can you help crying out in yourself: 'O the wonder of it! The Almighty God has laid His heart upon me, the least of His creatures! What dost Thou wish of me, O King of glory? What dost Thou expect of me, who am nothing but dust and ashes? I see clearly, O Lord my God, in the light of Thy infinite love, that Thou hast but one desire, which most reveals the radiance of Thy love for me, namely that Thou desirest to give me the whole of Thyself as food and drink for no other purpose but to transmute the whole of me into Thyself, not because Thou hast any need of me, but because I have extreme need of

Thee; for in this way Thou dwellest in me and I in Thee; and through this union of love I become as Thou art. In human words: through the union of my earthly heart with Thy heavenly heart a single divine heart is created in me.'

Such thought cannot but fill you with wonder and joy, when you see yourself so highly valued by God and so beloved by Him, and understand that in His infinite love for you He seeks and desires nothing from you, save only to attract your love to Himself and thus to give you bliss, by delivering you from every passionate attachment to creatures and to yourself. For then you will be able to bring the whole of yourself as a burnt offering to Him, your God, and from then onwards, for all the rest of your life, only love of Him and an ardent desire to please Him will possess your mind, your will, your memory and all your senses. Every favour coming from God's love for you can produce this effect in your soul: but this effect is most natural if you look with understanding on the most blessed sacrament of the divine Eucharist. While you look at it with your mind, open your heart to it, and pour out the following devout prayers and loving sighs: 'Oh, heavenly Food! When shall the hour come when I am totally immolated for Thee and consumed, not by some other fire, but by the fire of Thy love? O uncreated Love, O Bread of Life! When shall I live by Thee alone, for Thee alone and in Thee alone? When, O my life, beautiful, sweet and eternal, when, O Manna from heaven, shall I turn away from all other earthly food, when shall I desire only Thee and be fed by Thee alone? When will it be, O my all-satisfying sweetness, O my highest good! O my Lord, most desired and most good! Tear this poor heart of mine from every wrong attachment and tendency, adorn it with Thy holy virtues and fill it with that good disposition which would make me, in all sincerity, do all things solely to please Thee! Then, at last, I shall attain to opening to Thee my heart, no longer unworthy of Thee, and, invoking Thee with love, shall make Thee enter it. And then, my Lord, having entered it, Thou wilt not meet with resistance and wilt perform therein all the actions Thou art wont to perform in souls devoted to Thee.'

In such loving thoughts and feelings you may spend the evening and morning, preparing for communion. Then, when the sacred hour of communion draws near, imagine most vividly, with humility and warmth of heart, Whom you are about to receive into yourself, and who are you, who are about to receive Him.

He is the Son of God, clothed in inconceivable greatness, before Whom tremble the heavens and all the powers: He is the Holy of holies, brighter than the sun, purity beyond all comprehension, compared with which all created purity is filth. In His love for you He took the form of a slave, chose to be despised, scorned and crucified by the malice of the lawless world, and at the same time remained God, holding in His hand the life and death of the whole world. And who are you? You are—nothing, who in your corruption, evil and malice have become less than nothing, worse than the least and most unclean of all creatures, the laughing stock of the demons of hell. Carried away by your fantasies and lusts, you have scorned your great Lord and Benefactor and, instead of giving thanks to the bountiful God for so many and such great favours, you have trodden under foot His priceless blood, spilt for your sake. Yet, in spite of it all, He is calling you to His divine supper in His unceasing and unchanging love for you. At times He even forces you to approach it by fearful admonitions, reminding you of His words said to all: 'Except ye eat the flesh of the Son of man, and drink his blood, ye have no life in you' (John vi. 53); and just as He does not shut to you the door of His mercy, so He does not turn His face away from you, even though, in your sins, you are a leper, weak, blind and poor, a slave to all passions and vices.

The only things He demands of you are:

(1) That you should grieve in your heart at having offended Him; (2) that you should abhor sin above all things, any sin, great or small; (3) that you should give yourself up to Him entirely and care for one thing only, with all the love and longing of your heart —to conform to His will always and in everything you do, and be for ever fully obedient to Him alone; (4) that you should have a firm faith in Him and an unshakeable trust that He will have mercy upon you, will cleanse you of all your sins and will protect you from all your enemies, both visible and invisible.

Fortified by this ineffable love of God for you, approach the Holy Communion with holy fear and love, saying: 'I am unworthy, O Lord, to receive Thee; for many and many a time have I angered Thee by my sins, and have not yet mourned all my wicked deeds. I am unworthy, O Lord, to receive Thee; for I have not yet cleansed myself of the dispositions and attachments to what is not pleasing to Thee. I am unworthy, O Lord, to receive Thee, for I have not yet surrendered in all sincerity to Thy love, Thy will and obedience to Thee. O my God, all-powerful and infinitely good! In Thy merciful loving-kindness, do Thou Thyself make me worthy of receiving Thee, for I run to Thee with faith.'

After this, when you have received the Holy Communion, shut yourself in the secret depths of your heart and, forgetting all created things, address to God these or similar words: 'Almighty King of heaven and earth! Who made Thee enter my unworthy heart, when I am accursed, and poor, and blind, and naked? No one, of course, but Thy immeasurable love for me. O uncreated love! O love most sweet! What dost Thou want of me, beggar that I am? Nothing, as I see and understand, except my love for Thee; nothing, except that no other fire should burn on the altar of my heart but the fire of my love for Thee, which would consume all love and all desire other than that of bringing myself to Thee as a burnt offering and fragrant incense. Nought else didst Thou ever desire or seek from me, and nought else dost Thou desire or seek from me now. So hear now, O Lord, the vows of my heart! See, I combine my desire with Thy desire; and as Thou hast given the whole of Thyself to me, so I give the whole of myself to Thee, to be wholly in Thee. I know, O Lord, that this cannot be, unless I renounce myself wholly; it cannot be if any trace of self-love remains in me, if I harbour some sympathy or disposition towards a will of my own, thoughts of my own, or some self-pandering habits of my own. Therefore I desire and I strive from now onwards to oppose myself in all that is not acceptable to Thee, but which my soul may desire, and to compel myself to do all things pleasing to Thee, even if everything in me and outside me should rebel against it. By myself, I have not strength enough to succeed in this. But since from now on Thou art with me, I daringly trust that Thou Thyself wilt accomplish in me all that is needed. I seek and strive that my heart may be as one with Thy heart; and I trust that Thy grace wilt grant me this. I seek and strive to see nothing and to hear nothing, to think of nothing and have sympathy with nothing, except that which Thy will, determined by Thy commandments, leads me to and shows, and I trust that it will be granted me by Thy power working in me. I strive and I seek not to let attention stray from the heart, where Thou dwellest, there to gaze at Thee unceasingly and be warmed by the rays of

177

light issuing from Thee; and I trust that this will be given me by the touch and embrace of Thy hands. I strive and seek for Thee alone to be henceforth my light, strength and joy; and I trust to be given this by Thy saving action on my inner man. It is of this that I pray and shall always continue to pray. O merciful Lord, grant me this, grant me this.'

Then strive to increase from day to day your faith in this most holy sacrament of the Eucharist, and never cease to wonder at the miraculous mystery of it, reflecting on how God manifests Himself to you in the guise of bread and wine, and becomes essentially present in you, to make you more holy, righteous and blessed. For blessed are they who do not see, yet believe; according to the words of the Saviour: 'Blessed are they that have not seen, and yet have believed' (John xx. 29). And do not wish that God should manifest Himself to you in this life under any guise other than this sacrament. Try to set alight in yourself a warm desire for this sacrament and to make progress every day both in your fervent readiness to do only God's will, and in spiritual wisdom, making it the queen and ruler over all your actions of the spirit, the soul and the body. Every time you take communion, while partaking of this bloodless sacrifice, offer yourself as a sacrifice to God, that is, profess your complete readiness to endure every affliction, every sorrow and every wrong you may meet in the course of your life, for the sake of the love of God, Who sacrificed Himself for us.

St. Basil the Great describes more fully the duty imposed on the communicant by the Holy Communion, basing it on the words of St. Paul that those who eat the flesh of the Lord and drink His blood show the Lord's death (I Cor. xi. 26). This death was suffered by the Lord for the sake of all men, and so also for the communicants. For what purpose? 'That they which live should not henceforth live unto themselves, but unto him which died for them, and rose again' (II Cor. v. 15). So those who approach the Holy Communion with faith, love and such readiness to be faithful to God's commandments and to every clear manifestation of His will, that they are prepared to lay down their lives for it, undertake the task no longer to live either for themselves, the world or sin, but for the Lord God they receive into themselves in the Holy Communion, Who died and rose again for them.

Finally, having received through the Holy Communion the Lord, Who sacrificed Himself for you, and having partaken of the force of this sacrifice, after glorifying the Lord and rendering thanks to Him, send in the name of this sacrifice prayers and supplications to your heavenly Father about your own needs, of the spirit, the soul and the body, then about the holy Church of God, your family, your benefactors and the souls of those who died in faith.

Being connected with the sacrifice through which the Son of God has obtained mercy for us all from God the Father, this prayer will be heard and will not be left without fruit.

CHAPTER FOUR

Communion of the spirit

Communion with the Lord through the sacrament of flesh and blood is possible only at definite times, according to one's possibilities and zeal, but never more than once a day. But inner communion with the Lord, in the spirit, is possible every hour and every minute; that is, through His grace, it is possible to be in constant intercourse with Him, and to be aware, when He so wishes, of this intercourse in one's heart. According to the Lord's promise, by partaking of His flesh and blood we receive Him Himself, and He enters and dwells in us with all His blessings, allowing the heart, that is prepared for it, to be aware of this. True communicants are always in a palpably blessed state after communion. Then the heart partakes of the Lord in spirit.

But since we are constrained by our body and surrounded by external activities and relationships, in which duty forces us to take part, so, by the splitting of our attention and feeling day by day, the spiritual partaking of the Lord is weakened and becomes overlaid and hidden. The sense of partaking of the Lord becomes hidden; but intercourse with the Lord is not broken, unless unfortunately some sin enters and destroys the state of grace. Nothing can compare with the delight of partaking of the Lord; therefore the diligent, when they feel it weaken, hasten to restore its full power, and, when they have restored it, they feel themselves again partaking of the Lord. This is spiritual communion with the Lord.

179

It is in this way that it takes place in the times between making communion with Him through the Holy Mysteries. But it can also be unceasing—in a man who always keeps his heart pure and his attention and feeling constantly directed towards the Lord. All the same, this is a gift of grace, granted to a man struggling on the path of the Lord, if he is diligent and pitiless to himself.

Even if a man partakes of the Lord in spirit only from time to time, this partaking is still a gift of grace. All that we can bring is thirst and hunger for this gift, and diligent striving to obtain it. There are, however, works, which open the way to this communion with the Lord and help to obtain it, although it always seems to come as it were unexpectedly. These works are pure prayer, with child-like crying of the heart, and special acts of self-denial in the practice of virtues. When no sin pollutes the soul, when no sinful thoughts or feelings are tolerated, that is, when the soul is pure and cries to God, what can keep the Lord, Who is present, from letting the soul taste Him, or the soul from awareness of this taste? And so it happens thus, unless the Lord deems it better, for the good of the soul, to prolong its thirst and hunger for Him before satisfying it. Amongst acts of self-denial the most powerful of all for this purpose is humble obedience and casting oneself under the feet of all men, stripping oneself of acquisitiveness and suffering injustice with a good heart, all this in the spirit of complete surrender to the will of God. Such actions liken a man to the Lord more than any others, and the Lord, present in him, allows his soul to taste Him. Also pure and diligent fulfilment of all God's commandments bears fruit in the abiding of the Lord in the heart, together with the Father and the Holy Spirit (John xiv. 23).

Spiritual communion with the Lord should not be confused with mental memory of communion with Him in the Mysteries of flesh and blood, even if this memory is accompanied by strong spiritual sensations and an ardent longing for actual communion with Him in the Holy Mysteries. Neither must it be confused with what the worshippers present in the church receive when the Eucharist is celebrated. They receive divine sanctification and benevolence, as participants in the bloodless sacrifice through faith, contrition and readiness to sacrifice themselves to the glory of God: and they receive in the measure of these dispositions. But it is not the same as communion, although communion can also take place here.

180

CHAPTER FIVE

On giving thanks to God

Every blessing we possess, and every good deed we do is of God and comes from God. It is therefore our duty to give thanks to Him for everything:—for every blessing we receive from His munificent hand, whether visible or invisible, for every right action, for every right effort and for every victory over the enemies of our salvation, as we were directed: 'In every thing give thanks: for this is the will of God in Christ Jesus concerning you' (I Thess. v. 18). So take care to keep feelings of gratitude to God warm from the first moment of awakening from sleep and throughout the day, and go to sleep with words of thanks on your lips. For you are immersed in Divine blessings, one of which is sleep itself.

God does not need your thanks: but you stand in extreme need of Divine blessings. And the place to receive and store these blessings in you is a grateful heart. 'The best way of preserving the benevolence of a benefactor,' says St. Chrysostom, 'is remembrance of his favour and constantly giving thanks.' And St. Isaac writes: 'The gratitude of the receiver encourages the giver to bestow greater gifts than before. He who is not grateful for little will be disappointed in his hopes of much. A gift is always increased, except when there is no gratitude.' St. Basil the Great adds to it a useful warning, saying: 'If we do not give thanks for the blessings given by God, it becomes necessary to withdraw these blessings in order to bring us to our senses. As the eyes fail to see what is too near, but need a suitable distance, so ungrateful souls, when deprived of blessings, often become aware of former mercies: and while they had no gratitude to the Giver when they enjoyed the gifts, they glorify the past when they have lost it' (ch. On giving thanks, p. 74, Vol. 4).

Giving heed to my words, you will ask: 'How can I set the feeling of gratitude alight in myself and always keep it?' Examine all God's favours to mankind—to our race—and to you yourself, and go over them frequently in your thought, rehearsing them in your memory; and if you have a heart, you will not be able to refrain from singing your thanksgiving to God. You will find examples of such hymns in prayers and in the writings of the

181

saints. Hear how St. Basil the Great describes God's munificence towards us. 'From non-being we were brought into being, were created in the image of the Creator, were endowed with mind and speech, which constitute the perfection of our nature and give us knowledge of God. To diligent study, the beauties of creation are like a book showing us the greatness of God's Providence in all things, and His Wisdom. We can discern good from evil; nature itself teaches us to chose what is useful and turn away from the harmful. Being estranged from God by sin, we are recalled to communion with Him, freed from ignominious slavery by the blood of His Only-begotten Son. And what of the hope of salvation and the delights of angelic bliss; what of the kingdom of heaven and the promised blessings, surpassing all word or understanding!' (ibid. p. 51). Read this description of God's favours towards us, or choose another one, or compose one yourself, including in it the blessings which God has given you personally. Repeat them often in word and thought, not only every day, but many times a day, and you will always have the feeling of gratitude to God.

But, once provoked, a feeling does not like to stay hidden: it seeks manifestation and expression. How, then, can you fittingly express to God your feelings of gratitude to Him? By doing what God wants of you, when He surrounds you with His munificent gifts. And what does God want? Surrounding you with His blessings, God wants that in seeing them you should constantly remember Him—so remember; He wants you wholly to cleave to Him with love—and so cleave; He wants you never to digress from His will in anything you do, and to strive to please Him in every way—so do so; He wants you to rely on Him alone in all things—so rely; He wants you to remember the many occasions when you have offended your Benefactor by your evil and shameful deeds, so that you are filled with contrition, repent and weep, until you make peace with your conscience and receive the assurance that God has completely forgiven you—so do this.

Do you see how wide is the field of thanksgiving and how many the means to fulfil this duty? Learn from this how unpardonable is the sin of those who are remiss in this, and strive not to stain yourself with this sin. Ingratitude among men is called black. What word can you find for ingratitude to God? So take care and always keep the feelings of gratitude to God warm in yourself, especially in church during the liturgy when the bloodless sacrifice, called the Eucharist, is offered to God, for Eucharist means giving thanks. Do not forget that here the only worthy thanks you can render to God is full readiness to sacrifice both yourself and all you have to the glory of His holy name.

CHAPTER SIX

On surrender to the will of God

When a man has repented he gives himself up to the service of God; and immediately begins this service by walking in His commandments and His will. This work and labour begins in the sweat of the brow. Commandments are not hard in themselves, but there are many obstacles to practising them in the external circumstances of the struggler, and especially in his inner tendencies and habits. With God's help a tireless struggler overcomes everything in the end and achieves peace within and a calm flow of events without—relatively, of course.

The struggler always acts himself, although with the help of God. But the experience of the first days makes him realise that in spite of all his efforts if anything good is done, it is done only because he is given force from above to do it. The further he goes, the more this conviction grows and becomes deeply rooted. When comparative peace is established within, this conviction is emphasised and takes command, until finally it ends in complete submission to God's will, or in total surrender to His influence. God's influence begins to act in those who struggle for salvation from the first moments of their turning to God, and it effects the turning itself. But it begins to grow as the struggler turns further and further away from himself and cleaves to God and, realising his own impotence, has an ever firmer trust in God's power. When at last he surrenders himself entirely to God, God is actively present in him, both in showing what he must do and in fulfilling it. This is the summit of Christian perfection, in which 'it is God which worketh in you both to will and to do' (Phil. ii. 13). As was said in the beginning, the seed of this perfection lies in non-reliance on oneself and in hope in God; but here it is shown in full maturity.

183

What constitutes the essence of total submission to the will of God can be learnt when it manifests itself in full force. It comes of itself and there are no special rules for acquiring it, so it is impossible to say: do this and do that and you will receive it. It grows imperceptibly under non-reliance on oneself and hope in God. I have mentioned it here simply because it has to be mentioned somewhere, and what was said, at the end of the previous chapter, of sacrificing oneself to God offered an opportunity to mention it now. Total surrender to the will of God actually is this sacrificing of oneself as a burnt offering to God.

The proof of this state is dying to oneself,—to one's own opinions, wishes and feelings or tastes, in order to live by Divine intellect, in conformity with the Divine will and in partaking of God. In the forefront of all this endeavour is our Lord and Saviour. He surrendered the whole of Himself to God the Father, and us in Himself, 'For we are members of his body, of his flesh, and of his bones' (Eph. v. 30). So let us hasten in His footsteps, since He gave to God the Father an undertaking for us (John xvii. 19), in the hope that we shall indeed be such and act so.

Why is this sacrifice made at the end, and not in the beginning? Because an offering to God must be perfect, without blemish. And in the beginning perfection is sought, but not yet attained. When in the end it is attained, then it is fitting to offer oneself as a sacrifice. At first man only dedicates himself to this sacrifice, but at the end he actually makes the sacrifice of himself. Indeed, it is impossible to sacrifice oneself as a burnt offering before attaining perfection. Other sacrifices can be offered, such as propitiatory offerings, offerings of purification, of thanksgiving, but not the burnt offering. One can attempt it, and one can talk about it, but it will be words and not the actual deed. This deed is accomplished without words.

Know that as long as you are still attached to something earthly, as long as you still lean on something within or outside you, that is not God, as long as you find flavour in something created and enjoy it, you are unfit to be a burnt offering. First endeavour to renounce all this, make all the lives in you stop and only one life remain—life in God. In other words, make it so that you no longer live, but instead God, our Lord Christ and the Holy Spirit live in you. Then immolate yourself to God, or then you will be immolated to God. And, until this comes to pass, have as

184

an offering to God a contrite spirit and a contrite and humble heart, and be content with this for a time, but not for ever. For in the end you will have to come to sacrificing yourself wholly as a burnt offering to God.

CHAPTER SEVEN

On warmth of heart, and on cooling and dryness of heart

Spiritual warmth of heart is the fruit of feeling for God and for everything divine. It is born at the time when a man turns to God in repentance. In the course of tasks of penitence to purify the heart it acquires more and more strength, and from intermittent feelings of warmth visiting the heart from time to time it gradually becomes constant, until finally it becomes a permanent state of the heart.

When in one place in his writings St. John of the Ladder advised: 'Strive always to have feeling towards God and divine things', he meant this warmth. Every object which delights the heart, warms it; so warmth of heart can be of many kinds. Spiritual warmth is born from the influence of spiritual things upon the heart, which takes place in the order of spiritual life. Its distinctive feature is renunciation of all created things, when the attention is wholly fettered by God and by all things divine. This feature makes it as far removed from warm feelings of soul and of body as heaven is removed from earth.

The feeling of spiritual warmth is concentrated and appears simple and single; but in its essence it is the fusion of many spiritual movements, just as a ray of light is the fusion of the seven colours of the spectrum. It contains reverence, contrition, tenderness, prostrating oneself before God, worship, holy zeal and love of God. Since these spiritual feelings cannot all become established in the heart at once, spiritual warmth does not immediately become an attribute of our heart.

Until spiritual warmth of the heart has become a permanent state, it comes and goes. Either it comes of itself, as a heavenly guest, or it is a fruit of spiritual exercises—reading, meditation, prayer, acts of self-denial and doing good. It goes when attention strays from spiritual subjects, following which the heart partakes of things which are not of the spirit, and delights in them. This quenches spiritual warmth, as water quenches fire.

Do you wish to preserve this spiritual warmth in your heart? Keep your attention within and stand praying in your heart before God; do not allow your thoughts to wander, distracting your attention, let no sympathy for things of the soul or the body enter the heart, cut off at once all cares and worries at their inception, keep alive your zeal to please God and to save your soul. In external affairs, observe the order dictated by reason, direct them all towards your chief aim and, while doing the one, do not burden your thought by cares about the many. But I will add that when once you have experienced this warmth, you cannot but strive to keep it; striving, you will use suitable methods to this end; using them you will see the best way to keep it. If you carry out this work with good judgment, spiritual warmth will become your trusty guide, teaching you how to control your inner life and how to behave in external affairs and control your whole conduct—in order to keep this very thing.

Just as the presence of spiritual warmth in the heart is sweet, so is its absence bitter, wearisome and frightening. It has been said already that it goes when attention and heart deviate from things of the spirit and turn towards things not of the spirit. By this is meant not something sinful—since a man who has had a taste of spiritual warmth is no longer attracted by sin—but all the soul–body realm, vain, earthly, created. As soon as attention inclines towards it, spiritual warmth immediately declines; but when the heart also cleaves to it, it withdraws altogether, leaving behind coldness towards all things divine and towards God Himself, accompanied by indifference to all spiritual works and occupations, practised for the purpose of preserving this warmth. If a man recollects himself at once and hastens to re-establish his habitual warmth-producing order, this warmth returns quickly or not so quickly. But if he pays no attention to it and, through being dispersed, infatuated with something or self-reliant, deliberately allows himself to linger in this cooling atmosphere, and especially if he takes the risk of satisfying in actual deed his non-spiritual tastes resurrected by it, his very zeal for spiritual life becomes undermined, if not completely deadened. The latter is

186

the forerunner of falling into former habitual sins, which will not fail to overcome the negligent. But if a man recollects himself, he has no difficulty in returning to his spiritual state, even from there.

This is how cooling always happens; it is always through our own fault, since it is produced by weakening of attention and of watchfulness over oneself. This weakening is caused either by the temptations of a man's worldly surroundings, when forms of worldly prelest stupefy a man and abduct him from his own self; or by the wiles of the enemy, who contrives to induce a man to come out of his inner self, which the enemy sometimes succeeds in doing, merely by adding his own more attractive pictures to the natural flow of images of fantasy, and sometimes by somehow affecting also the body. But, whatever the cause, the action of cooling begins with attention coming out of the inner depths, and its further progress is established by the heart cleaving to something, at first vain and empty, and later passionate and sinful. And in every case it is a man's own fault. For neither the world nor the devil can violate man's freedom; they can only subject it to temptation.

Sometimes cooling is due to the action of grace. In its true aspect, spiritual warmth is the fruit of grace present in the heart. When grace comes, the heart is warm, when it goes—it is cold. Grace also leaves a man, when he comes out of himself attracted by wrong things. Then this cooling is and is called punitive. But sometimes grace withdraws of its own accord, for the purpose of assisting the spiritual progress of the servants of God. And in such cases this withdrawal is and is called instructive. But in this instance the consequences are still the same—cooling, a sensation of emptiness in the heart; for the guest and visitor has gone. The difference between these coolings is that the guilty cooling weakens the very zeal for spiritual life, whereas cooling due to an instructive withdrawal of grace makes it burn with even greater fervour, which is also one of the purposes of such withdrawal.

Divine grace withdraws of its own accord for purposes of instruction for the following reasons: to excite zeal, which sometimes slackens through a long period of calm;—to make a man examine his situation with greater attention and reject the attachments and occupations not directly connected with a life acceptable to God and not leading to Him;—to increase and strengthen

187

the consciousness and feeling that everything good in us is the fruit of God's grace;—to make us value more highly the gifts of God in the future, care more about preserving them, and be more deeply humble;—to make us surrender with greater sincerity into the hands of Divine providence, with complete self-denial and self-belittlement; to force us not to become attached to spiritual delights themselves, thus dividing our heart in two, since God wishes the whole of it to belong to Him alone; to prevent us from relaxing our efforts when Divine grace works in us, but to make us toil without sleeping on the path of God, straining all the powers with which He has endowed us precisely for this purpose.

Thus, even when cooling results from an instructive withdrawal of Divine grace, you yourself are the cause of it, since, although Divine grace withdraws of its own accord, it does so with its eye on you. So when you feel a cooling for spiritual things and occupations and generally for all divine things, enter deeply into yourself and examine carefully why it has happened; and, if it is your fault, hasten to eliminate and efface it, not so much because you are anxious for the return of spiritual delights, but rather because you want to destroy in yourself all that is unfitting and not pleasing to God. If you find nothing of this kind, submit to God's will, saying to yourself: 'God has so decided: let Thy will be done on me, O Lord, weak and unworthy as I am.' Then be patient and wait, never allowing yourself to deviate from the habitual order of your spiritual life and spiritual works and exercises. Overcome the lack of taste for them, which has assailed you, by forcibly making yourself practise them, paying no attention to thoughts which try to distract you from your efforts by suggesting that this occupation is useless; drink willingly your cup of bitterness, saying to the Lord: 'See my humility and my efforts, O Lord, and deprive me not of Thy mercy,' and let your efforts be inspired by the faith that this cup comes from God's love for you, because He desires you to attain a greater spiritual perfection.

Follow willingly in the footsteps of the Lord not only to Mount Tabor, but also to Golgotha, in other words, not only when you feel divine light and spiritual joys and delights within you, but also when you are assailed by darkness, afflictions, stress and bitterness, which the soul has to experience at times from the temptations of the demons, both inner and outer. Even if this cooling is accompanied by such darkness and confusion that you

188

do not know what to do and where to turn, have no fear. Stand firm in your place, remain submissively on your cross and cast far away from yourself every earthly comfort, which the world or the flesh choose to offer, prompted by the enemy. Try also to hide your sickness from all other people, and speak of it to no one but your spiritual Father; and this, not to complain about the affliction which has visited you, but rather to seek guidance about how to avoid it in future and how to suffer it with a good heart now, for as long as God pleases to keep you in it.

Continue to practise your prayers, communion and other spiritual exercises as usual, but not for the sake of spiritual joys, not in order to be taken down from your present cross, but to be given strength to remain nailed to this cross with soul untroubled, to the glory of Christ our Lord, crucified for us, and to live and act always as is pleasing to Him. If at times your condition makes it impossible for you to pray and have good thoughts, as you had done before, owing to a great darkening and confusion of your mind, do all this as well as you can, so long as you do it without laziness and self-indulgence. Then what lacks perfection in execution, will be accepted as perfect for the sake of your desire, effort and seeking. Remain in this desire, effort and seeking, and you will see its wonderful fruits—inspiration and strength, which will fill your soul.

I offer you here an example of how to call to God in times of such darkening of the mind. Call to Him: 'Why art thou cast down, O my soul? and why art thou disquieted within me? hope in God: for I shall yet praise him, who is the health of my countenance, and my God' (Ps. xliii. 5). 'Why standest thou afar off O Lord? Why hidest thou thyself in times of' (my) 'trouble?' (Ps. x. 1). 'Forsake me not, O Lord: O my God, be not far from me' (Ps. xxxviii. 21). Remembering how Sarah, the beloved wife of Tobias, was inspired by God to pray in her trouble, cry: 'Every man working for Thee, O Lord, knows truly that if this life is a trial, it will be crowned, and if it is filled with afflictions, it will be redeemed and, by Thy mercy, will not cease even in corruption. Thou dost not rejoice in our perdition; but Thou bringest calm after storm, and joy after tears and weeping. Blessed be Thy name for ever, O God of Israel!'

Recall also to your mind Christ our Lord, Who, through His immeasurable sufferings felt Himself abandoned by His heavenly

Father in the garden of Gethsemane and on the cross, and when you feel yourself as it were crucified in your present position, cry from your heart: 'Thy will be done, O Lord!' 'Not as I will, but as thou wilt' (Matt. xxvi. 39). If you do this, your patience and your prayer will rise on high to God's presence, as the flame of your heart's sacrifice. And you will prove yourself filled with love as strong as death, and ardent readiness of will to shoulder your cross and follow after Christ our Lord on any path, by which He chooses to call you to Himself. This is true life in God! To desire and seek God for the sake of God, and to possess Him and partake of Him in the way and measure that He wishes. If men entered the path of godly life with this attitude, and measured their progress by its strength, instead of by the tides of spiritual joys and delights, they would not be so easily overcome by temptations, which come of themselves, or through the wiles of the enemy, neither would they languish uselessly, nor complain, when times of cooling and dryness come. On the contrary, they would accept such times thankfully and suffer them gladly, convinced that if it is God's will it must be for their own good. So, disregarding them, they would continue along the path of a life pleasing to God, observing all the established ordinances with still greater zeal, greater self-denial and greater urging of themselves.

It happens sometimes that while the soul languishes in this state of coolness and absence of taste for anything spiritual, the enemy attacks with greater vigour, inciting evil thoughts, shameful impulses and seductive dreams. His aim is to provoke hopelessness from the sense of being abandoned by God and to make a man give up the struggle, and incline towards something passionate, in order to lead him back with ease into the vortex of sinful life. Being aware of this, stand firm. Let waves of sin roar round the heart; but as long as your heart is filled with aversion to sin and with desire to be faithful to God, your little craft is safe. Divine grace has withdrawn its comforts from you, but it stands watching nearby, and will not leave you without help, so long as your will is on the side of good. So stand firm, inspired by the certainty that this storm will soon be over and with it your dryness will leave you. Believe that this is allowed for your own good; since, if you endure this time of trial and temptation, you will come out of it with greater knowledge of your own weakness, greater humility and a stronger conviction

190

that God's help is always ready at hand. I have already had occasion to speak to you about such tempestuous attacks of the enemy. Read again what I said there.

CHAPTER EIGHT

On guarding and examining conscience

Use all means, brother, to keep your conscience pure; in thoughts, words, and deeds, let it always remain blameless; let it never reproach you and gnaw at you for anything. If you do this, it will gain strength both in your inner and outer actions and, becoming mistress over all your life, will govern it rightly. A pure conscience will make your life blameless, for then it will be sensitive and strong for good against evil. Conscience is the law, inscribed by God in the hearts of men, to shed light on their path and guide them in righteousness, as the Apostle Paul teaches, calling it 'the work of the law written in their hearts' (Rom. ii. 15). On the basis of this saying, St. Nilus gives the following advice: 'In all your works follow the guidance of conscience like a lamp.'

There are four relationships in which you should keep your conscience blameless: in relation to God, to yourself, to your neighbours, and to everything, which is in your hands.

All this you know; yet I will remind you of the most important points: *In relation to God*—abide in remembrance of God and walk in the presence of God; be aware of yourself being carried and protected by God's power, and led towards that end, for which He called you to existence; dedicate yourself and all you have to the service of God and the glory of His name; live in Him, have trust in Him and surrender to Him your fate, both in time and in eternity.

In relation to yourself—be just to yourself and give its due to every part of your being: let your *spirit*, which seeks the heavenly and eternal God, rule over soul and body, whose joint function is to organise the temporal life; let the *soul* obey the dictates of the spirit and bend the neck of the mind to truth revealed by God, and so illumine the whole scope of its knowledge,—let it keep the

191

will in the ordinances of Divine commandments, not allowing it to turn aside towards its own desires, opposing them—let it teach the heart to find flavour only in divine matters and in those which bear the divine imprint and are its expression,—and in this spirit let it order and conduct its affairs, both public and those of daily life; to *the body* give what it needs, observing a strict measure, and establish for yourself the rule to 'make not provision for the flesh, to fulfil the lusts thereof' (Rom. xiii. 14) ever and in anything. If you keep to this, you will be a good ruler and true benefactor of yourself.

In relation to your neighbours—respect them all as being images of God, wish them all well and do good to them as much as is in your power; be humble before all and seek to please them all within the limits of what is good, rejoice with those who rejoice and grieve with those who grieve; judge and humiliate no one, even in thought or feeling; do not conceal the truth, if you know it, from those who seek from you guidance and advice, but do not impose yourself upon anyone as a teacher of your own accord, and above all keep peace and harmony with all men, ready on your part to make any sacrifice to this end, and take every care to lead no one astray.

In relation to things—respect all things as God's creations; preserve and use to the glory of God those, which God has placed in your possession; be content with what you have, whatever its measure, and give thanks to God for it,—form no passionate attachments for anything and regard all things as external means and instruments, so as to be free in your dealings with them, without their becoming ties and obstacles in your righteous endeavours; do not allow yourself to lean on these fragile supports, do not boast of your possessions, nor envy those of another, avoid avarice and do not be prodigal in things which are not good.

Every man is obliged to observe all this every day in one form or another, almost at every step. Thus, if you 'live honestly', you will have a 'good conscience', imitating St. Paul (Heb. xiii. 18).

Those 'willing to live honestly' and zealous for salvation behave as I have indicated, trying not to go wrong in any of these things and not to stain their conscience. Yet, in spite of all their efforts, now wrong thoughts and feelings, now wrong words, now wrong actions slip through, at times unnoticed, at others even observed, and cover with dust the pure face of conscience, so that, towards the end of the day, hardly anyone escapes looking like a wayfarer, who has walked along a dusty road, with dust clinging to his eyes, nose, mouth, hair and covering his whole face. This is why every man zealous for salvation is given the task of examining his conscience in the evening and, seeing all the wrong things which gained admittance to his thoughts, words and actions, to wash them off with repentance: in other words, to do what the dusty traveller does, for the latter washes himself with water, while the former cleanses himself with repentance, contrition and tears.

This self-examination must put everything to the test, both good and bad, right and wrong, from all the sides indicated above. If you see something right in itself, look whether it was right as regards impulse and intention, right in the mode of putting it into practice and the attitude towards it after its completion, that is, whether it was done for effect, for gaining favour with men, or for self-indulgence,—whether it was fitting, timely and in the right place,—whether having done it you had blown your own trumpet before yourself and praised yourself, without giving praise to God. A right deed is truly right when it is done from obedience to God's will and to the glory of God, with complete renunciation of self and forgetfulness of self.

If you find something wrong, examine how you happened to do it, when you keep a constant desire to do only what is right; find the external and internal causes that led to it, how you should have controlled yourself on this occasion so as not to sin, and why you have not done so; then, without blaming things or people, but only yourself, determine sensibly how you should behave in future to avoid sinning in these or similar circumstances, and establish a firm rule for yourself to carry out your decision without deviation, self-indulgence or seeking favours, thus using even impurities to fertilise the field of your heart.

At the end of this examination, give thanks to God for all things that were right, without awarding any part in it to yourself, for indeed 'it is God which worketh in you both to will and to do' (Phil. ii. 13) and without Him we can do nothing good (John xv. 5). So render thanks to God and, imitating St. Paul, forget it, and follow his example increasing your zeal and 'reaching forth unto those things which are before' (Phil. iii. 13). As to wrong things, repent and be contrite before the Lord, blaming yourself that the loaves you bring Him as your offerings are never quite pure, but always mixed with chaff and impurities, and make a firm resolution to watch yourself closely the following day, and allow nothing wrong to slip through, not only in words and deeds, but also in thoughts and feelings.

Those who watch themselves perform all this, that is, the examination and the action that results, actually during the course of the day's happenings, so that in the evening the examination of their conscience is only a repetition of that made in the course of the day, its correction and amplification. It is impossible not to agree that this latter method is better and more natural. No wrong which was allowed can be hidden from conscience: and having once noticed it, conscience immediately becomes troubled. Is it not more natural to calm it at once by self-condemnation, contrition and decision to behave rightly in future, than to leave all this till evening?

I would like to add one or two more words on this subject.

Examine your actions with the utmost strictness and explore deeply into their causes, pronouncing thereupon a merciless verdict against yourself. The more deeply you explore into all that happens in you and comes from you, eliminating all wrong things and affirming right things, the more quickly you will cleanse your conscience; just as the deeper the well, the purer the water.

Once conscience has learnt what is right and wrong, it will not cease to demand actions corresponding to the former, and pursue with condemnation and remorse any allowing of the latter. But, until it reaches full knowledge of the one and the other, or until it has its 'senses exercised to discern both good and evil' (Heb. v. 14) thus possessing in itself eyes to see,—it remains in this sense to some extent dependent on the other powers of the soul, and especially on the judgment of reason. But until the heart is purified of passions, reason is often bribed by them and so produces many justifications, which cloud the eye of conscience and mislead it into taking black for white. Therefore, so long as you are still struggling with passions, in examining yourself place your deeds before the mirror of the word of God and be guided by this in determining their quality and value. Moreover, do not be lazy or diffident in paying frequent visits to your spiritual Father.

Begin and end the examination of your deeds with a diligent prayer, asking the Lord to give you eyes to see the innermost depths of your heart, for 'the heart is deceitful above all things, and desperately wicked: who can know it?' (Jeremiah xvii. 9). No one but God, Who is 'greater than our heart, and knoweth all things' (I John iii. 20). 'For thou, even thou only, knowest the hearts of all the children of men' (I Kings viii. 39). There are wrong feelings deeply hidden in the heart; at times they slip into a man's actions, at times they are not even noticed and pollute them with the stench of sin. So pray with David the Prophet: 'Cleanse thou me from secret faults' (Ps. xix. 12).

CHAPTER NINE

On preparation for battle with the enemies in the hour of death

Although our whole life on earth is an unceasing warfare and we have to fight to the very end, the chief and most decisive battle awaits us in the hour of death. Who falls at that moment cannot rise again. Do not be surprised at that. For if the enemy dared to approach our Lord, Who was without sin, at the end of His days on earth, as the Lord Himself said: 'The prince of this world cometh, and hath nothing in me' (John xiv. 30); what can prevent him from attacking us, sinful as we are, at the end of our life? St. Basil the Great says in his commentary on the words of the 7th Psalm: 'Lest he tear my soul like a lion, rending it in pieces, while there is none to deliver' (Ps. vii. 2), that the most tireless fighters who have struggled unceasingly with the demons through-out their life, have avoided their nets and withstood their on-slaughts, at the end of their life are subjected to an examination by the prince of this age, to see whether anything sinful remains in them; and those who show wounds, or the blots and imprints of sin are retained in his power, whereas those, who show nothing of this, freely pass him by and attain rest with Christ.

If this is so, it is impossible not to keep it in view and prepare oneself beforehand to meet that hour and to pass through it successfully. The whole of life should be a preparation for this. You will prove well prepared for that hour, if in the whole course of the temporal life allotted to you, you fight with courage against the enemies of your salvation. Having acquired during life the skill to overcome your enemies, you will easily gain the crown of victory in the hour of death.

Moreover, think often of death with attention, bringing to mind everything which must then happen. If you do this, that hour will not catch you unawares, and so will not frighten you, or will not frighten you too much, and your soul, not weakened by fear, will show itself more firm and strong to undertake the struggle and overcome the enemy. Men of this world flee from the thought and memory of death, so as not to interrupt the pleasures and enjoyments of their senses, which are incompatible with memory of death. This makes their attachment to the blessings of the world continually grow and strengthen more and more, since they meet nothing opposed to it. But when the time comes to part with life and all the pleasures and things they love, they are cast into excessive turmoil, terror and torment.

To make this thought of death bear its full fruit, you must put yourself mentally in the place of a dying man and, in the pain and straitness of mortal agony, must vividly imagine the enemy temptations which may assail you, at the same time reproducing such thoughts and feelings as have the strength to repulse them. I shall now describe to you the enemy's onslaughts possible at that moment, and ways of repulsing them, so that you should, while still alive, get used to rehearsing them in your mind, and be able to put them into practice when your hour of death comes. For this war and this battle comes but once, and, since it is inevitable, a man must learn how to meet it and engage in it with skill, lest he makes a mistake and suffers losses which cannot be repaired.

CHAPTER TEN

The four temptations which come from the enemy in the hour of death. The first temptation, against faith, and the means to overcome it

The four chief and most dangerous temptations to which our enemies, the demons, usually subject us in the hour of death are: (1) wavering of faith, (2) despair, (3) vainglory, (4) various images assumed by the demons which appear to the dying.

As regards the first, when the evil enemy begins to sow in you thoughts of unbelief or, appearing in a visible shape, speaks to you against faith, do not enter into argument with him, but affirm within yourself faith in what he attacks, and say to him with holy indignation: 'Out of my sight, Satan, father of lies. I refuse to listen to you; with my whole soul I believe and have always believed in what my mother, the holy Church believes. And this is enough for me.' Admit no thoughts of unbelief, and stand firm, according to the Scriptures: 'If the spirit of the ruler rise up against thee, leave not thy place' (Ecclesiastes x. 4). Be vividly aware, and keep this awareness, that this is nothing but the guile of the devil who strives to confuse you in the last hour. If you cannot stand firm in your mind, keep alert in desire and feeling, do not let them incline towards the suggestion, even if it is served up under the cover of texts from the Scriptures, which the destroyer of souls introduces. For whatever text of the Scriptures he may remind you of, he does so with the aim of leading you to perdition by a distorted interpretation and perversion of the true words of God.

If this evil snake asks you: what does the Church teach? do not answer, and pay no attention to his words, ignoring him altogether. Aware that he is nothing but lies and deceit, and that he has begun talking to you to confound you with words, plunge deep into the contemplation of faith in your believing heart. Still, if you feel yourself firm in faith and strong in thought, and wish to confound the enemy, answer him that the holy Church believes in what alone is the truth. If he asks again: what is this truth? say that the truth is that in which he believes, namely, that by the cross, our Lord Christ has stricken his head and has abolished his power. Then cleave with the eye of your mind to the contemplation of the Lord, crucified for us, and pray to Him: 'O my God, Creator and Redeemer! hasten to my aid and do not let me be shaken, however little, in the truth of Thy holy faith. Since, through Thy loving-kindness, I was born in this truth, let me abide in it and so end my mortal life to the glory of Thy name.'

CHAPTER ELEVEN

Second temptation in the hour of death— through despair

The second temptation in the hour of death, by which the enemy strives finally to strike us down, is fear at the memory of the multitude of our sins. This fear cannot be avoided; but it is mitigated by belief in the redemption of our sins by the death on the cross of Christ our Saviour. The enemy obscures this faith and fans the fear of our sins, so as to stifle all hope of salvation and strike us down with hopelessness and despair. So, my brother, prepare yourself beforehand to repulse this attack, and resolve even now to grasp firmly in your hand our victorious standard— the cross of Christ, when you approach the gates of death. In other words keep firmly in your heart the faith in the redeeming power of our Lord's death on the cross. If, entering the gates of death, you actually experience attacks of hopelessness, hasten to realise, first of all, that they are works of the enemy, and not the natural results of the recollection of your sins. This recollection brings humility, contrition and heartfelt grief at having offended the just and merciful God; therefore, although it brings fear, this fear does not extinguish the hope of God's mercy, and being mixed with it, produces a daring trust in salvation, removing all sense of being cast out. If you know this, you will always recognise, as coming from the devil, every recollection of sins, which has the power to oppress and cast you into despair, extinguishing all hope of salvation and striking you down through fear of being cast out. Once aware of this it will not be difficult for you to have hope beyond hope, which will banish all despair.

Hope beyond hope plunges a man into contemplation of the Divine mercy, into whose infinite depths a man endowed with it casts the great multitude of his sins, with a firm conviction that God desires and seeks not our ruin but our salvation. The only sure foundation on which this conviction can gain strength at any time, and particularly at that time, is the boundless power of the death of our Lord and Saviour on the cross. Therefore, since we must always seek the protection of this cross, how much more must we do so then! Here is a fitting prayer to address to your

Lord and God on entering the gates of death: 'O Lord! Many are the reasons for me to fear that, in Thy justice, Thou wilt condemn me and cast me out for my sins; but still greater is my daring hope of Thy forgiveness according to Thy infinite mercy in Christ Jesus, our Saviour and Redeemer. So I beseech Thee to spare me, Thy poor creature, in Thy infinite goodness, for though condemned by my sins, I am washed by the priceless blood of Thy Son and our God, to glorify Thee for ever. I give the whole of myself into Thy hands: deal with me in Thy mercy. Thou alone art Lord of my life.'

CHAPTER TWELVE

Third temptation in the hour of death— by vainglory

The third temptation in the hour of death is through vainglory and self-appreciation, which moves a man to rely on himself and his own works. Therefore never, and especially in the hour of death, let your attention dwell on yourself and what is yours, giving way to satisfaction with yourself and your works, even if your progress in virtues were greater than that of all the saints. Let all your satisfaction be in God, and place your hope wholly on His mercy and the sufferings of our Lord and Saviour; belittle yourself in your own eyes to your last breath, if you wish to be saved. If some good deed of yours happens to come to your mind, think that it was the work of God in you and through you, instead of your own, and that it is entirely due to Him.

Take refuge in the protection of Divine mercy; yet do not allow yourself to expect it as a reward for the many and arduous struggles endured or for the victories you have gained. Stand always in saving fear and sincere conviction that all your efforts, struggles and endeavours would have remained vain and fruitless, if God had not taken them under the wing of His benevolence and had not helped them and worked in them. So put now your trust in this merciful benevolence.

If you follow this advice of mine, be sure that in the hour of death the enemies' attacks will fail and a free road will open before you, by which you will pass with joy from the earthly valley to the heavenly Jerusalem, the home you longed for.

CHAPTER THIRTEEN

Fourth temptation in the hour of death—
by phantoms

If our evil, cunning and tenacious enemy, who is never tired of tempting us, should attempt to seduce you in the hour of death by some phantoms, visions or transformations into an angel of light, stand firm in the consciousness of your poverty and utter nothingness. And say to him from a courageous and fearless heart: 'Return accursed one, to your darkness. I am unworthy of visions and revelations. Only one thing I need—the infinite compassion of my Lord Jesus Christ, and the prayers and intercessions of our Lady, the Mother of God, the Virgin Mary and of all the saints.' Even if certain clear signs make you think that you see true visions sent by God, do not be too quick in believing them, but rather hasten to plunge deeply into the realisation of your nothingness and unworthiness. Do not fear to offend God by this; for our humble feelings are never unpleasing to Him. If you have need of such visions, God knows how to prevent you from closing your eyes to them, and will forgive the reluctance of your belief that they come from Him. He Who sends grace to the humble, does not take it away for actions inspired by humility.

Such are the more usual weapons used by our enemy to attack us in our last mortal hour. But he also uses for the same purpose any other passion, which possessed the dying man during his life, and to which he is most addicted, and the enemy tries to provoke it, so that the man may leave this life in a passionate state, which would then decide his fate. This is why, beloved, we should be armed against our strongest passions before this great battle is upon us and, fighting against them with courage, should overcome them and cleanse ourselves of them, to make victory more easy at our last hour, which may come at any moment. In this connection the Lord says to all men: 'Fight against them until they be consumed' (I Sam. xv. 18).

CHAPTER FOURTEEN

On spiritual peace of heart

Your heart, beloved, is made by God for the sole purpose of loving Him alone and of serving as a dwelling for Him. So He calls to you to give Him your heart, saying: 'My son, give me thine heart' (Prov. xxiii. 26). But since God is peace passing all understanding, it is quite indispensable for the heart, which wishes to receive Him, to be peaceful and free of all turmoil. For only in peace is His place, as David says. So strive above all things to establish and make firm the peaceful state of your heart. All your virtues, all actions and endeavours should be directed towards achieving this peace, and especially your valiant feats of struggling against the enemies of your salvation; as the great practiser of silence, Arsenius, says: 'Make it your whole care that your inner state should be in accordance with God, and you will vanquish your outer passions.'

Peace of heart is disturbed by passions; so if you do not allow passions to approach the heart, it will always remain at peace. In the unseen warfare, the warrior stands fully armed at the gates of the heart and repulses all those who attempt to enter and disturb it. While the heart is at peace, victory over the attackers is not difficult. Peace of heart is both the aim of spiritual warfare, and the most powerful means to achieve victory in it. So, when passionate turmoil steals into the heart, do not jump to attack the passion in an effort to overcome it, but descend speedily into your heart and strive to restore quiet there. As soon as the heart is quietened, the struggle is over.

Human life is nothing but unceasing warfare and endless temptation. Temptation provokes struggle, and so warfare ensues. Owing to this warfare you should always keep awake and do your utmost to guard your heart and watch over it, to keep it peaceful and quiet. When some disturbing movement arises in your soul, strive with zeal to stifle it and pacify the heart, lest this confusion makes you stray from the right path. For the human heart is like a weight on a clock or like a boat's rudder. If you make the weight lighter or heavier, this will immediately change the movement of all the wheels, and the hands will cease to show the correct time. If you move the rudder to the right or left, the course of the boat is at once altered, so that it no longer stays on its former course. In the same way, when the heart is thrown into turmoil, everything within us is brought into disorderly movement and our very mind loses the capacity of right thinking. This is why it is so necessary not to delay in quietening the heart as soon as it becomes troubled by something internal or external, whether in time of prayer or at any other time.

And you must realise that you will know how to pray rightly only when you have really mastered the task of guarding your inner peace. So direct your attention to this subject and try to find out how to achieve a state of affairs when every action is done in peace of heart, with pleasure and joy. I should say, in brief, that preserving peace of heart should be the constant endeavour of your whole life; you must never allow it to be cast into disorderly turmoil. Then, doing all your business tranquil in the shelter of this peace, as it is written: 'My son go on with thy business in meekness' (tranquillity) (Ecclesiasticus iii. 17) you will attain the bliss promised to the tranquil: 'Blessed are the meek; for they shall inherit the earth' (Matt. v. 5).

CHAPTER FIFTEEN

On the means of preserving inner peace

To preserve inner peace:

(1) First of all keep your outer senses in order and flee all licentiousness in your external conduct,—namely, neither look, speak, gesticulate, walk nor do anything else with agitation, but always quietly and decorously. Accustomed to behave with decorous quietness in your external movements and actions, you will easily and without labour acquire peace within yourself, in the heart; for, according to the testimony of the fathers, the inner man takes his tone from the outer man.

(2) Be disposed to love all men and to live in accord with everyone, as St. Paul instructs: 'If it be possible, as much as lieth in you, live peaceably with all men' (Rom. xii. 18).

(3) Keep your conscience unstained, so that it does not gnaw at

you or reproach you in anything, but is at peace in relation to God, to yourself, to your neighbours, and to all external things. If your conscience is thus kept clean, it will produce, deepen and strengthen inner peace, as David says: 'Great peace have they which love thy law: and nothing shall offend them' (Ps. cxix. 165).

(4) Accustom yourself to bear all unpleasantness and insults without perturbation. It is true that before you acquire this habit you will have to grieve and suffer much in your heart. through lack of experience in controlling yourself in such cases. But once this habit is acquired, your soul will find great comfort in the very troubles you meet with. If you are resolute, you will day by day learn to manage yourself better and better and will soon reach a state when you will know how to preserve the peace of your spirit in all storms, both inner and outer.

If at times you are unable to manage your heart and restore peace in it by driving away all stress and griefs, have recourse to prayer and be persistent, imitating our Lord and Saviour, Who prayed three times in the garden of Gethsemane, to show you by His example that prayer should be your refuge in every stress and affliction of the heart and that, no matter how faint-hearted and grieved you may be, you should not abandon it until you reach a state when your will is in complete accord with the will of God and, calmed by this, your heart is filled with courageous daring and is joyfully ready to meet, accept and bear the very thing it feared and wished to avoid; just as our Lord felt fear, sorrow and grief, but, regaining peace through prayer, said calmly: 'Rise, let us be going: behold, he is at hand that doth betray me' (Matt. xxvi. 46).

CHAPTER SIXTEEN

Peace of heart is established little by little

Your constant care should be not to let your heart become agitated or troubled, but to use every effort to keep it peaceful and calm. Seeing your efforts and endeavours, God will send you His grace and will make your soul a city of peace. Then your heart will become the house of comfort as is allegorically expressed in the following Psalm: 'Jerusalem is builded as a city' (Ps. cxxii. 3). God has required only one thing from you, that every time you are disturbed by something, you should immediately restore peace in yourself, and should thus remain undisturbed in all your actions and occupations. You must know that this requires patience; for just as a city is not built in a day, you cannot expect to gain inner peace in a day. For gaining inner peace means building a house for the God of peace and a tabernacle for the Almighty, and in this way becoming a temple of God. You must also know that it is God Himself Who builds this house in you, and without Him all your labour will be in vain, as it is written: 'Except the Lord build the house, they labour in vain that build it' (Ps. cxxvii. 1). You must know too that the main foundation of this peace of heart is humility and avoidance of actions, works and occupations which bring worry and care. As regards the first—who does not know that humility, peace of heart and meekness are so closely related that where one is, the other is too. A man whose heart is at peace and who is meek is also humble, and a man who is humble in heart, is also meek and at peace. This is why our Lord joined them indissolubly together, saying: 'Learn of me; for I am meek and lowly in heart' (Matt. xi. 29). As regards the second, we see its prototype in the Old Testament, namely, in the fact that God wished His house to be built not by David, who spent almost all his life in wars and tribulations, but by his son Solomon, who, by his name, was a peaceful king and fought no one.

CHAPTER SEVENTEEN

To preserve peace of heart one must avoid honours and love humility and poverty

Thus, my brother, if you love peace of heart, strive to enter it by the door of humility, for no other door but humility leads therein. And in order to acquire humility, strive and force yourself to welcome all afflictions and tribulations with a loving embrace, as beloved sisters, and to flee all fame and honours, preferring to be unknown and scorned by everyone, and to receive no care or consolation from anyone but God. Convinced of its beneficence, establish firmly in your heart the thought that God is your only good and your sole refuge, and that all other things are but thorns, which will cause you mortal harm if introduced into your heart. If you happen to be put to shame by someone, do not grieve, but bear it with joy, convinced that then God is with you. Seek no honour and have no desire other than to suffer for the love you bear to God and to those things that enhance His glory.

Urge and force yourself to rejoice when you are insulted, blamed or scorned. For this ill-treatment and dishonour conceals a great treasure and if you willingly accept it, you will soon become rich in spirit, unbeknown to the man who has done you this service, that is, who brought this dishonour upon you. Never seek to be loved or honoured in this life, so that you may be more free to suffer with the crucified Christ, for then you will meet no hindrance to this from anyone or anything. Beware of your own self as your bitterest enemy, and do not follow your own will, mind, taste or feeling, if you do not wish to get lost. Therefore always be fully armed against yourself, and when your desire inclines towards something, however holy, strip it naked of everything extraneous and place it, alone, before your God, with the greatest humility, imploring Him that in this His will and not your own may be done. Do this with a sincere and heart-felt surrender of yourself to the will of God, with no trace of self-love, knowing that you have nothing in yourself and can do nothing by yourself in your work for salvation.

Guard yourself from thoughts, which appear holy and inflame an unreasonable zeal for themselves, of which the Lord speaks allegorically: 'Beware of false prophets, which come to you in sheep's clothing, but inwardly they are ravening wolves. Ye shall know them by their fruits' (Matt. vii. 15, 16). Their fruit is the languishing and breaking of the spirit. Know that everything which draws you away from humility and from inner peace and quiet, however beautiful it may seem, is nothing but false prophets who, under the cover of sheep's clothing, that is, of a hypocritical zeal to do good to their neighbours without discrimination, are in truth ravening wolves who raven you of your humility, peace and quiet, so necessary to every man who desires steady progress in spiritual life. The more the external aspect of an action seems holy, the more carefully it must be examined, but without heat or agitation. If you happen sometimes to fall into error in this, do not be dejected but humble yourself before God and, conscious of your weakness, use it as a lesson for the future. For it may be that God has allowed it to happen, to break some concealed feature of your pride that you do not suspect.

If you feel your soul pricked by a barb of the poisonous thorn, that is by passion, or a passionate thought, do not become agitated, but redouble your attention and strive not to let it reach your heart. Meet them face to face, and resist them, keeping your heart behind you, out of their reach and pure before God. Thus, because of its purity, you will always have God present in the depths of your heart. At the same time, fill your inner man with the conviction that all that befalls you and happens in you is a test and an education, to teach you in the end truly to discern things, which lead to your salvation, so that, in following them you may be worthy to receive the crown of truth, prepared for you by God's loving-kindness

CHAPTER EIGHTEEN

It is essential that the soul remain secluded in itself, for God to encompass it with His peace

Since the God of gods and the Lord of lords was pleased to create your soul that it might be a dwelling place and a temple for Himself, you should hold it in great respect and not let it be debased by inclining towards something lower than itself. Let your whole desire and hope be always centred on this invisible visitation of God. But you must know that God will not visit your soul, if He does not find it secluded in itself. God wishes it to be secluded in itself, that is, to be as far as possible empty of all thoughts and desires, and above all of its own will. In connection with this last, you must not undertake any severe feats of endeavour or voluntary privations of your own accord and without due deliberation, or seek opportunities to suffer for the love of God, obeying only the suggestions of your own will. For this you must have the advice of your spiritual Father, who guides you as God's deputy. Obey him in all things, and, through him, God will indeed direct

206

your will towards what He Himself wills and finds most useful for you. Never do anything solely from your own will, but let God Himself do in you only what He wants from you. Your wishing should always be free from yourself; that is, you should have no wishes of your own, and if you have a wish it must be such that whether it comes to pass or not, or even if what comes to pass is opposed to it, you are not in the least grieved thereby, but remain serene in spirit, as though you wished absolutely nothing.

Such a disposition is true freedom of the heart and seclusion, for then it is shackled neither by mind nor will in relation to anys thing. If you present to God your soul thus emptied, free and single in itself, you will witness the miraculous works He will perform in it. But above all He will encompass you with Divine peace, which gift will become in you a receptacle for all other gifts, as the great Gregory of Salonica says (in his Word to the nun Xenia, Greek Philokalia, p. 944). O wonderful unification, secret treasure-house of the Almighty, where alone He consents to listen to the converse you address to Him, and Himself converses with the heart of your soul! O desert and solitude which has become a paradise! For there alone does God allow a man to see Him and converse with Him. 'I will now turn aside, and see this great sight' (the bush) says Moses in the desert of Sinai, a physical place, yet rich in inner contemplations (Ex. iii. 3). If you wish to be worthy of the same, step in this place unshod, for this ground is holy. First bare your feet, that is, the dispositions of your soul, and let them be stripped and free of every earthly thing. Carry neither purse, nor scrip going on this way, as the Lord commanded His disciples (Luke x. 4). You should no longer desire anything from this world, and should salute no man by the way, as Elisha instructed his servant and the Lord commanded His disciples; your whole thought, whole disposition and whole love should be turned only to God and not to any creatures, 'let the dead bury their dead' (Matt. viii. 22); walk alone in the land of the living, and may death have no part in you.

CHAPTER NINETEEN

On good sense in works of love for your neighbours, for the sake of your peace of soul

The Lord said in the Gospels that He had come to send the fire of love on the earth of our heart, and that His great desire is that it be quickly kindled* (Luke xii. 49). Love for God has no measure, just as the beloved God Himself has no bounds nor limits. But love for one's neighbour must have its bounds and limits. If you do not keep it within the right limits, it may turn you away from the love of God, cause you great harm and cast you into perdition. You must indeed love your neighbour, but your love must not cause harm to your soul. Do all your works in a manner simple and holy, with nothing in view, except to please God; and this will protect you from any false steps in actions dictated by love for your neighbour.

The most important thing in these actions is assisting in the salvation of your neighbours. But these actions are often interfered with by injudicious zeal, which brings nothing but harm both to your neighbours and yourself. Be an example of sincere faith and of a life pleasing to God, and, like the Apostles, you will be the fragrance of Christ, drawing all men to follow Him. But do not importune all people indiscriminately with your words, for in this way you will only destroy your peace with others and in yourself. Have an ardent zeal and a strong desire for everyone to know truth in the same degree of perfection as you have it, and to be intoxicated with this wine, which God has promised and which is now given by Him without price (Isaiah lv. 1). This thirst for the salvation of your neighbours you must always have; but it must arise from your love of God, and not from ill-judged zeal. God will Himself plant such love for your brethren in your soul, when it has renounced all things, and will come in His own time to collect its fruit. But you must not sow anything of your own accord; all you have to do is to offer to God the earth of your heart, free of all tares and thistles, and He will sow the seed in it,

* The English version has, 'and what will I, if it be already kindled' but the Russian text means literally 'how I wish it were already kindled'.

how and when He wills. This seed will bring fruit in its proper time.

Remember always that God wishes to see your soul withdrawn from everything, in order to unite it with Himself. So leave Him to act in you, and do not hinder Him by the interference of your will. Make no plans for yourself, except one—always seek to please God by obedience to His will. The householder has already gone out to find labourers for his vineyard, according to the Gospel parable. Put away all care and all thought, strip yourself of all anxiety about yourself and all passionate attachment to anything temporal, and God will clothe you in Himself and will give you things you cannot even conceive. Wholly forget about yourself, as much as you can, and let only love of God live in your soul.

Moreover, you must use circumspection and moderate your zeal in relation to others, and the Lord will preserve you in peace and serenity of soul. Watch, lest your soul suffers loss in its chief blessing, peace of heart, from foolish worries about the profit of others. The source from which you can be enriched by this blessing is total obedience of your soul to God, together with renunciation of all things. Do this, but not in expectation of reward, and never admit the thought that you can do something worthy of it. God Himself acts in all things, and expects nothing from you, except humility before Him, and the gift to Him of your soul, freed from all earthly things, with only one wish in the depths of your heart—to have God's will fulfilled in you, always and in all things.

CHAPTER TWENTY

Stripped of its will, the soul should surrender to God

Brother, trust in God, Who calls all men, saying: 'Come unto me, all ye that labour and are heavy laden, and I will give you rest' (Matt. xi. 28), and follow this voice that calls you, at the same time hoping for the coming of the Holy Spirit. Plunge with eyes closed into the sea of Divine providence and benevolence; let the mighty waves of God's will carry you, like some inanimate thing, with your own will unresisting, thus quickly to be borne to the harbour of salvation and Christian perfection. Practice this many times a day, and seek inner and outer solitude as much as is possible, so as to consecrate all the powers of your soul to the practices, which have special power to produce in you a strong love of God, such as: prayer, unceasing invocation of the most sweet name of our Lord and Saviour, tears which flow from love for Him, a warm and joy-giving adoration of Him, and other spiritual works. Let these works be performed in you without forcing and coercing your heart, lest you foolishly exhaust yourself by compulsory exercises, and thus become hardened and incapable of receiving the influence of grace. Procure for this work the advice of the experienced and, with its help, strive to acquire the habit of constant contemplation of God's holiness and His countless favours. Accept with humility the drops of sweetness, which may fall into your soul from His ineffable goodness.

Yet do not importune God asking for such manifestations of His benevolence; but stay humbly in your inner seclusion, waiting for God's will to be done in you. And when God grants them to you without overstraining on your part, you will experience their sweetness and fruitfulness. The key, which opens the mysterious treasure-house of spiritual gifts of knowledge and Divine love, is humility, renunciation of self and surrendering oneself to God at all times and in every action. The same key locks the door of ignorance and spiritual coldness.

Love, as much as you can, silently to stand with Mary at the feet of Christ our Lord and to listen to what He has to say to your soul. Beware, lest your enemies, the greatest of whom is you yourself, hinder this holy standing in silence before the Lord. When you seek God with your mind, to come to rest in God, do not assign to Him any place or limits by your narrow and impotent fantasy. For He has no limit and is everywhere and in all things, or rather—all things are in Him. You will find Him within yourself, in your soul, every time you truly seek Him. God Himself desires to be with us, sons of men, to make us worthy of Him, although He has no need of us.

When you read the Holy Scriptures, do not have in mind to read page after page, but ponder over each word; when some words make you go deep into yourself, or stir you to contrition, or fill your heart with spiritual joy and love, pause on them. It means that God draws near to you; receive Him humbly with

210

open heart, as He Himself wishes you to partake of Him. If for the sake of this you fail to complete the spiritual exercise (i.e. reading) allotted to you, do not worry. For the purpose of this as of all spiritual exercises is to become worthy to partake of the Lord, and when this is granted, there is no point in worrying about means. In the same way, when you reflect on some divine subject, especially some instance of the passion of Christ our Lord, pause at the part, which touches your heart, and keep your attention longer on it, to prolong this holy feeling.

One of the great obstacles to preserving inner peace, my brother, is binding yourself as by some immutable law, by a set rule, to read so many Psalms and so many chapters from the Gospels and Epistles. Those who set such rules to themselves, are usually in a hurry to complete the reading, not concerning themselves as to whether the heart is touched by it or not, or whether spiritual thoughts and contemplations arise in the mind; and when they fail to finish the reading, they are agitated and worried, not because they were deprived of the spiritual fruit of reading, which they need in order to create a new man in themselves, but simply because not everything was read. Listen to what St. Isaac has to say about this (ch. 30): 'If you wish to gain delight in reading texts and understand the words of the Spirit you utter, brush aside the quantity and number of verses, so that your mind could be absorbed in studying the words of the Spirit, until, filled with wonder at the Divine dispensation, your soul is incited to a lofty understanding of them and is thus moved to praise of God or to sorrow that profits the soul. Slavish work brings no peace to the mind; and anxiety usually deprives the reason and understanding of the power of taste, and robs the thoughts like a leech, which sucks life from the body along with the blood of its members.'

If you sincerely wish to complete the course of your present life virtuously, have no other aim but to find God wherever He chooses to manifest Himself to you. When this is given you, stop all other activity and do not persist with it; forget all else and have rest only in your God. When the Almighty chooses to withdraw from you and ceases to manifest His nearness to you in some present instance, then you can again turn to your usual spiritual exercises and continue them, having still in view the same aim, to find through them your Beloved, and, having found Him, again to do what I said above, that is, stop whatever you are doing, to rest in Him alone. Take good note of what I have said, for there are many engaged in spiritual work, who deprive themselves of the saving fruits of peace, derived from their spiritual works, by the fact that they persist in them, afraid to suffer loss if they fail to complete them, convinced, wrongly of course, that this constitutes spiritual perfection. Thus following their own will, they coerce and torment themselves much, but receive no real quiet nor the inner peace, in which God truly dwells and has His rest.

CHAPTER TWENTY-ONE

Do not seek pleasures and comforts, but only God

Always choose what is difficult and painful, and do not love pleasures and comforts, which bring no profit to the soul. Love to be in a subordinate position, dependent upon the will of others. Each action should be for you a step bringing you nearer to God, and let no action of yours become an obstacle on this path. This should be your joy.—God alone should be for you the sweetest delight and all else bitterness. Offer to God every hardship you meet. Love Him and surrender all your heart to Him, without reflection or fear. And He will find the means to solve all your perplexities and to raise you if you have fallen. In a word, if you love God, you will receive every blessing from Him. So offer the whole of yourself as a sacrifice to God, in peace and quiet of spirit.

To help your progress on this path, and free it from weariness and confusion, place your will in God's will. The more completely you succeed in placing it there, leaving nothing for yourself, the more strength and comfort you will gain. Let your will be so attuned as to desire only what God desires, and to desire none of the things He does not desire. Always and with every action renew the intention and resolve of your soul to please God in all things. Make no plans for the future, since you do not know 'what a day may bring forth' (Prov. xxvii. 1), but keep yourself unbound and free. This does not forbid any man from taking reasonable care and pains about things required by his state and position, since such care is in conformity with God's will and does not interfere with inner peace, devotion to God or man's progress in the spirit. In everything you undertake, keep a firm resolve to do all you can, all that is needed and all that is obligatory for you, but be indifferent to everything else and humbly submit to whatever outer results may follow.

The thing that you can always do is to sacrifice your will to God; so wish for nothing more. As a result you will always enjoy freedom and, tied by nothing from any side, will always rejoice and be at peace in yourself. This freedom of spirit constitutes the great blessing, of which you hear in the writings of the saints. It is nothing but a steady abiding of the inner man in himself, with no desire emerging from his inner fastness to seek something outside him. As long as you keep yourself thus free, you will be partaking of that divine and inexpressible joy, which is inseparable from the kingdom of God, established within us, as the Lord says: 'The kingdom of God is within you' (Luke xvii. 21).

CHAPTER TWENTY-TWO

Do not lose heart when inner peace withdraws or is interrupted

Those who follow the path of God often experience times when the holy peace, the sweet inner seclusion and the freedom they love are interrupted and withdraw, and when sometimes movements of the heart raise such clouds of dust within that they cannot see the path they have to follow. When you happen to experience something of this kind, know that God allows it to happen for your own good. This is precisely the warfare for which God has rewarded His saints with radiant crowns. So, remembering this, do not lose courage in the trial you have met. And, as in any other trouble, look up to the Lord and say to Him from your heart: 'O Lord my God! Take care of Thy servant, and let Thy will be upon me. I know and profess that firm is the truth of Thy words and Thy promises are not false. I put my trust in them, and stand unwavering on Thy path.' Blessed is the soul which thus surrenders itself to the Lord each time it experiences trouble and hardship! If, in spite of this, the struggle persists and you cannot harmonise and unite your will with the will of God as quickly as you would wish, do not grieve or lose heart, but continue to surrender yourself to God, and bow down willingly to His decisions—and through this you will gain victory. Remember the battle, which our Lord Christ had to fight in the garden of Gethsemane, when His human nature, at first horrified by the cup to be drained, cried: 'O my Father, if it be possible, let this cup pass from me'; but later, coming back to itself and putting its soul in the hands of God, said from its full and free will, and with deepest humility: 'nevertheless, not as I will, but as thou wilt' (Matt. xxvi. 39).

When you are in difficulties, refrain from making any step before you raise your eyes to the crucified Christ, our Lord. There you will see written in large letters how you too should behave in the affliction which has befallen you. Copy it for yourself, not in letters but in actions; namely,—when you feel attacks of self-loving self-pity, do not pay heed to them and do not cravenly crawl down from your cross, but resort to prayer and endure with humility, striving to conquer your will, and to be firm in wishing for God's will to be done upon you. If you come out from your prayer with this fruit, rejoice and exult. If you fail to attain it, your soul will be left fasting, not having tasted its natural food. Try to let nothing dwell in your soul, for however short a time, except God alone. Do not grieve or be distressed by anything. Do not turn your eyes to the evil of others and to bad examples; but be like a little child which, in its innocence, does not notice them and harmlessly passes them by.

CHAPTER TWENTY-THREE

Many are the wiles of the enemy to despoil us of inner peace; so watch

Our enemy, the devil, rejoices when our soul is in confusion and our heart in agitation. So he uses all his cunning to try and perturb our souls. The first means in these attempts is to excite self-

love, resulting in withdrawal of the grace, which creates and pre
serves inner peace. For this purpose, he suggests the idea that all
things which are and appear good in us, are acquired by our own
labour and diligence and, banishing humility and simplicity, disposes us to put a high value on and ascribe great weight to ourselves, and to feel ourselves something important, shrouding in
forgetfulness the action of Divine grace, without which no one
can even say the Lord's name, as St Paul testifies, saying: 'No
man can say that Jesus is the Lord, but by the Holy Ghost'
(I Cor. xii. 3). This grace is given to all believers and its presence
is a sign that a man is a true believer. Having received it, a believer no longer does, nor can do, anything truly good without its
help; it remains always with him, according to the Lord's promise,
and the enemy can do nothing with him, while it is in him and
encompasses him. So the enemy strives by all possible means to
make it withdraw, and the first thing he does for this end, as was
said, is to suggest self-appreciation or feelings that we are not
nothing, but something, and something not without importance.
To him who accepts such suggestions, the enemy offers a new idea,
consisting in being sure that he is better than others, more zealous
and more rich in works. Having succeeded in implanting this
opinion, the enemy thereupon leads a man to judge and despise
others, which is invariably followed by pride. All this can take
place in the heart in the course of a single moment; but even so,
the action of grace is immediately reduced, which results in inattention to oneself, weakening of zeal, and arising of thoughts,
at first empty, and later passionate, which is followed by the
stirrings of passions themselves, and is indissolubly connected
with a storm raging in the heart—Inner peace is lost. Such a state
is not permanent, and if the sufferer remembers himself, he returns
to himself, and is filled with contrition, repents and by prayer re-
establishes his habitual inner order. The enemy is banished; but
he does not lose heart, and returns again and again with the same
suggestions for the same purpose—to destroy inner peace.

Knowing this, my brother, and in order to oppose these hostile
efforts, keep an alert watch over yourself, according to the words
of the Lord: 'Watch and pray, that ye enter not into temptation'
(Matt. xxvi. 41). Watch yourself with all diligence, lest the enemy
steals near and robs you, depriving you of this great treasure,
which is inner peace and stillness of soul. The enemy strives to

destroy the peace of the soul, because he knows that when the soul is in turmoil it is more easily led to evil. But you must guard your peace, since you know that when the soul is peaceful, the enemy has no access to it; then it is ready for all things that are good and does them willingly and without difficulty, easily overcoming all obstacles. To succeed more readily in this, try to foresee the advances of the enemy. An advance of the enemy is—a self-reliant thought. Make it a rule to regard as clearly coming from the enemy every thought, which tends to decrease your conviction that all good comes from God, that you can succeed in nothing without the help of His grace, and that, therefore, you must put all your trust in Him alone. You must regard all such thoughts as clearly coming from the enemy and wrathfully reject and chase them away, until they disappear. The action of the Holy Spirit in us is on all occasions to lead our souls towards union with God, to kindle in them a sweet love of Him, a blessed confidence and a firm trust in Him. Whatever is opposed to this is the work of the enemy.

He uses all the means and methods he can invent to disturb the soul: he introduces into the heart superfluous fears, increases the soul's weakness, prevents it from keeping the necessary dispositions and from delighting as it should in confession, in holy communion, or in prayer, but makes it go through all these not with humble daring and love, but fearfully and confusedly;—he makes the soul receive with hopeless sorrow and pain the impoverishment of religious feeling and the absence of inner delight, which often come in times of prayer or during other spiritual exercises,—by suggesting to it not that this impoverishment is allowed by God for its own good, but that it means that all its efforts and endeavours lead nowhere, and so are best all abandoned; by this he finally brings it to a hopelessness and confusion so great that it actually begins to think that everything it does is indeed useless and fruitless, and that God has completely forgotten and abandoned it.

But this is clearly a lie. A soul may experience dryness and an impoverishment of religious feelings and of spiritual sweetness; but, in spite of this, it can perform all kinds of good actions, moved by simple faith and armed with holy patience and constancy. Still, to help you better to understand it all, and to prevent you suffering harm when God finds it desirable, for your own good, to allow or to send you such impoverishment of spiritual feeling and of sweetness, I shall describe in the following chapter what blessings come from humble patience to those, who show it in times of dryness and coldness of heart,—in order that you may learn how not to lose your peace of soul and not be eaten up by sorrow, when you have to suffer either this or some other disturbing inflow of thoughts and passionate impulses.

CHAPTER TWENTY-FOUR

One must not be perturbed by impoverishment of spiritual feelings or by other inner temptations

Although I have already spoken in chapter seven of the dryness and cooling of the heart, and of the grief these bring to the soul, I shall now add something I did not say there,—namely, that this grief and this dryness of heart or impoverishment of spiritual joy and sweetness, bring much profit to the soul, if we accept and endure them with humility and patience. If a man knew of this profit beforehand, he would certainly not consider this state a burden nor be grieved if he has to experience it. For then he would not regard this bitter dearth of inner spiritual comforts as a sign of Divine displeasure, but would see it as the work of God's particular love for him, and so would gladly accept it as a great mercy.

Indeed, he may already draw comfort from the very fact that these states are chiefly experienced by such men as abandon themselves with particular zeal to the service of God, and give special attention to avoiding all things that may offend Him;—and they experience them not in the beginning of their conversion to God, but when they have worked for Him for a considerable time, when their heart is sufficiently purified by holy prayer and contrition, when they have felt a certain spiritual sweetness, warmth and joy, which made them consecrate themselves wholly to God, and when they have already begun to do so in practice. Neither do we see that sinners and people addicted to the vanities of the world and of daily life ever have such experiences or are subjected to such

217

temptations. This clearly shows that such bitterness is an honourable and precious food, to share which the Lord invites those He loves best, and even if its taste is not pleasant at the time of eating, yet it brings us great profit although this is not then evident. For when the soul is in this state of dryness, when it tastes this bitterness and suffers temptations and thoughts the mere memory of which makes one tremble, it poisons the heart and almost kills the inner man. But, when the soul finds itself in this state, it learns to distrust itself and not to rely on its own good state, and so acquires true humility, which God so much wishes us to have. Moreover it then becomes inspired with a desire to acquire a most ardent love for God, a most diligent attention to its thoughts and the greatest courage to endure such temptations without harm and comes out of this struggle with 'senses exercised to discern both good and evil' (Heb. v. 14) as St. Paul said. But since these good fruits are hidden from the sight of the soul, I repeat, it is troubled and flees from this bitterness, for it does not wish to be deprived of its spiritual comforts even for a short time, and regards every spiritual exercise not accompanied by them as wasted time and useless labour.

CHAPTER TWENTY-FIVE

Every temptation is sent for our good

In order to make you understand better that all temptations in general are sent us by God for our own profit, pay attention to what I have to say. The tendency of man's corrupted nature is to be proud, to love self-glory and self-display, to hold fast to his own opinions and decisions and always to want everyone to give him a much higher value than he actually has. This self-appreciation and high opinion of oneself are extremely harmful in the work of spiritual endeavour, so much so that even a shadow of them is enough to prevent a man from reaching true perfection. Therefore, in His wise dispensation for us all, and especially for those who have sincerely abandoned themselves to His service, our loving Father in heaven allows temptations to assail us, so as to bring us to a state in which we can easily escape this terrible danger of self-appreciation, and are almost compelled to reach a truly humble knowledge of ourselves. He did this with the Apostle Peter by letting him deny Him thrice, in order that he should realise his own weakness and not rely on himself. St. Paul had a similar experience when, after being ravished to the third heaven and shown the ineffable divine mysteries, God made him endure a certain wearisome and troublesome temptation, so that he should bear in himself this indication of his own impotence and nothingness and so progress in humility and boast only of his weaknesses, lest the magnitude of the revelations granted to him by God should make him puffed up with pride, as he himself testifies: 'And lest I should be exalted above measure through the abundance of the revelations, there was given to me a thorn in the flesh, the messenger of Satan to buffet me, lest I should be exalted above measure' (II Cor. xii. 7).

Thus, moved by compassion for this unfortunate and lawless tendency of ours (always to think highly of ourselves), God allows all kinds of temptations to assail us, at times very grievous, so that knowing our weakness we should be humbled. In this the Lord shows His loving-kindness as well as His wisdom; for by humbling us He makes us derive the greatest benefit from things which appear most harmful, since of all things humility is what is most necessary and useful to our soul. Thus, if all temptations are given us to teach us humility, it follows that every servant of God who tastes these bitter states of the heart—dryness, lack of spiritual savour, dearth of spiritual comforts in his heart—experiences this in order to learn humility through thinking that they were brought about by his own sins, that no other soul could be so lacking in all things, or work for God so coldly as his soul, that such states only visit those who are abandoned by God, and consequently that he too is abandoned and abandoned deservedly. From such humble thoughts is born this good: a man, who formerly thought of himself as something, and something very important, now, having tasted the bitter medicine sent him from above, begins to regard himself as the most sinful man in the world, unworthy even to be called a Christian. And indeed he would never have arrived at so base an opinion of himself and such deep humility, if he were not moved to it by those special temptations and this great sorrowing and bitterness of heart. So they are a great mercy, which God shows in this life to a soul, which surrenders itself to Him with wise humility, to let Him cure it as He wills and by the remedies He alone knows perfectly and deems necessary for healing and bringing it to a good state.

Besides these fruits, brought to the soul through these temptations by impoverishment of spiritual comforts, there are also brought many other fruits. Made contrite by these inner burdens, a man forces himself with renewed vigour and zeal to run to God and beg for His speedy help, does diligently everything deemed useful to cure the grief of his soul and banish the bitterness from his heart, and, to avoid this torment of soul in future, makes a firm resolution to walk henceforth on the path of spiritual life, paying the strictest attention to all movements of the heart, and to avoid even the merest shadow of sin and the slightest negligence capable of separating him from God and God from him in any way whatsoever. Thus the grief he considered so contrary to his aims and so harmful, becomes for him a spur, inciting him to seek God with greater warmth and to avoid more strenuously all things incompatible with God's will. In brief—all sorrows and torments, which the soul suffers during inner temptations and the dearth of spiritual comforts and delights, are nothing but a purifying remedy; by their means God in His loving-kindness cleanses the soul if it endures them with humility and patience. And these torments ensure for such patient sufferers a crown which is gained only through them, a crown the more glorious the more painful the torments suffered by the heart.

It is clear from all this that we must not torture ourselves too much or be sorely troubled either by other temptations which assail us from without, or by the aforesaid temptations within, as are those who have little experience in the matter. For, in their inexperience, they regard what comes from God as coming from the devil, or from their own sins and imperfections; they take signs of Divine love for signs of Divine wrath, interpret His gifts and favours as blows and scourgings, brought upon them by extreme Divine displeasure, and regard all they have done and are doing as useless and worthless labour and their present loss as beyond repair. For if they believed that these temptations bring no loss of virtue, but, on the contrary, greatly increase it when the soul accepts them with humility and suffers them with thankfulness; if they believed that they are arranged by God's loving benevolence towards us, they would not be excessively troubled and would not lose their peace of heart from the fact that they experience such temptations, have unseemly and shameful thoughts, and are cold and dry during prayer and other spiritual exercises. All this would only make their soul more deeply humble before God and would make them resolve in their heart to fulfil God's will in everything they do, since it is only in this way that God wishes to be pleased in this world; they resolve too to strive by all means to keep themselves peaceful and calm in accepting all things that befall them, as coming from the hand of our heavenly Father, from whence also comes the bitter cup they have to drain at the present moment. For whether a temptation comes from the devil, from other men or is caused by sins, it still depends on God and is sent by Him for our good and to turn some other great temptation away from us.

CHAPTER TWENTY-SIX

Remedy against being perturbed by small transgressions and weaknesses

If you happen to fall into some pardonable transgression by word or deed, for example, if you are perturbed by some accidental happening, or criticise, or listen to criticisms by others, or enter into argument about something, or are at times impatient, flustered, or suspicious of others, or if you neglect something,— you must not be too perturbed, sorrowful and despairing in thinking about what you have done; above all you must not aggravate your perturbation by sad thoughts about yourself, that evidently you will never manage to be free of such weaknesses, that your will to work for the Lord is too weak, or that you are not progressing on the path of God as you should,—for every time you do this you burden your soul with thousands of other fears produced by faintness of heart and sadness.

For what follows? You are ashamed to stand daringly in the presence of God, since you have proved unfaithful to Him, you waste time in examining how long you had lingered in every transgression, whether you were identified with it and had begun to desire it or not, whether you had rejected this or that thought or not, and so on. And the more you thus torture yourself, the more your spirit is disorganised, and the greater becomes your stress and unwillingness to confess your sins. Even if you go to confession, you do so with a disturbing fear, and after confession you still find no peace; for it seems to you that you have not said everything. Thus you live a life that is bitter, disquieted and of little fruit, and you waste much time uselessly. And all this happens because we forget our natural weakness and lose sight of the attitude the soul must have to God. In other words, we forget that when the soul falls into some pardonable sin that is not mortal, it should turn to God with humble repentance and hope, and not torture itself with excessive sorrow, bitterness and stress.

I say this about pardonable sins, for only these are excusable for a soul, which has embraced the strict life described here. We address ourselves here to those who lead a spiritual life and actively seek to make progress in it, exerting every effort to avoid mortal sins. Those who do not lead a strict life, but take life as it comes and remain untroubled even if they offend God by a mortal sin, require other advice. The remedy given above is not for such men. They must grieve deeply and weep bitterly, always strictly examine their conscience and confess all their sins without self-pity, and they must neglect no means which can cure and save them.

In small everyday transgressions, repentance must always be inspired and imbued with firm trust in God, and still more must it be so in sins more grievous than ordinary, into which even a zealous servant of God sometimes falls by God's leave. For a penitent distress, which so tortures the heart and gnaws at it, can never re-establish hope in the soul, if it is not accompanied by a firm trust in Divine goodness and mercy. This trust must always fill the heart of those wishing to reach the highest degrees of Christian perfection. It animates and tautens all the powers of the soul and the spirit. Yet many who have entered the path of spiritual life fail to pay attention to this, and so stop in their progress with heart weakened, and move no further; thus they become unsuitable for receiving the blessings of grace, which the Lord has distributed along this path and which usually reward only those whose efforts never slacken and who move steadfastly on and on.

But above all, those who experience some perturbation of the heart, or some perplexity, or a split in their conscience, must turn to their spiritual Father or someone else experienced in spiritual life, at the same time trustfully begging the Lord to reveal the truth through them and send them a reassuring solution of their troubles and perplexities. Thereupon a man should be wholly set at rest by their word.

CHAPTER TWENTY-SEVEN

If a man is perturbed, he must immediately re-establish peace in his soul

Every time you fall into some pardonable transgression, even if it happens a thousand times a day, as soon as you notice it, do not torture yourself and so waste your time without profit, but at once humble yourself and, conscious of your weakness, turn to God with hope and call to Him from the depths of your heart: 'O Lord my God! I have done this because I am what I am and so nothing can be expected of me but such transgressions or even worse, if Thy grace does not help me and I am left to myself alone. I grieve over what I have done, especially because my life has no righteousness responding to Thy care of me, but I continue to fall and to fall. Forgive me and give me the strength not to offend Thee again and in no way to digress from Thy will. For I zealously wish to work for Thee, to please Thee and be obedient to Thee in all things.' Having done this, do not torment yourself with thoughts as to whether God has forgiven you. The Lord is near and listens to the sighings of His servants. So calm yourself in this certainty and, having regained your calm, continue your usual occupations as though nothing had happened.

You must do this not once but, if necessary, a hundred times and every minute, and the last time with the same perfect trust and daring towards God as the first. In doing this you will render due honour to the infinite goodness of God, Whom you must always see as full of infinite loving-kindness towards us. Then you will never cease to make progress in your life and will go on moving forward without waste of time and labour.

Another way of protecting your inner peace when you succumb to these trespasses, is the following: combine the inner action of realising your worthlessness and your humility before God, with a warm remembrance of the great mercies, which God has shown you personally, and thus reviving your love for Him, rouse in yourself a desire to thank and glorify Him; and then actually thank and glorify Him warmly from the depths of your soul. Since thanking and glorifying God is the highest manifestation of our living union with God, if you take your downfall rightly, its fruit will be, with God's help, your rising higher towards Him. This should be kept in view by those who are too sorely troubled and tormented by small transgressions, to make them see how great is their blindness in this matter, and how much they harm themselves by their ill-judgment. So it is really to them that this last advice is directed. It puts into our hands the key with which the soul can open the great treasure-house of the spirit and can in a short time be enriched by the grace of our Lord Jesus Christ, to Whom be glory, honour and worship, together with His Father Who has no beginning, and the Holy Spirit, now and for ever and ever.

Amen.

A HISTORY OF
UNSEEN WARFARE

A HISTORY OF
UNSEEN WARFARE

By Professor H. A. Hodges

I. *History and significance of the Unseen Warfare*

The work which is here offered to the English reader has a striking history, and occupies a peculiar position in the world of Christian spiritual literature.

In its original form it is the work of a Roman Catholic priest who lived and worked in Italy in the sixteenth century. The *Combattimento spirituale* of Lorenzo Scupoli was first published in 1589, and was afterwards enlarged by the author himself to many times its original size. It is a classic of spiritual writing of the Counter-Reformation period. It has been translated into many languages, and to English readers it has been accessible in one form or another for over three hundred years. It was reprinted in English as recently as last year (1950). It is a book whose merits have commanded a constant public in every age since it first appeared.

The present edition, however, is not merely another reprint of the familiar text. It is the first presentation in English of a very interesting variant upon it.

In the eighteenth century a copy of Scupoli's work fell into the hands of a monk named Nicodemus, an inhabitant of the famous Orthodox monastic settlement on Mount Athos. Nicodemus was so impressed by it that he translated it into Greek, combining it with a shorter work also by Scupoli, and giving it the title of *Unseen Warfare* ('Αόρατος Πόλεμος). In translating it he made various changes and adjustments to adapt it to the needs of Orthodox readers, and added copious notes and illustrations drawn from the Bible and the Fathers of the Eastern Church. He made clear that the original author was another than himself, but he did not reveal his name or nationality.

The *Unseen Warfare* in Nicodemus' version was a success. It won for itself a place in the spiritual life of the Greek Church, and at the present day it is held in high esteem on Mount Athos.

From there, in turn, it made its way to Russia in the nineteenth century. Bishop Theophan the Recluse, a director of souls and an ascetic theologian of note, who was acquainted with Nicodemus' writings, was moved by his admiration of them to translate the *Unseen Warfare* from Greek into Russian. Like Nicodemus, and on an even greater scale, he allowed himself in translating it to make various changes and adaptations. The resulting version, supported by the double authority of Nicodemus and Theophan, took an assured place in the spiritual literature of the Russian Church. It is from Bishop Theophan's Russian text that the present translation into English is made.

While the *Spiritual Combat* as Scupoli wrote it will always repay direct study, the Greco-Russian *Unseen Warfare* has an interest and value of its own. The fact that Nicodemus translated it in the first place is a testimony to the extent of common ground which, in spite of centuries of schism and estrangement, still unites the Christians of East and West. In Nicodemus' Greek and in Theophan's Russian the book has been absorbed into the thought and life of the Orthodox Church, and has obtained the sanction of the great centre of Orthodox spirituality on Mount Athos. On the other hand, it has not gone through the process of translation altogether unchanged. While the main body of the book remains as Scupoli fashioned it, certain sections have been modified or even totally rewritten, and this has been done with a purpose. The most drastic changes occur in the chapters dealing with the ways of prayer, and they amount, in sum, to a criticism of Scupoli's teaching at that point. Nor is the criticism merely personal; it is rather a conflict of traditions. It is not merely Nicodemus or Theophan substituting his own views for Scupoli's; it is the Orthodox Church criticising the Counter-Reformation and quietly but firmly adhering to its own more ancient traditions in the life of prayer.

It is not only for its intrinsic value, therefore, that this translation of the *Unseen Warfare* deserves to be studied, but also as a document illustrating the play and counterplay of influences between East and West in this vitally important sphere of ascetic theology. For that growing number of people who take to heart the scandal of schism, and of that mutual ignorance and estrangement which is both cause and effect of schism, and who work and pray for a better understanding between the Christians of East and West, the lessons which this book can teach are of no small moment. It is not in the sphere of ecclesiastical organisation, of canon law and church government, that unity will be discovered and union achieved. Nor is it in the sphere of dogmatic discussion, severed as that so often is from the actual life of the Christian community and reduced to a battle of abstractions. It is where we fight and pray together, in the same spiritual combat against the same unseen enemies, that we shall find ourselves to be one army—not become one army, but discover that we are one. And when we discover that, the formulae and the institutions will be adjusted accordingly. It is as material for reflection on this theme, on the points of identity and difference between East and West in their conduct of the unseen warfare, that this book is offered to the Christians of this country.

II. *The spiritual teaching of the Fathers*

Christian ascetic theology is not something borrowed from extraneous sources, from eastern religions or from Greek philosophy. It is firmly based on the Bible. The ruling idea of it is familiar to all of us from St. Paul, for it is he who tells us that the Christian life is an athletic contest, and draws the conclusion that we must go into training for it. It is he, again, who likens the Christian life to a battle, and the Christian to a soldier; he describes the discipline to which the Christian is subject, his armour and his weapons of offence, and the enemies, internal and external, against whom he has to fight. Christian ascetic theology is simply the development of these Pauline conceptions into a systematic doctrine and a practical discipline, so that the Christian soldier or athlete may know exactly what he is contending for, and be well trained for the struggle.

The Bible is full of material for such a doctrine and discipline. If it contains the gospel of God's free grace, it also contains the new law, the law of liberty and love, by which God's people are to govern themselves. If it tells of the work that was wrought for us once for all by Christ on the Cross, it also tells of the work which is wrought in us every day by the Holy Ghost, and in that work it summons us to be 'fellow-workers with God'. We are told to work out our salvation in fear and trembling, knowing that we can do nothing unless God works in us, and yet that in Christ we can do everything.

The Bible, Old and New Testaments alike, is full of teaching which bears upon this theme. But, as is the manner of the Bible, it is presented piecemeal, and often in figurative and obscure language. Ascetic theology is the attempt to present it as an organised body of doctrine, with an agreed terminology and accepted principles, and to relate it to the experience gained through a practical discipline. Such an organised body of doctrine has come down to us by continuous tradition and development from its first beginnings, which can be traced back to the third century.

The intellectual formulation begins with Clement of Alexandria. He, and after him Origen, taught Christians to think of the Christian way of life in terms which could be understood by educated Greeks. They began the construction of a theory of Christian living, by establishing certain fundamental conceptions and providing the beginnings of a terminology. The practical discipline, however, and the experiential content, came from the deserts of Egypt and Syria. There hermits living in solitude, and monks in communities of various kinds, set themselves to create a perfect pattern of Christian living. 'If you wish to be perfect,' said Christ to the rich young man, 'sell all that you have and give it to the poor, and come and follow me.' The men of the Desert obeyed the command and claimed the implicit promise. They aspired to that perfection which Christ commands.* They sought the Kingdom of God, the pearl which the merchant in the story sold all his possessions to buy. They did not say that no one can be a true Christian in the world. They told stories of holy lives lived in the world, to shame the lazy monk. But for themselves they chose to withdraw from worldly temptations and distractions, in order to devote themselves wholly to the spiritual combat. It is therefore not surprising that, from daily meditation on the Scriptures and from their own daily experience, they came to know a great deal about it.

* Matt. v. 48, 'You therefore shall be perfect'.

Their doctrine was codified in Greek by Evagrius of Pontus (d. 399), and a generation later in Latin by John Cassian, as well as by various other writers. It is the starting-point of all subsequent development in ascetic theology. A short summary of it will enable us to see how faithfully the *Unseen Warfare* follows the primitive models.

The goal of the Christian discipline is union with God by loving contemplation. This is the Kingdom of God, and this is eternal life. For this we were created, but from this we have fallen; our minds are distracted and fascinated by created things, our wills are held in bondage to finite and transient goods. The purpose of our discipline is therefore to turn the mind and will back into their proper alignment, so that they may receive in full measure the illumination of divine grace. They cannot do so while they are inordinately attached to the creatures; it is the pure in heart who shall see God, and therefore the immediate aim of our discipline must be to attain to purity of heart. This is what Abbot Moses explained to Cassian: 'The goal of our profession is the Kingdom of God or the Kingdom of heaven; but our immediate aim or target is purity of heart, without which it is impossible for anyone to reach that goal.'

The way which leads to the goal can be considered under three aspects.

1. It is a moral way, a discipline of the will and character, and this has naturally two sides: a purgation of what is evil and a cultivation of what is good.

(*a*) The beginning of wisdom is the fear of the Lord. At first, while the passions are strong and liable to carry us away, we are governed and kept in order mainly by the fear of God, together with shame and repentance for past sin. These motives lead gradually to the building up of self-control, and patience under temptations and difficulties. This in turn kindles hope. Drawn on by hope and guided by a growing experience, we set to work not merely to control, but to 'eradicate' the passions. It is a lengthy process; but gradually the bodily appetites are weakened and the soul purged, until at last we arrive at purity of heart, or freedom from passion ($\dot{\alpha}\pi\dot{\alpha}\theta\epsilon\iota\alpha$). This does not mean that we cease to have any feelings; it means that we are no longer ruled by our feelings, but remain untroubled and tranquil in all circumstances. The heart or will, no longer swayed by emotions or

231

carried away by its own self-will, is 'sober', 'awake', 'attentive' to God.

(b) As we purge ourselves of passion, we also grow in virtue. The seeds of all the virtues are latent in us from the start; it is they which constitute the likeness of God in the soul, which sin has defaced but not destroyed. We must set to work methodically to cultivate them, until at last, by constant practice, they become easy and congenial to us. As passion weakens, virtue grows, and at length the heart which is pure from all passion is also adorned with all the virtues; or rather, at this stage, the separate virtues are united and summed up in the all-sufficient virtue of love. Love toward God, and love of our neighbour for the sake of God, becomes the ruling power in the heart.

From Scriptural study and from long experience the Desert Fathers built up an unsurpassed body of moral teaching. They classified and analysed the various types of sin and of virtue; they found out effective ways of mortifying the one and strengthening the other; all subsequent Christian teaching on these matters is under their influence.

2. Parallel with the moral discipline, helping it on and helped on by it, runs the discipline of the mind, *i.e.* of the senses, the imagination, and the intellect. Here too there is a negative and a positive side.

(a) The senses, the memory, and the imagination must be guarded, not only against things which are a direct temptation to sin, but against everything which may engage the mind in passing interests when it should be bent upon the unseen realities. The intellect too must be called off from all vain curiosity, from all learning or enquiry pursued merely for its own sake.

(b) Instead, we must teach ourselves to see God in all things and all things in God. This is done by stages. First we learn how to contemplate material things and the face of nature; we come to see these things with the eyes of the Psalmist, to whom they all declare the glory of God. Then we can rise to contemplate the glory of God in immaterial things, especially in the human soul, which bears His image and likeness. Next we go on to contemplate God's actions in history, His judgments and His saving acts and the whole 'economy' or 'dispensation' of our redemption. The mind becomes penetrated with the meaning of these things, so that whatever we see or hear speaks to us of them. In time a great simplification takes place. Instead of contemplating all these things separately and in detail, we come to see them all as summed up in Christ, from Whom are all things, and in Whom is fulfilled the whole counsel of God toward us. When the heart becomes pure and love reigns in it, then also the contemplation of Christ becomes habitual in the mind. The soul has become Christ-centred.

There is a stage beyond this. However the imagination and the intellect may be disciplined, we cannot truly apprehend God while we cling to visible things and let our minds dwell upon images of such things. Even Christ Himself, Who is the heart and centre of the visible universe, is not truly known if we stop short at His human nature, not recognising in Him the Eternal Word, the Second Person of the Blessed Trinity. A time must come when the mind turns from all objects of sense and clears itself of imagery. The eye of the body and the imagination being then shut, the inward eye of the spirit is opened; the soul, recollected and concentrated within herself, can see herself for what she is, and rise above herself to the vision of God, Whose image and likeness she bears. There is a supreme mode of contemplation, indeed, in which the soul, seized and uplifted by God, forgets all created things, including herself, being involved, so far as they are concerned, in an 'infinite ignorance'; but this ignorance of creatures is at the same time a luminous knowledge of God, a formless contemplation of Him Who is without form or mode. The soul which has enjoyed this high contemplation has reached the summit of 'knowledge' (γνῶσις) and 'wisdom' (σοφία). She has attained to the Kingdom of God. Even when not engaged in actual contemplation, such a soul is permanently 'settled' on God, and lives in the light of a perpetual awareness of Him, accompanied by an abiding joy.

3. Officially the Fathers recognise only two ways, the moral and the contemplative; but in fact they also show us a third way running parallel with these two. It is the way of prayer.

In I Tim. ii. 1 we are bidden to practise 'petitions, prayers, intercessions, and thanksgivings';* the Fathers take this as a progressive series marking out the road of prayer. 'Petitions' are confessions of sin and prayers for pardon and restoration, and the prayer of beginners is dominated by these. In them the fear

* δεήσεις, προσευχάς, ἐντεύξεις, εὐχαριστίας.

233

of God finds voice. 'Prayers' are taken to mean requests for the virtues and graces, and acts of self-dedication and renunciation of the world. These are expressions of hope; they are characteristic of the soul which is beginning to be led forward in the paths of righteousness. As time goes on, this soul will begin to spare more time, in charity, to intercede for others. By the time that purity of heart is attained, even intercession will have been transcended, and the prayer of the pure soul will be predominantly thanksgiving and adoration. Of course it is not meant that the soul, in passing from one form of prayer to another, leaves the old one behind and ceases to practise it. No one can outgrow penitence; and the earliest and lowliest of all prayers, the prayer of the publican, will accompany the soul to the very end of her journey. Nor can she ever cease to make requests for herself and for others. It is a question of where the emphasis lies; and the pure heart, which lives in the contemplation of Christ, cannot live predominantly in fear and shame. It is ruled by thankfulness and love.

Prayer and contemplation are closely joined together; and as in contemplation, so in prayer, a time comes when we must rise above the colourful imagination and the busy intellect, and approach God in 'pure prayer'. By this is meant a kind of prayer in which the mind does not run from image to image, or from one consideration to another, nor work out its prayer in a coherent texture of words, but stands still in unmoving attachment to God. The various elements of prayer, penitence, supplication, intercession, thanksgiving, adoration etc., are not separately expressed in successive sentences; they are all present at once in the unity of this prayer. The soul may use a few pregnant words which say much in little, *i.e.* in modern western terminology an 'aspiration'; or the prayer may be wordless altogether, *i.e.* what in modern western terminology is called the 'prayer of simplicity', or 'prayer of faith'. The Fathers class all such types of prayer together under the name of 'pure prayer' (καθαρὰ προσευχή) or 'quietness' (ἡσυχία). In the pure heart, such prayer becomes habitual, and so fulfils the apostolic command to 'pray without ceasing' (I Thess. v. 17). Such a soul may also be visited by moments of 'burning prayer', or 'infused' prayer as modern writers would say; these are a gift which God gives when it pleases Him. But the abiding state of the pure soul is one in

234

which pure love, habitual contemplation, and perpetual prayer are all united; for though the three ways are distinct all along their courses, they become one and the same when they reach their common goal. Pure contemplation is inseparable from perfect love, and this pours itself out in pure prayer.

The foregoing is a summary of the spiritual teachings of the Desert. It is not a full account of the ascetic theology of the Eastern Church. I have said nothing about that body of teaching which stresses above all the transcendent mystery of God, and which speaks of the contemplation of God not as light, but as darkness. That teaching is known to the whole Christian world, East and West, through the writings which bear the name of Dionysius the Areopagite. Its influence in some quarters has been very great indeed, but on the other hand it has never been universal. Christian ascetic theology was already an organised body of thought, accompanied by the appropriate practical discipline, before the Dionysian teaching was accepted into it, and it was not accepted everywhere. The *Unseen Warfare* shows little trace of specifically Dionysian phrases or conceptions. It stands firmly on the basis of that earlier tradition, fundamental alike to East and West, whose main points are summarised above.

III. *Hesychasm and the Jesus prayer*

In contrast with the set forms of prayer which are proper to public worship, and the private extempore prayers and colloquies with God, which may be of considerable length, there is another mode of prayer which is distinguished by its brevity; it consists in the use of a short formula, never more than a couple of sentences, sometimes no more than a single word. The value of such a formula lies in the fact that, if well chosen, it can be pregnant with meaning, saying much in little space. It can be used on special occasions—a sudden temptation, or danger, or other challenging situation—when there is no time for lengthy prayer. Or it can be used habitually, by repeating it over and over again, until the repetition becomes automatic and self-perpetuating; and this can be a powerful means of penetrating the soul with the spirit of prayer, and promoting recollection.

Such prayer has been recognised in the Christian tradition from the beginning. It is called 'one-word prayer' (μονολόγιστος εὐχή) or 'javelin-prayer' (*oratio jaculatoria*). Cassian gives an account of it in his interview with Abbot Isaac. The Abbot told him of a 'formula', handed down by an esoteric tradition in the Desert, which was a sure means of attaining to the state of perpetual prayer. It consists of the words: 'O God, make speed to save me; O Lord, make haste to help me.' These words, says Abbot Isaac, sum up all worthy affections and are appropriate to every situation. They express on the one hand humility, fear, and self-distrust, and on the other hand trust and confidence in God. They can be used on particular occasions of all kinds, and they can be used habitually. So used, they ultimately penetrate the mind and soul, and bring it into a permanent state of prayer.

Abbot Isaac's formula was widely used. Through Cassian's recommendation, it has passed into the public prayers of the western Church. Other formulae, however, were also in use, and everyone was free to use whatever words he found helpful to himself. One method, of ancient origin, has in the course of time obtained an overwhelming predominance over all rivals in the affections of Christian people; that is the use of the Name of Jesus, or of some short form of words including that Name. The formula: 'Lord Jesus Christ, Son of the living God, have mercy on me a sinner', or some close variant upon it, is especially popular in the Orthodox Church, and is known there as the Jesus Prayer. There are several references to it in the *Unseen Warfare*, and one whole chapter (Part I, chap. 51) is devoted to an account of it.

The prayer of the Holy Name can be traced as far back as the 4th century, in Ephraim the Syrian and in Chrysostom. In the 5th century Hesychius writes 'Let the Name of Jesus cling to your breath and your whole life.' His contemporary, Diadochus of Photike, tells us to keep the intellect occupied by the perpetual interior repetition of the formula 'Lord Jesus'; the Holy Spirit recites it with us like a mother teaching her child to say 'Father'. The Holy Name, thus kept in mind by ceaseless meditation, becomes a devouring fire which consumes all the sin that disfigures the soul, and leads us to the loving contemplation of God. Similar teaching continues in the 6th century, in Barsanuphius and in John of the Ladder.

In the last named it is possible to see foreshadowed a peculiar form of spiritual discipline which in later years, under the name

of 'hesychasm', has found a large following in the Orthodox
Church. The literal meaning of the word 'hesychasm' is 'quietism'; but Orthodox hesychasm has little in common with what was
called 'quietism' in the West in the 17th century. It is simply a
form of spiritual discipline, based on the teachings of the Fathers,
and meant to bring the soul to that state of repose in God
(ἡσυχία) which we have seen is identified with the state of
perpetual prayer. It took shape gradually, and at first was handed
down by oral tradition. It was first put into writing by St.
Simeon the New Theologian (949–1022), Abbot of St. Mamas,
and ultimately found in Mount Athos a local habitation and
centre of diffusion.

We may consider the hesychast teaching under four heads.

1. In the hesychast discipline, the repetition of the Jesus
Prayer plays an essential part. The repetition should be regular
and rhythmical, and there are degrees in the practice of it. (a) At
first the words of the prayer are deliberately repeated by the voice,
or at least by the lips and tongue, at such times and for such
periods as the aspirant finds opportune. (b) In course of time the
prayer becomes more internal and spontaneous; the mind takes up
the rhythm of it and keeps repeating it silently without a conscious
act of will. (c) Later still, the prayer comes to dominate the whole
personality; it becomes identified with the movement of the heart,
and controls that movement by its own rhythm, and the whole
mind and will of the devotee are governed by the prayer, which is
now truly perpetual. This final stage of the prayer is known as
'spiritual action'.

2. The practice of the prayer brings the soul at last to the state
of quiet (ἡσυχία), in which there are no sensible images and
no discursive movements of the intellect, but only an imageless
intuitive apprehension of the soul itself and of God.

3. Then the 'flame of grace' is kindled in the soul, bringing
with it a feeling of 'warmth' and a perception of the 'light of
Mount Tabor'. This 'warmth' and 'light' are not merely meta-
phorical terms signifying peace and joy and similar emotions.
Peace and joy are included in the experience, but there is something more. It is a perception, not indeed a 'finite organical perception' as William Blake would say, but nevertheless a genuine
perceptual apprehension of that which eye has not seen nor ear
heard. The ascetic, now united with God and made effectually a

'partaker of the divine nature' (II Peter i. 4), *sees* the divine glory in and about him, as the three disciples were permitted to see it in Christ at the Transfiguration. This state of supersensible perception is the normal state, according to Orthodox conceptions, of 'perfect' souls. It has nothing to do with 'ecstasies' or 'raptures' or 'visions', which are momentary occurrences of an extraordinary character. On the contrary, it is the ordinary, normal, permanent state of those who live in constant union with God. To adapt again a phrase from Blake, their 'senses discover the infinite in everything', and they move open-eyed where most men are blind.

4. These results flow principally from the use of the Jesus Prayer, and can be obtained by that discipline alone, with of course the appropriate dispositions of will and character. It is thus that the *Unseen Warfare* presents them to us. Historically, however, hesychast teaching has often inculcated certain physical postures and processes, as conducive to concentration and recollection. The aspirant is taught to control his breathing, and to keep his head down and his eyes fixed on his heart or navel. This is sometimes referred to as 'confining the soul within the body', and it is meant as a physical parallel to the process of introversion, by which the eyes of the soul are turned away from outward things and directed inward upon the soul itself, and upon God Who indwells it.

Hesychasm obviously has features which invite criticism, and it has in fact been criticised. It was challenged as early as the 14th century, when the hesychasts of Mount Athos were attacked by the monk Barlaam of Calabria and various humanist scholars, while St. Gregory Palamas, Archbishop of Salonica, defended them.

Into one aspect of that controversy we need not enter, viz. into the question whether the light which the perfect soul perceives, granting it to be a reality and not a delusion, is something created or uncreated. That is a question of dogmatic theology: in what sense can a human soul 'partake of the divine nature', and in what sense can it see or know God? The hesychast need not worry about the answer to this question, providing it is agreed that he does see God, and does partake of the divine nature, in some real and objective way, and not merely in fantasy.

But does he see, and does he partake? That too was called in question in the 14th century. It was said that the hesychasts, by their breathing exercises and their postures, were in fact hypnotising themselves into a state of trance, and mistaking their experiences in that state for a perception of divine reality. It was said that they deceived themselves into thinking that the soul, and indeed the divine glory, is located in the navel, and that by intense concentration they could make themselves see it there. How much better, it was said, if they would stop this unhealthy concentration on the body, and recognise that spiritual realities are to be discerned by separating the soul from, not by enclosing it within, the flesh.

This attack on hesychasm, like many similar campaigns throughout Christian history, was part of a wider controversy. It was the work of humanists and philosophers, men who, by virtue of what they were, had but slight sympathy with ascetic disciplines and the contemplative life and were almost predestined to misinterpret these things. Their charges have been echoed by their successors in modern times, and hard things have been said about an alleged infiltration into Christianity of mistaken and dangerous practices from India. We need not deny that there may have been foolish persons in the hesychast ranks, whose utterances would provide ammunition for the humanist critics. They, however, are not the real issue. Do we really think that the discipline of concentration and contemplation, as taught in the Desert, is a right and good way to treat the mind? If not, the case is settled against hesychasm and against all forms of ascesis. But if we do think so, we must consider fairly the sober and reasoned defence of hesychast methods made by Palamas.

He points out that holding one's breath is often an involuntary result of keen absorption in something, and urges that the breathing exercises are natural and normal if taken as what they are meant to be—an aid to concentration for beginners. He points out too that bodily posture does affect our mental attitudes, and refers to the publican in the parable, who prayed with downcast eyes, and to Elijah, who sank his head between his knees. In general it is right, he says, if the body is the temple of the Spirit, that we should learn to worship with bodily attitudes and rhythms, and especially with the ruling organ of the body, the heart; and all the more since these things are an aid to spiritual recollection.*

* G. Palamas, *On those practising holy silence.*

Everyone who kneels or bows his head to pray has conceded the main point of this defence. He cannot quarrel with the hesychasts on principle, but only on details, on the particular postures and other exercises which they adopt. He may think that they give too much emphasis to these (in themselves legitimate) things, and that this may prove a distraction from the matter chiefly in hand. Or he may think that the particular postures adopted by the hesychasts are not the most suitable. The reader will find that the *Unseen Warfare* takes a moderate view of all these things, saying that they are not essential, but may be useful, and that we should not dismiss them too light-heartedly.

The really essential thing is of course the Jesus prayer itself, the constant repetition of the Name. But here too there are doubts and suspicions which must be fairly met.

In the present century a tendency has appeared, among some Orthodox writers on Mount Athos and elsewhere, to ascribe supernatural powers and dignity to the Name JESUS itself, and to make it an object of worship in the strict sense ($\lambda\alpha\tau\rho\epsilon\iota\alpha$). To a western observer this seems parallel to a similar over-veneration (as it seems to be) offered by some Orthodox to the icons of God and the saints. One may ask whether this exaggerated reverence for the Name and the icons is connected with the absence from Orthodox worship of any cult of the Sacred Elements, in which western Catholicism recognises a real *shekina* and focus of devotion. However this may be, the tendency in question is that of one group or party, not of the Orthodox Church as a whole, and we may dissent from it without thereby dissenting from the Orthodox Faith itself, and without condemning the use of the Jesus prayer. Of course it must be added that a very high degree of reverence, short of $\lambda\alpha\tau\rho\epsilon\iota\alpha$, has been paid to the Name of Jesus from the earliest times. We have seen how Diadochus speaks of the Holy Name, and his attitude is not untypical.

As for the Jesus prayer itself, it has obviously two dangers. If it is repeated without attention to what it means, it is a vain repetition such as Our Lord denounces. (The same would apply to any other formula, if unintelligently used.) If on the other hand the mind is kept concentrated on the actual words of the prayer, or on some one definite idea of 'Jesus' which is bound up with them in our mind, then they may become an incantation, a formula which imprisons the mind instead of setting it free. It may lead to the wrong kind of Christocentrism, in which the soul's devotion is centred on Christ not as what He is, the Word of the Father, but as Himself in isolation. It is evident, however, that these dangers lie not in the prayer as such, but in the wrong use of it. They point to the necessity of keeping the mind's eye fixed on its divine Object, beyond all words and images and concepts, and to the necessity of adequate dogmatic instruction as to Who that Object really is. The practice of spiritual disciplines is always dangerous when it is not governed by a sound rule of faith. Granted this, the repetitive rhythm of the prayer is indeed a most valuable aid to recollection. It keeps the unruly imagination busy with something which is true and of central importance, while it stimulates the higher levels of the soul to apprehend God after their manner. In some, it sets the intellect to work to meditate on divine things. In others, who have passed beyond intellectual meditation, the prayer leads the spirit on to the silent contemplation of Him Who is without form or mode. The western use of the rosary is an application of the same principle. And there are western parallels to the actual Jesus prayer itself.

The practice of short repetitive prayer has of course been well recognised in the West. Human nature would have led to its discovery, even if there had been no tradition; and in fact, through Cassian, the teaching of the Desert on this subject was made accessible to the Latin world. St. Benedict, following Cassian, says that prayer should be 'short and pure', and in mediaeval times a saying was current that 'short prayer pierces heaven'. The story is told of St. Francis spending a whole night repeating the formula: '*Deus meus et omnia.*' In 14th-century England Walter Hilton (d. 1396) offers for our guidance a formula: 'I am nought, I have nought, I covet nought, but One', and he explains, very much in the spirit of Abbot Isaac, that the first two clauses are an expression of humility and the last two of love (*Scale of Perfection*, bk. II, chap. 21). The contemporary *Cloud of Unknowing* recommends the use of a word of one syllable, such as 'God' or 'love', for the 'work' of interior prayer, and speaks of it as a weapon, echoing a phrase of Abbot Isaac's. Another passage in the *Cloud* suggests 'good Jesu', 'fair Jesu', 'sweet Jesu' as phrases which may be used; and generally in the western world the use of the Holy Name has been widespread. In its honour the Feast of the Holy Name was instituted; and well-known hymns such as 'To the name that brings salvation' (15th century) or 'How sweet the name of Jesus sounds' (18th century, Protestant) tell their own tale.

It should be said, however, that the western writers do not aim at making the repetition of such formulae automatic and perpetual. Frequent it may and should be; and during the time of 'the work' the repetition should be constant and unceasing; but beyond that the teaching does not go. The state of recollection is not said to rest upon the perpetual internal repetition of the formula; rather it is conceived as an imageless and wordless awareness of God. Hilton, in describing his own formula, says that the meaning of the words should be 'in thine intent and in habit of thy soul lastingly'; he does not say 'the words', but 'the meaning of the words'. The *Cloud* suggests that even in the 'work' of prayer itself a 'naked intent' of the will, a 'loving stirring and blind beholding' of God can suffice, without the aid of a repetitive monosyllable. As we shall see, the *Unseen Warfare* itself reckons with the possibility that, in the end, the words of the prayer may vanish from consciousness, and only its meaning be left. But the *Unseen Warfare* regards this only as a possible stage beyond that of automatic and perpetual repetition; and this seems to be a peculiarly eastern view.

Finally, what is to be said about the 'warmth of heart' and the 'light of Mount Tabor' which the advanced soul is said by the hesychasts to perceive? Has this any western parallel? The first thing which springs to mind is the description by Richard Rolle of a 'fire of love' in the breast, which as he means it is no mere emotion metaphorically described, but a real perception of heat. Here is a real parallel to the hesychast doctrine, but it is exceptional in western writing; and there seems to be no western parallel at all to the doctrine of the 'divine light'. The *Cloud of Unknowing* (chap. 45) gives a strong warning against trying to play tricks with one's physical heart, and against feelings of warmth in the breast, which it says are often diabolical deceptions, or else morbid symptoms due to unhealthy exercises.

It must be frankly recognised that in these matters we are apt to experience what we have been led to expect to experience. Every religious tradition, Christian or non-Christian, has its habitual expectations, its recognised pattern of spiritual life, and the experiences of its adherents normally run true to this pattern. The hesychast pattern creates an expectation of light and heat, and these are accordingly perceived. This does not mean that the hesychast adept does not truly apprehend God, and enjoy His manifest presence, as he supposes. It means that the presence of God is manifested and enjoyed as light and warmth, not because that is the one proper way in which it can be manifested and enjoyed, but because that is how God is manifested to minds which have been moulded by hesychast teaching. Western ascetics are not so moulded, and their experience of God takes other forms.

On the main point, however, that the advanced soul enjoys an abiding sense of God's presence, and lives in joy and peace in constant communion with Him—on this, apart from the manner of His manifestation, the West naturally agrees with the East and with the undivided Church. Western writers also speak of 'light' and 'fire'. They can hardly help it, for these are Biblical terms; and even if they were not, they would still be obvious and unavoidable images symbolising knowledge and love. In that sense we all know that the Holy Ghost is the Giver of light and fire, and that the soul which is truly one with God lives in the abiding possession of these gifts. That the constant devout use of ejaculatory prayer, and in particular of the prayer of the Holy Name, may be expected at last to lead to this consummation, is not a point which anyone should wish to dispute.

IV. *New tendencies and methods in the West*

The spiritual discipline of the western Church was based originally on eastern models. The teaching of the Desert and of the eastern Fathers generally was the common inheritance of East and West. It is true that in the Dark Ages, when a knowledge of Greek and an understanding of eastern conditions became rare, Latin Christendom was driven to depend more on its native authorities, and especially on St. Augustine, who is an army in himself. Yet the authority of Cassian remained high, and the Benedictine rule, so influential in the Latin world, was partly based on his writings. Later, in the mediaeval period, the influence of 'Dionysius' was strongly felt. And not only were individual eastern teachers still studied in the West; the general body of ideas which took shape in the Desert can be recognised, unaltered in its main structure and emphases, at least as late as the 13th century. The *De Triplici Via* of St. Bonaventura is based on the traditional pattern of the threefold discipline of will, thought, and prayer; though it is overlaid by personal idiosyncrasies of the author, and the course of later developments is foreshadowed in it.

Of course, from an early date Latin Christendom found a voice of its own. Not only the ecclesiastical organisation and the liturgical forms, but also the spiritual flavour of the western Church was something distinctive. Among the Fathers especially St. Augustine stands out, the channel of transmission for so many Greek philosophical influences, but also the fountain-head of a stream of devotion by which the whole western Church is watered. But differentiation need not mean opposition, and the appearance of a peculiarly western type of spirituality does not imply a departure from the common basis of tradition. The same may be said to a large extent of the Cistercian, Victorine, and Franciscan types of spirituality, whose rise in the West corresponds in date with that of hesychasm and Palamism in the East. Even after the schism has hardened, the West does not suddenly cut itself off from the common past of Christendom. Inherited wisdom survives, the Fathers are still read, ancient rules are still followed. Later, in the many-sided movements of the 16th and 17th centuries, there is still much which can be regarded as an enrichment of the common tradition, not a departure from it. But there is also, it must be acknowledged, a good deal which from an Orthodox point of view seems new and strange.

It has often been observed that western theology and devotion in mediaeval and modern times has given to the Cross a more exclusive centrality than has the Orthodox Church. In mediaeval Europe the Crucifixion was regularly presented to the eyes of the faithful in the rood screens of their churches, overshadowing the way to the Altar and imposing an interpretation of the meaning of what is done there. Western theories about salvation, however various in other respects, have in common the tendency to talk more about the death of Christ than about His Resurrection. Union with Christ, for western saints, has tended to mean participation in His sufferings, a participation made visible in the stigmata of St. Francis; whereas the eastern saint is invested

244

rather with the glory of the risen Christ, and shines with divine light as did St. Serafim of Sarov. We must not exaggerate this difference, or talk as if the East knew nothing of the Cross and the West knew nothing of the glory. Nor need we be hasty to judge that one of these two ways is better than the other. But, with all due qualifications, the fact of their difference must be acknowledged.

Moreover, the difference is reflected in ascetic theology. East and West do not give wholly the same impression of the higher rungs of the spiritual ladder. The Fathers, whom Orthodox teaching still follows, describe the soul's progress as a way of continual purgation, but also of continually increasing illumination, until, with the attainment of purity of heart and perpetual prayer, the soul lives in the light and warmth of God's presence, in continual joyous communion with Him. But some of the principal western writers lay great stress upon the trials which the soul has to undergo through inner darkness, aridity, and seeming alienation from God. If the doctrine of warmth of heart is characteristically eastern, the doctrine of the night of the soul is characteristically western. The night of the soul is characterised by loss of sensible or emotional fervour, difficulty in prayer, and a continual feeling that God is absent. According to the prevailing western doctrine this state of darkness and dryness is partly punitive, but more especially educative ; it strips the soul bare of all dependence upon created things, even upon its own experiences, however lofty and spiritual they may be, and teaches it to look beyond religious experience to God Himself. It is added that the soul passing through the dark night should accept its sufferings as its allotted share of the Passion of Christ ; it is precisely here, in the darkness of the spiritual night, that the soul is most effectively made one with Christ Crucified.

It is consonant with this, that modern western writers always make a point of warning their readers against being captivated by 'sensible devotion', i.e. by the emotional fervour which sometimes accompanies meditation and prayer. We are told that this fervour is especially characteristic of beginners, and its drying up should be welcomed as a sign that we are getting beyond the first stages. To try to retain it, or to long for its return in the midst of dryness, is to refuse to grow up. It is to refuse the Cross. By our steady adherence to God when the affections are dried up, and nothing is left but the naked will clinging blindly to Him, the soul is purged of self-regard and trained in pure love.

This certainly seems different from the Orthodox teaching with its emphasis on the divine light and warmth of heart. Modern writers on both sides call attention to the difference. Yet we must not exaggerate. A difference can be important, even if it is only a difference of emphasis ; and it may be doubted whether the East-West difference is anything more than this.

We must recognise first of all that the 'sensible devotion' which is characteristic of beginners, and from which the modern western writers say we must learn to detach ourselves, is not the same thing as the 'warmth of heart' which the Orthodox ascribe to the purified soul. The western writers here are not contradicting the eastern, they are talking about something else. Further, what they say is not new. It can be found already in Diadochus (*Spiritual Perfection* 60, 86, 87). He distinguishes clearly between the joy of beginners, imaginatively excited and emotional, and the calm imageless joy of the advanced soul. Between these comes the discipline of aridity, of spiritual 'trials' and the feeling of being abandoned by God; a discipline which is partly punitive but mainly educative, and teaches us humility. It is true that Diadochus does not emphasise the severity of the trials, or their duration, as the moderns tend to do. He speaks of a 'blessed sadness', of 'tears without sorrow', of 'little desolations and frequent consolations'. Other eastern writers, however, are more explicit about these sufferings and more emphatic about their severity. In sum, the night of the soul is recognised well enough in the primitive teaching. But it is recognised as an incident in a way which is, on the whole, a way of light and joy.

This is the general teaching of the early Church, and it persists in the mediaeval West, even at a time when the special devotion to Christ Crucified begins to make its way in. On the whole the teaching of St. Bernard, St. Francis, St. Bonaventura conforms to the primitive type. The last-named in particular presents the spiritual way as a way of continually increasing illumination. The 14th-century English school keep up the same tradition. Thus Hilton explains that what is night to the senses and the passions, *i.e.* the turning away from the world to God, is *ipso facto* light to the spirit.

The modern concentration of attention upon the dark night

begins in late mediaeval times, in writers like St. Catherine of Siena, and comes to a head in the writings of St. John of the Cross. To him we owe the careful analysis of the experience in question, and the fixing of the terminology in which it is discussed. In St. John himself, and in his contemporary St. Teresa, we seem to see the doctrine expressed in an actual life. Yet, even here, it is equally true that St. John and St. Teresa are favourite sources for the study of the grades of infused prayer and contemplation, up to the very highest. Even with them, the way of the Cross is still a way and not a goal ; and if their account of the suffering has a peculiar and distinctive intensity, so has their account of the glory.

It may well be that, in God's design for His Church and for the world, the western Church has been called to explore particularly the mystery of suffering. If this is so, it may have something to do with the course which the history of society and civilisation has taken in western Europe. Many and various energies have been released, strong forces have been set in motion both for good and for evil, and even on the secular plane Europe pays in suffering for the achievements of the Renaissance and the modern period. The Church's life is mysteriously interwoven with that of the surrounding world, and somewhere in this relation may be found the explanation and the justification of those western emphases which seem alien to the Orthodox. However that may be, there are two mistakes which we must avoid in speaking of these differences between East and West. We must not assume that one side is necessarily right and the other wrong ; and we must not elevate what is a difference of emphasis into a conflict of principle. In the last resort, whatever their differences of approach, the greatest ascetic theologians of East and West tell the same tale. It is the tale of the soul's progress from the slavery of the passions and the sensible world into the light of God's presence, known and felt.

This is true of the greatest on both sides. When we come to lesser men, it is not so clear. There is at least one western tendency, in the last three or four centuries, which really does run counter to primitive tradition. I mean the tendency in many quarters, since the Counter-Reformation, to warn people off the more intuitive and contemplative forms of prayer, and to make analytical meditation the norm of devotion for ordinary people. This has been the predominant tendency in Catholic writing through much of the modern period, and it is nothing less than a revolution.

It arose in the Counter-Reformation period, and must be explained by reference to the circumstances of that time. The age of the Counter-Reformation came on the heels of the High Renaissance, and was heir to the achievements and aspirations of that brilliant period. It was an enlightened age, conscious of centuries of recent achievement in social and political life, in art and science, and justly proud of the powers of human reason, inquisitive and critical. Philosophically it had been tutored by Plato, not without some tincture of the more sceptical philosophies which followed his in the ancient world. Men looked back upon the Middle Age as a time of darkness from which they had escaped; and monasticism, and the disciplines associated with it, were part of that outgrown system. Asceticism was rejected, the contemplative life was suspect, except of course in the sense in which Plato or Aristotle would have understood the term—the life of a scholar or cultivated man. The mind was too active in enquiry and invention, too eager in the assertion of its autonomy, to be able to understand what the ascetic discipline was aiming at. If there is an element of exaggeration in the emphasis placed upon self-negation by a writer like St. John of the Cross, it is perhaps no more than the necessary counterpoise to the ruling tendency of his age, which was an age of unbridled self-assertion.

It is intelligible that at such a time there should have been voices within the Church criticising the doctrine of contemplation, much as hesychasm was criticised in the Orthodox Church three centuries earlier. Such a movement of criticism will always have the support of activists, who are the majority of mankind, and of Christians, and also of those scholars and intellectuals whose minds run on analytical rather than intuitive lines. In the 17th century the cultural atmosphere was favourable to such a movement, and there were also reasons of policy to be urged on its behalf. There was a fear of illuminism and individualism in piety. It was seen, rightly, that the most fervent devotion will go wrong if it is not kept under the control of a sound rule of faith. In a world of busy questioning and conflicts of doctrine, it was necessary to capture and discipline above all the imagination and the discursive reason; for that was the level on which most of the faithful in fact lived, and on which they were exposed to the assaults of false teaching. To teach them to meditate regularly and in detail on the mysteries of the Faith, especially of the Passion, and on the capital sins and the virtues, was to arm them against the errors of the time.

Accordingly we find the spiritual writers of the Counter-Reformation period vying with one another in the production of 'methods' of meditation, which are often of an astounding complexity. There are remote and proximate preparations, and preliminaries, and preludes; readings, and points for consideration; affections and colloquies, reflections, resolutions, and much else. All the methods presuppose a long time for their full deployment. All of them are in startling contrast with the command to 'be still, and know'. But it is clear what their purpose is, and they fulfil that purpose very well.

What is hard to view with equanimity is the attempt to make such methods normative for Christian devotion. Several of the most outstanding figures in the spiritual life of the time got into difficulties through their use of contemplative prayer: among them St. Teresa of Avila, and her confessor, Fr. Bartholomew Alvarez. As individuals, they were finally granted indulgence, but it was held that such prayer is only for a few exceptional souls. Meditation was made compulsory for members of the Society of Jesus, and at one time they were forbidden to read Ruysbroek, Tauler, and other masters of contemplative prayer. Attempts were made to explain away what these authors say. The Jesuit theologian Suarez admitted that infused contemplation can occur, but only very rarely, and in the greatest saints. Others maintained that contemplation is merely the culminating stage in an intellectual process, when the mind, having thought round its subject and marshalled its reasons in an orderly way, ends by having an intuitive grasp of the truths to which these reasons lead. What was thought of the affective side of prayer, of 'spiritual warmth' etc., can be gathered from the languishing and contorted attitudes of the saints in baroque painting and statuary. Altogether we may say that the idea of contemplation was vulgarised and made empty and superficial.

This unfortunate attitude was usual in Roman Catholic circles from the beginning of the 17th century down to the end of the 19th. The 20th century has seen a powerful reaction against it.

Renewed study of the classics of the spiritual life has corrected many misrepresentations, recovered many forgotten truths, and made clear to our generation what the genuinely traditional teaching in these matters has been. Western scholarship has at last recognised where the truly memorable teaching of the Counter-Reformation period is to be found; the eminence of St. John of the Cross is now admitted and his teaching holds a position of authority. But at the same time we learn to look behind him and his age, and behind even the great age of the 13th century, to the earlier sources of western tradition, to St. Bernard and ultimately to St. Augustine. From St. Augustine an easy transition brings us to Cassian and so to the Desert. Meanwhile the growing desire, among some western students, to understand the spiritual life and thought of the Orthodox Church, leads us back to the same place. We find ourselves renewing acquaintance with the common source from which all our divergent traditions have sprung, and it can hardly fail to result from this that we understand better both one another and ourselves.

The deviation in western teaching and practice, therefore, though recent, is already largely an episode of the past. But it was precisely in the deviation period that the *Spiritual Combat* was written. That is why, when it was translated by Orthodox writers, they could not translate it just as it stood, but were constrained to alter it at certain points.

V. *Lorenzo Scupoli*

Lorenzo Scupoli (Francesco in secular life) was born at Otranto, of noble family, in 1529. No incidents are recorded from the first forty years of his life, but certain things can be inferred about him from what he later became. He comes before us as a man of striking appearance and winning manner, but not physically robust. His writings show a clear mind, with a great insight into human nature and a gift of forceful expression. His style of writing is clear, and free both from excessive adornment and from sentimentality.

In 1569 he sought and was granted admission to the Theatine Order, a community of priests and aspirants to the priesthood who devoted themselves to the cultivation of the spiritual life, to preaching and spiritual teaching, and to the care of the sick and of prisoners; and on the 25th January 1571 he was admitted to the solemn profession in the house of San Paolo in Naples. Even before he was ordained priest he was employed in the work of spiritual direction. In 1577 he moved to Piacenza, where he was ordained. In 1578 he was transferred to Milan, and in 1581 to Genoa. While working there, in 1585, he was accused of a grave and scandalous offence, and, on failing to clear himself, was degraded from his priestly functions and sentenced to a long and severe penance. It is not clear who the accuser was, or what was the nature of the charge, or how the odium of it was finally lifted. All that is clear is that Scupoli lived for a period of years in retirement, moving to and fro between Venice and Padua, held in dishonour by the members of his Order, and prevented from pursuing his work as a priest and a director of souls. Ultimately the ban was lifted, and his real innocence acknowledged. In 1599 he was transferred back to Naples, and died there, in the house of San Paolo, on the 28th November 1610.

Scupoli was strict in the observance of his rule, a man of great humility, constant in prayer, 'a great lover of solitude and silence'. His natural gifts, enhanced by his life of devotion, gave him an insight into spiritual things and a power of clear expression, which made him a skilful director of souls. This is manifest, apart from contemporary testimony, from the writings in which his wisdom has come down to us, the *Spiritual Combat* and the *Path to Paradise*.

The *Spiritual Combat* was not originally written for publication. A friend of the author, who saw it in manuscript, persuaded him to give it to the world. The first edition (Venice, 1589) was a short work of only 24 chapters; but, as edition followed edition, the book grew by constant additions from the author's own hand. By 1599 it had reached its present length of 66 chapters, and in 1610 there was added a *Supplement* of 37 chapters. This *Supplement* is really a complete work in itself, covering much of the same ground as the main body of the work, though of course not so fully. Scupoli also wrote a separate work of 15 chapters entitled *The Path to Paradise* (1600), in addition to other works which need not concern us.

The *Spiritual Combat* was published anonymously at first, and this gave rise to disputes about the authorship. On instructions from his superiors, the author revealed himself in the enlarged edition of 1599, by writing a dedication of his book to Christ and signing it with his name 'Lorenzo Scupoli, C.R.'* Other views of the authorship survived for a long time among people who had not seen this edition, especially outside Italy ; but ultimately the facts were placed beyond doubt, and Scupoli's authorship came to be universally acknowledged.

The book was recognised from the first as a masterpiece. Within the author's life-time it went through over 30 editions in Italian, and was translated into Latin, English, French, Spanish, German, and two Asiatic languages. In Europe as a whole there were more than 250 editions of it between 1589 and 1750, and its popularity continues to this day. But there can be no more striking tribute to the worth of the book than that which was paid to it, in the author's life-time, by St. Francis de Sales. When the first two editions came out, at Venice, in 1589, St. Francis was living as a student in Padua. A copy of the second edition (which contained 33 chapters) was placed in his hands by a member of the Theatine Order, with an intimation that the author belonged to the same Order. St. Francis was immediately captured by the book. In later years we find him repeatedly urging his correspondents to read it, and drawing their attention to particular passages in it. In 1607 he writes to Mme. de Chantal that he has carried it about in his pocket for 18 years, and in the following year he says the same in a letter to another lady. He said the same to the Bishop of Belley, adding that he read some part of it daily, and that the book had been in effect his spiritual guide. He said that it held a position in the Theatine Order analogous to that of the writings of St. Ignatius among the Jesuits. Comparing it with the famous *Imitation of Christ*, he said that the *Imitation* was better as a guide to prayer and contemplation, but the *Combat* was better as a guide to the moral life; one should read the *Spiritual Combat*, and not leave the *Imitation* unread. Accordingly we find that his own *Introduction to the Devout Life* (1608) is much influenced by Scupoli; we do not find the same influence in his *Treatise of the Love of God* (1616), which deals at much greater length with prayer and contemplation.

The first edition of the *Spiritual Combat*, with its 24 chapters, was indeed a compact little treatise with a strictly practical aim. In its first chapter, which is also the first chapter of the present

* *i.e.* Chierico Regolare.

version, it sets clearly before the reader the goal of the Christian life, which is the attainment of perfection and union with God; it says that to reach this goal requires a continual struggle; and it offers four weapons for use in the struggle, viz. distrust of self, trust in God, spiritual exercises or disciplines, and prayer. Self-distrust and trust in God are allotted a chapter each, and the main body of the treatise is devoted to the inculcation of spiritual exercises. These include, in accordance with tradition, a discipline of the mind (senses, imagination, intellect) and a discipline of the will (eradication of sinful tendencies, acquisition of virtues). Warnings are given against impatience and discouragement, and against various deceptions of the Devil. The work ends with two or three chapters on prayer, but this subject is not dealt with at any great length. The book is 'ascetic' in the strict sense, *i.e.* it is concerned above all with the struggle for self-mastery from which it gets its title.

The addition of nine fresh chapters in the second edition may have been made in response to a request for more guidance on prayer. The new matter includes several chapters on the art of meditation. It also includes several on the Holy Eucharist, on sacramental and spiritual communion. These matters were not dealt with in the original treatise, and are obviously an afterthought; the Holy Communion is introduced as a 'fifth weapon' in the spiritual combat, in addition to the four originally enumerated.

Subsequent additions, though they doubled the size of the book, introduced no fresh themes, except for a group of chapters on how to meet the approach of death. The *Supplement*, which the *Unseen Warfare* does not incorporate, is likewise devoid of novelty. The *Path to Paradise*, however, which is incorporated in the *Unseen Warfare* and forms the last 14 chapters of Part II, is held together by the recurring theme of 'interior peace', which is indeed its alternative title.

Scupoli has essentially a practical mind, and writes with a practical aim. His work contains no speculations on the higher mysteries; it is centred in what he himself calls 'the contemplation of a Crucified God', and the driving power of his ascesis is his response to the immeasurable love, humility, and patience which were manifested on the Cross.

His account of the ascesis is strongest in dealing with the control of the mind and will, the daily and hourly battle against evil passions within and evil spirits without, which is the everyday experience of the Christian. It is to his teaching on these matters that his work owes its reputation. It is clear, forceful, sensible teaching, true to tradition and yet always speaking from experience. He is himself evidently a man of disciplined mind and will, of clear ideas and firm purposes, and his advice, if we followed it, would make us the same. On the other hand, his teaching with regard to prayer reflects the teaching of his age and country in its most restrictive and unimaginative form. Out of nine chapters devoted to the subject, seven are wholly concerned with the practice of meditation, and there is no mention of the more contemplative forms of prayer except in one brief chapter entitled 'mental prayer'. It is here, above all, that his Orthodox translators have felt constrained to make changes, and to insert what seemed necessary to bring his work into proper balance.

His aim, in fact, in treating of prayer, is a limited one. He is not thinking of prayer in its inherent worth and dignity, as the adoration of God and the communion of the soul with Him, but as a weapon to be used in the spiritual combat. Prayer as he presents it therefore consists mainly of requests for deliverance from temptation and for the gift of the virtues. We have seen that this kind of prayer is recognised and given its place in the teaching of the Fathers. It is neither the prayer of beginners in the spiritual life, nor that of the perfect, but of those who are making progress; and it is for such souls that the *Spiritual Combat* was written. It is evident from the nature of the case, and from occasional remarks in the book itself, that Scupoli's own knowledge of prayer went deeper than this. But he was not concerned to tell all he knew; and his book devotes far more attention to the Christian's discipline and the battle he must fight than to the fruits of victory.

Something similar may be said of his attitude towards sensible devotion and spiritual aridity. He gives us the usual warnings against sensible devotion, but expands at considerable length on darkness and dryness of spirit, both as resulting from external troubles and as arising from something in the soul's own life. Here too the toil and trouble of the conflict are dwelt upon, and the fruits of victory are comparatively neglected; here too the Orthodox translators have felt it right to make additions which alter the total impression of the book. In some passages of

Scupoli we can guess that he is doing more than simply repeat the current teaching of his time ; he is speaking from personal experience, and the trials which he had to undergo, the experiences of injustice and contempt which he had to endure seem to be visible behind the text. Something else becomes visible too: the uncomplaining patience, the sincere humility and self-naughting, the dependence on God, the deeply rooted interior peace, which were the fruit of that trial. There are, however, no personal revelations or confidences to the reader. Scupoli's discipline of the mind had taught him objectivity, and his humility taught him reticence. The author stands well behind his work.

VI. *Nicodemus the Hagiorite*

After the Turkish conquest of Greece in the 15th century, the Church in Greece had to contend with many difficulties. Though the Turks did not attempt large-scale proselytisation on behalf of Islam, the Christian population was kept in a position of inferiority. All Christians had to pay a capitation tax. They were forbidden to build new churches, or even to rebuild such of them as were accidentally destroyed ; while it was always possible for an existing church to be taken over as a mosque. The Patriarch of Constantinople was driven in this way from three churches in turn, before he fixed his throne at the Phanar. It was made difficult to print Bibles, service-books, and other religious literature. When the Patriarch Cyril Lucaris opened a press in Constantinople the government forced it to close. Few theological schools or centres of learning survived, though the Patriarchal School in Constantinople continued to function. In short, while the Church was not suppressed, it lived and worked under heavy and continuing disabilities.

These and other aspects of Turkish policy favoured the growth of western influences in the Orthodox Church. Ever since the Crusades the western world, and with it the Latin Church, had taken an aggressive interest in Greece and the Near East. Venice held possessions in the Greek islands and mainland before the Turkish conquest, and again for a short time at the beginning of the 18th century. The Turkish government, willing to sow division among its Christian subjects, encouraged the setting up of Uniat Churches, ecclesiastically subject to Rome and politically under French protection. It is a striking testimony to the strength of Orthodoxy that these manœuvres found, on the whole, so little success. But while the great mass of the Greek people were faithful to Orthodox traditions, they were driven to seek abroad the higher education and theological learning which was so hard to obtain in their own country. Priests and theologians who were able to do so would go to western centres to study, and especially to Italy. Pisa, Florence, Padua and Venice were their places of study ; and a great deal of Orthodox literature was printed in Venice. In these circumstances they inevitably came under Latin and Catholic influences, to which they did not totally close their minds.

Since, moreover, Greeks enjoyed a predominance in the hierarchy of the whole Orthodox Church in the Turkish dominions, these influences were more widely diffused, and affected ecclesiastical pronouncements at the Synodical and Conciliar level. A Greek theologian took up and revised a Latinising Confession of Faith which had been drawn up by Peter Mogila, the Metropolitan of Kiev, and in 1643 this was approved by the four Orthodox Patriarchs. In 1672 the Council of Jerusalem, under the presidency of Dositheus, the Patriarch of Jerusalem, sanctioned this Confession, and further accepted a great deal of Roman Catholic doctrine and terminology in matters relating to the canon of Scripture, the Eucharist, the cult of the saints, and the doctrine of penance and purgatory. This Council represents the high water mark of Latin influence in the Orthodox Church. Indeed, it provoked a reaction. The Holy Synod of the Russian Church, when it discussed the acts of this Council in 1838, accepted them only after the removal of the most characteristically Latin phrases and doctrines.

The reliance of the Greeks on Italy for educational and printing facilities continued well on into the 18th century. Yet in the latter half of that century there were signs of better conditions in Greece. New opportunities were opened up for Greeks in trade and in government service. Schools and colleges were founded in some of the Greek towns, and a new spirit began to stir in the nation, which grew until it bore fruit in the 19th century in the Wars of Liberation. The new spirit showed itself intellectually in two movements which seem at first sight to be antithetic, but are really complementary to one another: the one, a movement to recover lost ground by learning all the new lessons which western science and philosophy had to teach, and the other to revive the traditions of Greece itself, and especially of the Orthodox Church.

Both these tendencies found expression on Mount Athos. On the one hand was the Athonite Academy, founded about 1750, offering to Orthodox Greeks a higher education in which ancient Greek philosophy, Locke, Leibniz, and modern physical science all had their place. Eugenius Bulgaris, perhaps the most eminent Greek theologian of the 18th century, was head of this Academy for a time. On the other hand was the careful study of the laws, customs and literature of the Orthodox Church, and the deliberate revival on Mount Athos of the hesychast doctrines and practices of earlier times. It is with this latter movement that the translation and adaptation of the *Spiritual Combat* for Greek readers is connected.

The translator was Nicodemus the Hagiorite* (1748–1809), one of the most prolific and influential writers in the Greek Church of that time, and a leader in the revival of hesychasm. His name in secular life was Nicolas, and he was a native of the island of Naxos. In 1775, about the age of 27, he took the first vows in the monastery of St. Dionysius, one of the many monastic settlements which together constitute the community of Mount Athos. In 1783 he proceeded to the higher degree of μεγαλόσχημος in a *skete* belonging to the monastery of the Pantokrator. Later still he moved into the so-called '*kellion* of St. George', under the authority of the Lavra ; and there he died on the 14th of July 1809.

Nicodemus has been described as 'an encyclopaedia of the Athonite learning of his time' ; he was at once a hymnographer, hagiographer, and Biblical commentator, a canonist, liturgiologist, and ascetic theologian. While his outlook was conservative, it was not narrow or obscurantist, and he had a reasonable acquaintance with ancient philosophy and modern science. On account of his learning he was chosen by the Patriarch and Synod to undertake, with assistance, the responsible task of bringing out a new edition of all the Conciliar decrees and canons of the Orthodox Church, with a commentary ; this work appeared in 1800, under the title of the *Rudder of the Orthodox Church*, and still carries authority. He also wrote a large manual on the

* ‘Αγιορείτης=inhabitant of the Holy Mountain (ἅγιον ὅρος), *i.e.* Mount Athos

practice of confession. But it is his spiritual writings, including original works, anthologies, and translations, which are the real basis of his enduring fame and influence.

Nicodemus was deeply read in the Fathers, and in the hesychast writers of mediaeval times. He wished to make their teaching a living force, both in the monasteries and among Orthodox people generally. To this end he compiled the great *Philokalia*, an anthology of passages from the ascetic writings of the Fathers of the eastern Church, in which the doctrine of pure prayer is set forth in the words of recognised masters of the spiritual life, from the earliest times down to the time of Palamas. It was published in Venice in 1782, and ran to more than a thousand folio pages. Nicodemus was its principal author, though he had the assistance of Macarius Notaras, Archbishop of Corinth, in the work. Nicodemus also expounded the doctrine of mental prayer in original works of his own, such as the *Handbook of Counsel* (1801),* which is a statement of hesychast doctrine in a form intended for the secular clergy and the general public. And he published collections of prayers and meditations which met with a popular response.

His adherence to hesychasm was not bigoted or exclusive. Nor did he despise or neglect the more discursive forms of prayer. He could appreciate effective teaching on that level, when he met it, even in the writings of a Roman Catholic, and was ready to turn it to account. His *Spiritual Exercises* (Γυμνάσματα πνευματικά) are in fact an adaptation from the *Esercizii spirituali* of the Jesuit Pinamonti, which are a series of meditations and self-examinations constructed according to the Ignatian method. From these, and from other works by the same author, Nicodemus selects what he considers useful, and translates it into Greek without substantial alteration, only enriching the text with a series of notes drawn from the Bible and the Fathers. The resulting work he presents to the public not as his own, but as 'adorned, corrected, and illustrated with various notes' by himself; he suppresses the real author's name and nationality, and the reference to Loyola in the Italian title, thus leaving no explicit indication that the original source was not Orthodox.

He adopts a similar method with the *Spiritual Combat*. Here

---

* Συμβουλευτικὸν ἐγχειρίδιον περὶ φυλακῆς τῶν πέντε αἰσθησέων τῆς τε φαντασίας τοῦ νοὸς καὶ τῆς καρδίας.

too is a work of Italian origin, a work obviously of high merit, though reflecting in some points the characteristic attitudes of the Counter-Reformation. Nicodemus decides to translate it, but in order to secure for it a favourable reception he conceals the name and nationality of the author. He feels free to combine it with other work by the same author, to add, omit, and alter, and generally do what is necessary to bring it into line with his own beliefs and the outlook of its intended readers.

He takes the *Spiritual Combat* in its complete form, as in the 1599 Naples edition, but without the *Supplement* of 1610. To it he attaches the *Path to Paradise*, suppressing its title and its separate identity, and making it run straight on from the end of the *Spiritual Combat* so as to form one continuous work. The resulting whole is re-divided into two parts, as may be seen in the present version, where the *Path to Paradise* is represented by chapters 14 to 27 of Part II, the rest of the matter being derived from the *Spiritual Combat*. He omits chapter 8 of the *Path* and chapter 61 of the *Combat*, without putting anything in their place, and for no very obvious reason—perhaps because they merely repeat what is said elsewhere. He prefixes a short Introduction explaining the purpose of the book. He enriches the text by adding to it many footnotes, consisting of passages from the Bible and the Fathers. These serve to reinforce the teaching of the book, and to show how it accords with Scripture and Orthodox tradition. He also makes a number of textual alterations, whose nature and significance is examined in detail later in this Introduction.

The *Spiritual Combat*, thus enlarged and altered, was published at Venice in 1796, under the title of *Unseen Warfare* (Ἀόρατος Πόλεμος)*. It was made clear on the title-page that Nicodemus is not the author of the work, but has merely 'adorned and corrected' it. The real author was described as 'a certain wise man'. His identity does not seem to have been suspected, and his very existence has often been ignored. The *Unseen Warfare* has taken its place in general estimation as one among Nicodemus' own works. It has even been printed under his name, without reference to his disclaimer of authorship. Perhaps the disclaimer was regarded as a literary artifice.

* Βιβλίον ψυχωφελέστατον καλούμενον Ἀόρατος Πόλεμος, συντεθὲν μὲν πρὶν παρά τινος σοφοῦ ἀνδρός, καλλωπισθὲν δὲ νῦν καὶ διορθωθὲν . . . παρὰ τοῦ . . . κυρίου Νικοδήμου.

The Holy Mountain in Nicodemus' time was a scene of animated controversy on issues of very various kinds. Sometimes it was a question of rites and ceremonies, sometimes of devotional practices, sometimes of articles of faith, and all the time there was the opposition between the conservatives and the modernising group associated with the Academy. Each party regarded its opponents as disloyal to Orthodoxy, and the methods of controversy were at times somewhat unscrupulous. Nicodemus was a leading conservative. He took the conservative side in one lengthy dispute about the manner of commemorating the departed ; and of course the whole meaning of his activities as an exponent of hesychasm was to bring about a return to ancient traditions and practices. Yet there have always been anti-hesychast voices in the Orthodox world, and among the modernists of his time such voices were heard, deprecating his teaching as a departure from the true way. On the other hand, he could incur criticism equally by his readiness to absorb ideas from the West. In translating Roman Catholic books he wisely concealed their authorship, and annotated them from the Greek Fathers. Yet he was not able to keep altogether out of controversy, and the purity of his faith was called in question.

There was a long-standing dispute about the practice of frequent communion, which then, as now, was being authoritatively encouraged in the Roman Catholic Church. It was encouraged also by the conservative party in the Orthodox Church; the private devotion of the hesychast was thus to be nourished from the Church's sacramental feast. Nicodemus' friend, Archbishop Macarius, wrote a book in 1783 in favour of frequent communion. But this book was denounced by an Athonite monk to the Patriarch, who condemned it; and those who attempted to communicate more frequently than was customary were sometimes repelled. Now, there are passages in Scupoli which bear upon this question. He too recommends frequent communion; and he alludes to the possibility that one's spiritual director may not allow one to communicate as often as one would wish. Nicodemus reproduces this passage in the *Unseen Warfare*, and adds a note referring to such action on the part of spiritual directors as an 'evil and perverse custom'. This may be the reason why, at the close of his life, he was himself accused of heresy in the matter of the Eucharist. Oddly enough, the accusation was not on the ground of excessive conformity to Catholic ideas; he was accused of 'freemasonry', which in the language of the time was a name of Protestantism, and a letter of his was falsified to make it appear that he adhered to a Protestant doctrine of the Lord's Supper. He appealed to the Synaxis, the governing body of Mount Athos, and was triumphantly vindicated (19th of May 1807). In a public statement the Synaxis declared that his writings contained no trace of heresy, and called upon the whole community to recognise him as 'most devout and most orthodox'.

This verdict of his own community has been recognised as just by the whole Orthodox world. Nicodemus stands to-day as a pillar of Orthodoxy, and the *Unseen Warfare* is not the least of his gifts to the Orthodox Church.

VII. *Nicodemus and Scupoli*

The Greek *Unseen Warfare* is a translation of two works by Scupoli. Out of a total of 81 chapters in the original, two are omitted, and the rest are translated substantially as Scupoli wrote them. They are, however, amplified by the addition of an Introduction and a considerable body of notes, and at certain points modifications are made in the text. These additions and alterations are not all of equal extent and importance.

The Introduction, in a somewhat rhetorical style, elaborates the conception of the Christian life as a warfare with many quotations from Scripture, and exhorts the reader to play his part manfully in the struggle. It is in the nature of a general advertisement of the contents of the book, and there is nothing in it over which we need linger.

The notes consist mainly of passages from the Bible and the *Philokalia*, chosen to illustrate and confirm what is said in the text. These call for no comment. A certain number of the notes are more positive than this; they expound doctrines which are not in Scupoli, but which his translator brings in to amplify his teaching; or they argue controversial points on which Nicodemus himself takes a stand. These are in effect additions to the substance of the work. The fact that they occur at the foot of the page does not detract from their importance.

Several of Nicodemus' changes are small ones, of a kind which are appropriate in adapting a Roman Catholic work for use by

Orthodox readers. Thus when he finds in Scupoli a reference to purgatory, or to the cult of the Sacred Heart, he quietly expunges it. He changes 'images' into 'icons'. But he is not systematically a'nti-Latin. His notes include several quotations from St. Augustine and other western Fathers. He retains Latin terms and phrases like 'ejaculatory prayers' (ἀκοντιστικαὶ καὶ σαΐτευτικαί) or the 'merits' of Christ (μισθός, ἀξιομισθία). He couples contrition and confession with 'satisfaction' (ἱκανοποίησις). He translates unchanged a paragraph in which Scupoli expounds the doctrine of sufficient grace. When Scupoli recommends a particular use of the devotion of the Angelus, Nicodemus renders what he says almost literally, only removing a reference to the 'three strokes' of the angelic salutation, which would be inapplicable in a country where the Angelus bell is not rung. Conversely, in one chapter he finds occasion to insert two brief references to the Jesus Prayer, which of course are not found in Scupoli.

The *Spiritual Combat* is written in the form of an address to a pupil or friend, who is thought of as feminine and is occasionally addressed as 'daughter'. Nicodemus addresses his reader as 'brother', as is natural in writing for a public of monks. Other similar changes seem less necessary. In one passage, faults attributed by Scupoli to devout but foolish women are ascribed by his translator to foolish men. A vision of Christ, seen by a woman, appears in Nicodemus unaltered except that the recipient of the vision becomes a man. It seems as if here the traditional anti-feminism of Mount Athos is in evidence.

These are changes arising from the place and circumstances in which the translation was made. They are not important changes. All of them together amount to very little. But this is not all. Apart from these special motives, the translator feels free on many occasions to rearrange, expand, or condense his author's text, or even to alter the substance of a passage here and there, or to insert something of his own. Often, when he does this, the change is of slight importance; it is just a question of giving more clarity and force to what Scupoli says, by presenting it in a more systematic order. At other times, when Nicodemus feels that he can add something from his own experience and reflection, he does so; and then what he does deserves examination, for in it we can often read something of his mind.

The most important changes which he makes are found in two

places: in chapters 21 to 24 of the *Spiritual Combat* (in the present version, Part I, ch. 21 to 26), which deal with the discipline of the senses and the imagination, and in a later group of chapters which are concerned with prayer. Let us take these in order.

Chapters 21 to 23 of the *Spiritual Combat* are concerned with the custody of the senses. The teaching given is sound, traditional, and in no way remarkable. Since the senses are the primary stimuli both of desire and of thought, their custody is a necessary part of the discipline both of the will and of the intellect. They must be freed from the evil suggestions and associations which cling about them, and made to carry suggestions and associations of a different kind, so that whatever we see or hear or otherwise perceive may remind us in some way of God. Scupoli tells us how to bring this about by deliberately meditating our way through the sensible world, bringing each class of object into relation with God, and attending especially to everything which can serve to remind us of the Passion of Christ. Chapter 24 follows with advice on the control of the tongue and the practice of silence, not only for the sake of discretion and humility, but also as an aid to interior recollection.

Nicodemus translates chapter 21 on the whole faithfully,* only rearranging some of Scupoli's points in order to present them in a more logical sequence. He takes us one by one through the four elements, the order of nature, and the five senses, showing how all created things can be to us a treatise of God ($\mu\acute{\iota}\alpha$ $\theta\epsilon o\lambda o\gamma\acute{\iota}\alpha$). He translates chapters 22 and 23 without alteration, only adding at the end of 23, somewhat inconsequently, a paragraph on the dangerous power of the imagination over the mind and body.

He translates chapter 24, on the control of the tongue and the practice of silence; but, again rather inconsequently, inserts into it a long section on the government of the senses, seen from a fresh point of view. There are some, he says, who have not the 'knowledge, discretion, and power of thought to correct their own senses' in the manner set forth in the preceding three chapters, viz. by meditating and establishing a positive relation in the mind between sensible things and God. Such people must put

---

* Theophan (*not* Nicodemus) inserts at the beginning of this chapter a brief exposition of the traditional doctrine of introversion. Man was created to find his delight in the inward presence of God; the Fall deprived us of our interior life and enslaved us to external things; our restoration must involve returning 'from without to within, and from within to God'.

all their strength into a negative discipline, turning the senses away from everything which may be hurtful to the soul.* He then takes the five senses in order, and warns against their misuse, where the preceding three chapters have taught us their proper use.

After this he inserts an entirely new chapter (*A.M.* I 25)† dealing with the 'correction of the imagination and the memory' He begins by explaining the function and power of the imagination, and goes on to put forward the theory that men and angels in their unfallen state were independent of any such faculty. In consequence of sin they fell from a purely spiritual and intellectual mode of being and consciousness into the bondage of images and fantasies ; and if man is to return to freedom and communion with God, the mind must first be stripped bare of imagery. Nicodemus goes on to speak of 'turning the mind about' and 'collecting it in the narrow place of the heart', inwardly reciting the Jesus Prayer, or else 'contemplating itself, or rather through itself intuiting God, and reposing'. The mind, thus concentrated on one point, becomes pure and luminous, and sloughs off from itself all images and passions and creaturely attachments. When the mind tires of this concentration, it may be allowed to look outward for a time, and then the various meditations on the natural world, or on the life of Christ, suggested in chapters 21, 22, and 23, are in place; but they are a second best, to be used only as a relief from the strain of inward prayer and contemplation. To that, whenever possible, we must return. Nicodemus adds a warning 'not to believe, or receive it in any way as true, if you see, while waking or sleeping, within the heart or without, any visible form such as light, or fire, or as it were the appearance of an angel, or a saint, or any other similar appearance, whatever it be.'‡

* Similarly in a footnote to chapter 13, on how to fight temptations, Nicodemus says that the proper way to deal with temptations is to confront the evil and destroy it by 'right reason', aided by the Jesus Prayer; but that those who cannot do this must fight their temptations 'obliquely', *i.e.* by running away from them and taking refuge in prayer.

† Theophan alters the arrangement of the chapters at this point. Down to the end of chapter 23 he follows Scupoli and Nicodemus. Then he takes the new sections on the negative discipline of the senses, added by Nicodemus to Scupoli's chapter 24, and makes them into a separate chapter, which is chapter 24 in the Russian text. Scupoli's chapter 24, on the control of the tongue, becomes Theophan's chapter 25; and Nicodemus's new chapter on imagination, which is 25 in the Greek text, becomes 26 in the Russian.

‡ Theophan omits this warning. But cf. Diadochus, *Spiritual Perfection*, chs. 36 and 40, where the same warning is given.

It is clear what has happened. Scupoli, moving as usual on the discursive level of consciousness, tells us how to purge the senses of evil suggestions and make them speak to us of God, and there his ascesis ends. Nicodemus, while not at all rejecting or despising this degree of discipline, regards it as only a first stage. His own ascesis aims higher, undertaking to raise the mind above the sensory and imaginative level altogether, and to settle it in pure prayer. That is the theme of his *Handbook of Counsel*, published five years after the *Unseen Warfare*, and the additions which he makes here in the *Unseen Warfare* are in effect a brief summary of the later work.

In the chapters dealing with prayer a similar pattern emerges. Scupoli's text is translated entire, or nearly so; but additional matter is inserted which gives expression to a different point of view.

Scupoli's discussion of prayer is found in a group of nine chapters (*Sp. C.* 44–52). A single ruling idea is manifest throughout ; prayer is regarded as a weapon to be used in the spiritual combat, and is therefore assumed to consist primarily of requests for deliverance from sin and the gift of the virtues. The principal method held out to us is meditation.

Chapter 44 opens the discussion with a list of points to be observed in order that our prayers may be effective. We must be sincerely devoted to the service of God, and have a living faith and trust in Him. We must seek to bend our will to God's will, and not His will to our own. We must practise the virtues we pray for. We must mingle thanksgiving with our petitions. We must plead the mercy of God, the merits of Christ, and the prayers of the saints. We must persevere in face of all discouragement. Nicodemus translates this chapter as it stands, and we need not linger over it.

Chapters 46 to 52 are all concerned with methods of meditation. Chapter 46 suggests that, if we wish to spend half an hour or an hour in prayer, a good way of using the time is to make a meditation on the life and Passion of Christ, with special reference to the particular virtue which we desire to obtain. As an example we are given a detailed meditation on the scourging of Christ, considered with special reference to the virtue of patience. We are to feel in our own senses, detail by detail, the physical sufferings of Christ, and we are to dwell upon His interior sufferings, in all this seeing Him pre-eminently as a pattern of patience; and the meditation will end with a request for the gift of this virtue. In chapter 47 Scupoli tells us how to consider the sufferings of Christ from the standpoint of their merit, and the satisfaction which they rendered to the Father, and to ask for grace by virtue of this. In chapter 48 we are given a detailed scheme of meditation on the Blessed Virgin, including a way of 'bringing to bear a sweet violence upon the Divine Son' by reminding Him of all that His Mother has done for Him. Chapter 49 sets forth reasons why we may confidently claim Mary's prayers. Chapter 50 follows with several suggestions as to ways of meditating and praying by reference to the saints and angels, especially St. Joseph. In chapter 51 Scupoli returns to the Passion of Christ, showing in detail how an imaginative reconstruction of it may be used, not as a basis for petition, but for the purpose of evoking various affections in ourselves, such as love, hope, joy, wonder, self-hatred, compassion. Finally, in chapter 52, we are shown how to meditate on the Crucifixion, once more as a pre-eminent example of patience. In conclusion Scupoli says that the Crucified Lord is the book, by reading which we may learn every virtue, and that no printed book can teach us so much as does 'the contemplation of a Crucified God'.* Here speaks the authentic voice of western Christocentric devotion, in terms which transcend confessional divisions.

Between the introductory chapter 44 and the series of chapters 46–52 on meditation stands chapter 45, whose theme is 'mental prayer'. Scupoli defines mental prayer as 'the lifting up of our heart to God, accompanied by an actual or virtual request for something we desire'. An actual request is a sentence or two, expressive of our petition, formed in the mind but not spoken by the lips. Scupoli gives examples, and they are mostly ejaculatory prayers. A virtual request is one in which we 'show God our need without moulding our thought into words or sentences', simply holding the thought of it in the mind, with a fervent desire and faith in God. Scupoli adds that 'there is another and swifter kind of virtual prayer, which consists of a mere glance of the mind towards God, so as to implore His help, which glance is as it were

* We may remember Charles Wesley's lines: 'Where saints in an ecstasy gaze, And hang on a crucified God'. Did Wesley know the *Spiritual Combat*? His brother John appears to have known it, in one of the versions which ascribed it to the Spanish Benedictine, Juan de Castaniza.

a silent remembrancer, asking for the grace which we had before prayed for'. We should form a habit of praying in this way, because it is a most effective weapon in the spiritual combat, and can be used at all times and seasons.

Here is something different in kind from analytical meditation. It is the μονολόγιστος εὐχή of the Fathers, the germ from which the doctrine and practice of the Jesus Prayer have grown. True, Scupoli thinks of it as primarily petitionary, as a weapon in the spiritual combat, a means to an end beyond itself. True, again, he says all too little about it; his chapter 45 is short. Nevertheless this chapter gives Nicodemus his opportunity, and he takes it. By weighting his translation of this chapter with fresh matter from the Fathers and the hesychasts, he gives full representation to an aspect of prayer which Scupoli treats somewhat cavalierly.

He defines mental prayer, or prayer of the mind and heart (ἡ νοερὰ καὶ καρδιακὴ προσευχή), as 'collecting the mind into the midst of the heart', and praying in silent words the μονολόγιστος εὐχή, the Jesus Prayer, controlling the breath while saying it. This is the true mental prayer, though in a broader sense all prayer without spoken words may be called mental. Prayer of the mind and heart is harder than vocal prayer, but much more effective. It cries aloud to God, as it is written 'Wherefore criest thou to me?' (Exod. xiv. 15). The formula 'Lord Jesus Christ, Son of God, have mercy upon me' calls down all gifts and graces; for the word 'mercy' does not mean merely pardon and remission of sins, but includes all the graces of the spiritual life. This one prayer, therefore, contains all petitions in itself. But of course you *can* ask for the different gifts severally. And of course, if the effort of silent prayer is too severe, you can utter the words of the Jesus Prayer aloud; so long as you keep well in mind what they mean.

In a footnote Nicodemus suggests that this kind of prayer is the only way in which we can fulfil the first commandment, to love God with all our heart and soul and strength and mind. For in this prayer the three constituent powers of the soul, the intuitive intellect (νοῦς), the discursive reason (λόγος), and the will or spirit (θέλησις, πνεῦμα), are united in a single act, and the soul, thus united within herself, is made fit for union with God. He refers to the opposition which the hesychast

A HISTORY OF UNSEEN WARFARE

doctrine has to face, and quotes in its defence the Συνοδικὸς Τόμος of 1351, in which Barlaam and his supporters were condemned and their doctrine declared incompatible with Orthodoxy.

Finally, he says, some recognise a form of mental prayer in which a man uses no words at all, not even silent ones, but 'with the mind alone he thinks and contemplates unchangingly how God is present before him', and responds to the divine presence with fear, or lively faith, or love and joy. This is what is meant in the Psalm: 'I have seen the Lord always before me'. And such contemplation need not be of long duration; it can be 'one. single unchanging glance of the mind towards God'.

In such manner Nicodemus expands Scupoli's brief chapter on mental prayer, making it into a statement of basic hesychast doctrine. Having done this, he goes on to say that, of course, meditation also can be recognised as a form of prayer, as St. Isaac of Nineveh declares. And then he proceeds to translate Scupoli's seven chapters on meditation, almost without alteration. He is not opposed to Scupoli's methods in their proper place, and at one point he even adds a new meditation of his own, on the theme of the Crucifixion. We see here very clearly what was Nicodemus' intention in the *Unseen Warfare*; not to substitute Latin methods of devotion for Greek, or Greek for Latin, but to marry the two, giving each its proper place in the scheme of the spiritual life.

He makes no other changes of equal extent or significance with these. There is nothing else over which we need linger, except in the chapter on spiritual communion (*Sp. C.* 56, *U.W.* II 4).

The phrase 'spiritual communion' is ambiguous. In its widest sense it can cover the whole interior life of the Christian, in so far as that life is one of conscious fellowship or communion with God in Christ. The Christian is always in fact united with God, so long as he is in a state of grace; and this union becomes communion when he becomes conscious of it. The ordinary Christian is conscious of it by fits and starts. He can become more conscious of it, and oftener, by practising acts of recollection. These may therefore be called acts of spiritual communion. In the state of permanent recollection and perpetual prayer, communion with God becomes constant and uninterrupted.

Christ is always present in the Christian soul, whether the soul is aware of His presence or not; but He becomes more effectively present as the soul grows in grace. The soul may be said to feed on Christ perpetually, by virtue of her perpetual dependence on His grace; but she can be said to do so more effectively as that dependence becomes more conscious and deliberate. Therefore, in any act of spiritual communion as defined in the preceding paragraph, we may say that Christ comes to the soul, bringing fresh gifts of grace and making Himself her food. It always makes good sense for the Christian to ask Christ to 'come' to him and 'feed' him in this way.

In the sacrament of Holy Communion, Christ 'visits' the soul and becomes her 'food' in a peculiar and distinctive manner, fully known only to Himself; and devout reception has the effect of increasing the closeness of our union with God, and also making us more conscious of it. This is not the whole meaning and purpose of the Holy Eucharist; but it is the reason why it is called Holy Communion. This sacramental communion is of course also a spiritual act. Every proper act of sacramental communion includes in itself an act of spiritual communion. If Christ is received orally but not spiritually, He is not received to any good effect at all.

In modern western usage, the phrase 'spiritual communion' has come to refer to a particular kind of devotional exercise, which we can perform on occasions when we should like to communicate sacramentally but are unable to do so. It is an exercise of love and aspiration, calling to mind the blessings of sacramental communion, and asking that they, or the essential part of them, viz. the spiritual reception of and feeding on Christ, may be granted to us now. 'Spiritual communion' in this sense is distinguished on the one hand from sacramental communion, because there is no reception of the Elements, and on the other hand from 'spiritual communion' in the broad sense previously defined, because it is a spiritual act of a definite kind, linked with the thought of sacramental communion and serving in a degree as a substitute for it when it cannot be had.

Scupoli treats spiritual communion explicitly as a way of 're-ceiving' the sacrament of the Eucharist. He contrasts sacramental communion, which cannot be more frequent than once a day, with spiritual communion, which can take place 'any hour and any moment'. It may take the form of an act of self-examination and penitence, with a prayer to Christ for fresh gifts of grace; or we may dedicate our mortifications and acts of virtue to Him, with the same request; or we may remember our last sacramental communion, and look forward with longing to our next. But Scupoli suggests also a 'more orderly manner' of spiritual communion, which is even more closely related to sacramental communion. There is a remote preparation and a proximate preparation, consisting of meditations on the meaning and value of sacramental communion; and these lead up to a prayer for grace to feed on Christ spiritually, since for the moment we cannot do so sacramentally. In other words, Scupoli recognises both the broader and the narrower sense of the phrase 'spiritual communion', and the value of each in its appropriate place. But his treatment of the subject is short and scanty, and there is no attempt to explain the underlying assumptions.

Nicodemus translates Scupoli's chapter almost literally, but adds fresh touches of his own. We can receive Christ, he says, spiritually and mentally (πνευματικῶς καὶ νοερῶς) at all times, 'by means of the practice of all the virtues and commandments, but especially of prayer to God, and above all of mental prayer'. For 'the Lord is found hidden in the virtues and in His holy commandments', and 'whoever fulfils one virtue or commandment receives into his soul the Lord Who is hidden in them', together with 'His Father Who is with Him, and His inseparable Holy Spirit; i.e. he receives into himself the entire Holy Trinity, and becomes His dwelling-place'. Nicodemus adds that, though the virtues render us like God and fit for union with Him, the union is actually wrought not by them, but by mental prayer, as Palamas writes: 'The power of prayer performs and accomplishes (ἱερουργεῖ καὶ τελεσιουργεῖ) the actual resurrection of man and his union with the Deity, being the bond between rational creatures and the Creator'.

VIII. *Athonite influences in Russia*

Orthodox Russia, like Greece, has had its share of Latin influences, and partly for the same reason, viz. oppression of the Orthodox Church by an alien power. The oppressor in this instance was Poland. From the year 1386, when the Grand Duke of Lithuania purchased the throne of Poland by becoming a

Catholic, for four hundred years the Ruthenians, White Russians and Ukrainians in the territories of the Grand Duchy were subjected to constant pressure from a Catholic government and an increasingly Catholicised nobility. Until 1667 the Metropolitan see of Kiev itself was under the Polish crown. After the Union of Brest in 1595, by which the Uniat Church was set up under Papal control, the Orthodox Church in Polish territory was legally non-existent. The mass of the people still clung to Orthodoxy, but they did so largely without schools or printing presses, and subject to all kinds of legal disabilities.

In such circumstances even those who spoke and wrote in defence of Orthodoxy were forced to seek help and inspiration abroad, and came to think and speak in a foreign idiom. When they were able to set up schools and theological colleges, they followed Jesuit models and introduced Catholic text-books, of course in Latin. Peter Mogila, who was Metropolitan of Kiev from 1633 until 1647, was a vigorous apologist for Orthodoxy in his writings, and did much to support the then recently founded Theological Academy at Kiev; but he himself had had a French education, and even in organising Orthodoxy for self-defence he unwittingly westernised it. His *Orthodox Confession* was written in Latin, and the Biblical quotations in it were from the Vulgate. This might be defended as an attempt to secure a hearing from western scholars. But even his catechisms and prayer-books show traces of Latin ideas and formulae.

In Orthodox Muscovite Russia, too, the westernising policy of the government after the time of Peter the Great produced similar results. There too, when theological schools were set up, the teaching was given in Latin, and the text-books used were western. In short, while Latin influences were at their strongest in the Church in Greece, a parallel wave of western influence was felt in Orthodox Russia. Not until the 19th century did Russian Orthodoxy find a clear voice of its own, largely through the teaching of Khomiakov. It was due to him in the first place that the essence of Orthodox faith and life was freshly seen and given positive expression. If in our own day Orthodoxy has proved capable of asserting itself as master in its own house, and of exercising a vigorous and growing counter-influence upon the West, it is to the revival of Orthodox theological and speculative thought in Russia during the 19th century that this result is mainly due.

This reinvigoration of Orthodox thought was in its turn made possible by a revival which had already begun in the spiritual life of Russia. The 19th century witnessed the spread of a tradition of spirituality which owes its origin to an 18th-century monk, Paissy Velichkovsky (1722–1794), one of the many Russians who lived and worked in exile at that time.

Velichkovsky was born at Poltava, an Ukrainian town which was then under Muscovite rule. In 1746 (nearly a generation before Nicodemus) he went to Mount Athos, and remained there for 17 years, learning the traditions of the place and studying the Fathers. Then he left Mount Athos and settled in Moldavia, where, after several changes of place, he ultimately became Abbot of Niamets. There he expounded the ascetic traditions of the Desert and of Mount Athos. Himself a great director of souls, he imparted his wisdom to others, who became the first of a long succession of elders (*startsi*) by whom the spiritual life of Russia was deeply influenced. Velichkovsky was also an active writer. He wrote a short book in defence of the Jesus Prayer, upholding it against detractors both at Mount Athos and in Russia. He made translations from the Fathers into Church Slavonic, and revised existing translations. In particular he translated a great part of the *Philokalia*, which was published in Slavonic, at Moscow, in 1793. By his labours, and those of his disciples who carried on the work, the treasures of the Orthodox ascetic tradition were made available to the Russian people in the language of their liturgy.

The tradition which Velichkovsky began was handed on in the 19th century to wider and wider circles in Russia. Many of his pupils gathered together in the monastery of Optino, near Kozelsk in the province of Kaluga. There a new *skete* or settlement on the Desert pattern, the Optino Pustyn, was founded in 1821, and there the tradition of spiritual direction and the work of writing and translating were carried on throughout the century. The influence of Optino was felt far beyond monastic circles. People of all kinds, from all parts of Russia, came there in search of instruction and guidance. Dostoievsky's portrait of Fr. Zosima in *The Brothers Karamazov* is a picture of the kind of men these elders were, and the kind of work they did. The Russian Church, and through it the whole of Christendom, is lastingly indebted to their teaching.

To this movement at a later stage belongs Theophan the Recluse (1815–1894), whose translation and adaptation of the *Unseen Warfare* is here rendered into English.

His name before his profession as a monk was George Govorov. He was born at Chernavsk, near Orlov, in the province of Viatka.* He was the son of a priest, and himself in due course became a priest. He was trained at the Theological Academy at Kiev. In 1841, at the age of 26, he became a monk. The next 18 years were a time of varied activities and travels. Twice he went abroad, once to spend seven years in Jerusalem, and once again to take up a post in connection with the Russian Embassy at Constantinople. Between these journeys abroad he was head of the theological school at Olonetz, and on his second return he became Rector of the Theological Academy in St. Petersburg. In 1859 he became Bishop of Tambov, and shortly afterwards of Vladimir. In 1866, however, he obtained leave to retire into seclusion at the Vychensky monastery. For six years he lived in quiet, devoting himself to writing and translating and to the work of spiritual direction, emerging from his solitude only in order to attend church services. In 1872 he ceased to do even this. He built himself a small chapel where he could celebrate the liturgy every day; and no one was allowed to see him except his confessor and the Prior of the monastery. In this close seclusion he remained, giving himself up to study and writing and to a voluminous correspondence with people who sought his guidance, until his death in 1894.

Theophan's literary work extends into various fields. While still in St. Petersburg he was president of the committee which was charged with the translation of the Bible into Russian. In addition to his work as a translator, he wrote commentaries on St. Paul's Epistles. But it is in the field of ascetic theology that his chief eminence lies, by virtue both of his personal wisdom and also of his spiritual writings and translations.

Among other things, he was chiefly responsible for a translation of the complete *Philokalia* from the original Greek into Russian. In this work he had the assistance of some of the monks of Optino and of the Moscow Theological Academy. It was a great work, and rather an adaptation than a translation; for the material is arranged in a different order from that of the Greek *Philokalia*, and additional material from the Syrian Fathers is

* Now Kirov.

273

brought in. The whole work came out, in five volumes, between 1876 and 1890.

His version of the *Unseen Warfare* is also to some extent an adaptation. He alters Nicodemus freely—more freely and extensively than Nicodemus altered Scupoli. He does not seem to have known the true nature and origin of the work he was handling, or recognised in it a product of the West. He knew that it was not Nicodemus' own work, for Nicodemus himself had said so, but he shows no sign of knowing who the real author was. He took it as a book by someone unknown, but guaranteed by the personal authority of Nicodemus and the corporate approval of Mount Athos. As such, and because he himself had a high sense of its value, he offered it to the Russian public. But he felt at liberty to make such alterations as would enrich and improve the book, and we shall see shortly what these alterations are. They have the same twofold motive as in Nicodemus, viz. to remove unnecessary Latinisms and to give a fuller expression to the patristic doctrine of pure prayer. In both directions Theophan goes further than Nicodemus did, and the book emerges from his hands so thoroughly modified that it may rightly be considered an Orthodox work and a witness to the Orthodox tradition of spirituality.

IX. *Theophan and Nicodemus*

Theophan's alterations of Nicodemus are of several kinds and degrees of importance. We are concerned mainly with those which seem to reveal differences of outlook and doctrine.

Theophan himself, in a short Foreword, indicates one change which he has made; the quotations from the Bible and the Fathers, which Nicodemus added as notes on Scupoli's work, are now (apart from a few which are omitted) incorporated in the text. This has made necessary a number of minor adjustments to make the text run smoothly, and Theophan tells us, ostensibly on this ground, to regard his work as a 'free rendering' rather than as a 'literal translation' of Nicodemus. This is misleading, for Theophan has in fact done both less and more than these words imply. On the whole, when he is translating Nicodemus, he translates him faithfully and accurately; but when he diverges from him, the divergences can be very drastic.

Nicodemus, as we saw, removed a number of Latinisms of

phrase and doctrine, though he retained perhaps more than he abolished. Theophan is much more thorough about this. He omits the sentences in which Scupoli expounds the doctrine of sufficient grace, which Nicodemus retained. Where Nicodemus links contrition and confession with 'satisfaction', Theophan alters this to 'purification by penance'. He removes Nicodemus' references to the 'merits' of Christ and the saints. He drops all but one of Nicodemus' quotations from Latin Fathers. Where Nicodemus speaks of 'ejaculatory' prayers under a translation of their Latin name, Theophan speaks of them in phrases drawn from the Psalms as the 'ways' to God's altar, or the 'cries' or 'pantings' of the soul after God.

In two passages in *U.W.* II 2 and 3 (*Sp. C.* 54 and 55) there is an interesting change of phraseology which bears upon the doctrine of the eucharistic sacrifice. In these chapters Scupoli suggests to us forms of devotion for use in connection with the Holy Communion. At the end of each chapter, among post-communion prayers, we are told to 'offer to the heavenly Father His Son' as a thank-offering, and also on behalf of ourselves and others. We are to make this offering in memory of, and in union with, the self-offering of Christ on the Cross, and in union with all other eucharistic offerings made throughout the Church on that day. Nicodemus translates this advice just as it stands. Theophan removes in each chapter the reference to 'offering' Christ to the Father. He tells us, having received Christ and 'partaken of the power of His sacrifice', to offer our supplications in the name of that sacrifice. He reminds us that, when Christ comes to us in Holy Communion, the Father comes too, and the Spirit sheds His graces upon us; and he bids us adore the Blessed Trinity, and make our good resolutions an offering to Him.

These are particular passages. When we come to consider whole chapters, we find several which Theophan has wholly or almost wholly rewritten in the light of his own experience and reflection, yet without revealing any important clash of outlook or teaching between himself and Nicodemus. Such are the chapters on the tactics to be followed in resisting temptation (*U.W.* I 13–14), two chapters on preserving peace of mind in face of troubles and disturbances (*U.W.* I 27–28), the chapter on how the Devil uses our virtues as weapons against us (*U.W.* I 34), and those on thanksgiving, on self-oblation, and on self-examination (*U.W.* II 5, 6 8).

Two consecutive chapters on the deceits of the Devil (*U.W.* I 32–33) are very thoroughly rewritten with a view to a different public. In Scupoli and Nicodemus, these chapters are of general application. They tell us of dangers which beset everyone who is resolved to enter upon the path to perfection. In Theophan's version they bear special reference to the temptations and difficulties met with by monks and recluses. We are told of the temptation to think that one can do without the guidance of an elder, the danger of presuming to make rules and dispensations for oneself, the monk's temptation to think he would do better in solitude, the solitary's temptation to think he would do better in a community, and so on. Theophan here is obviously writing from personal experience and observation, and for the benefit of others living in similar conditions to himself.

The most extensive change made by Theophan is also doctrinally the most significant. It occurs in the group of chapters dealing with prayer. We have already seen how Nicodemus deals with these, retaining Scupoli's lengthy account of meditation and simply adding to it an exposition of the hesychast doctrine of prayer. Theophan is much more thorough-going. Like Nicodemus, he keeps Scupoli's initial chapter (*Sp. C.* 44 = *U.W.* 46); but he makes a clean sweep of all the rest of Scupoli's work on the subject, together with most of Nicodemus' additions thereto. Eight whole chapters (*Sp. C.* 45–52 = *A.M.* I 46–53) are omitted, and seven new ones put in their place. It is here that the underlying significance of the whole revision comes out most clearly. Nowhere is Scupoli more a child of his age and country than in these chapters, where he sets forth a technique of meditation. Nowhere does the patristic discipline of pure prayer find clearer expression than in Theophan's substituted chapters here.

He begins with a short chapter on mental prayer (*U.W.* I 47), corresponding in position with Scupoli's chapter on the same subject. It is to this chapter of Scupoli that Nicodemus makes his additions, and some fragments of these are absorbed into Theophan's work. Theophan defines mental prayer as that in which a man 'collects his mind in the heart' and prays 'in silent words'. He distinguishes between praying with words, with the mind, and with the heart, and says that it is possible for everyone, and is required of everyone, to pray with both mind and heart, *i.e.* with both understanding and feeling. Anything less than this is not true prayer at all. Prayer which springs from the heart is truly effective prayer; it was when Moses prayed from the heart that God said to him 'Wherefore criest thou to me?'

If we pray persistently thus in mind and heart, we shall reach a higher state of prayer in which the soul, wholly concentrated within, wordlessly contemplates God as being present to her and within her, and responds to His presence with the appropriate affections. This is called 'standing in the presence of God'. Intermittent at first, this state can become permanent. Then it is called 'walking before God', and is the state referred to in the Psalm: 'I have set the Lord always before me'. This is the state of perpetual prayer.

Higher still, there is a 'prayer of the heart only', or 'spiritual prayer', which is not the soul's own act, but the act of the Holy Ghost in the soul; *i.e.* in modern western language, infused prayer. This is the prayer of the perfect, not of the ordinary Christian. But ordinary prayer of mind and heart is open to all and is demanded of all.

In chapter 48 Theophan tells us how to begin to cultivate it. He makes many wise comments and suggestions, but behind them all is the simple challenge: do we care enough about prayer to take the trouble necessary to make it a regular habit? A habit of thought and feeling, that is, and not merely of vocal exercises. If so, it needs only persistence and common sense. Chapter 48 shows us how to use set prayers composed by others. It is assumed that at the basis of our prayer life there will be a regular habit of using such prayers. The essential task herein is to keep our mind on what we are doing, so that what might be merely a mechanical rule of prayer-recitation becomes in fact a habit of prayer in mind and heart.

Chapter 49 shows how gradually, as the habit of true prayer is established, the soul will begin to find her own ways and pray in her own words, more or less formally, according to the heart's impulse. This is the point at which a modern western writer would begin to talk about the transition from 'vocal' to 'affective' prayer. But, apart from other differences, the modern western writer would almost certainly insert between these two a chapter on meditation and its methods; he would describe the discursive

277

Ignatian method, and by contrast perhaps one of the more intuitive methods; he would set forth the signs by which the soul may know that she is being 'called' to 'pass beyond' meditation, and would warn us not to try to do so until the signs are clear. Then he would go on to speak of affective prayer, and so to aspirations and the beginnings of contemplative prayer. This question of meditation occupies Scupoli, as we have seen, almost to the exclusion of everything else. Theophan on the contrary passes straight on from prayer in set forms of words to free prayer at the prompting of the heart; this is the nearest that he comes to our western category of 'affective' prayer. It is interesting to notice that he finds already on this level a discernible difference between what the soul herself spontaneously does, and what is wrought in her by the action of divine grace; this latter is the 'seed and germ' of 'spiritual prayer'.

The next stage, described in chapters 50 and 51, is in western language the building up of 'recollection'. Having learned from regular habits and exercises in prayer that the concentration of the mind and heart upon God is the matter of chief importance, the soul becomes desirous of having this concentration at all times; for then she would be in a state of perpetual prayer. The method of obtaining this is by constant use of the prayer of short phrases. Theophan illustrates this by reference to Abbot Isaac's formula as reported by Cassian, and various other formulae known to have been used by some of the saints. He encourages us to make ourselves familiar with a number of such short phrases, and to ring the changes on them. But of course the most famous of all such formulae is the Jesus Prayer, and chapter 51 is entirely devoted to describing it.

The prayer should be used, we are told, in whatever way is most likely to become habit-forming. It may be recited regularly at frequent intervals; or recited over and over again for a period, as long as the impulse lasts; or inserted into free moments, as opportunity arises, between one task and another in the day's work. However it is used, the mind and heart must be kept intent on what is being said, so that the habit of speech becomes also a habit of mind and heart. In the end, the words of the prayer may vanish from consciousness, and only the interior acts remain. The reader will notice that, although Theophan alludes to the postures and breath controls associated with this prayer, he emphasises that they are not essential, nor even suitable for everyone. He makes no such reservations about the practice of locating the prayer in the heart or breast. Most of all, however, he insists on the effort of attention, the conscious realisation of the meaning of the prayer as it is spoken. This is the really essential thing, and this it is which brings ultimately the 'warmth of heart' and 'flame of cleaving to the Lord' and 'peaceful ordering of the heart' of which he speaks. So far the soul can come by virtue of effort and discipline, with the help of that grace which is always bestowed on those who practise this discipline. He is careful to add that, beyond this acquired state of prayerful recollection, there lie the ways of prayer which cannot be acquired, but come as a gift of pure grace alone. To deal with these infused states, as the West would call them, is no part of his plan. He only mentions them to forestall misunderstandings.

He goes on in chapter 52 to discuss the concomitant discipline which is necessary to foster the life of prayer: abstinence, custody of the senses, reading and meditation, repentance and good works. Chapter 53 describes how, when the habit of prayer has been built up, it becomes a most powerful weapon in the spiritual combat. There is nothing here that calls for particular comment.

These seven chapters contain a much fuller statement of hesychast doctrine than Nicodemus gives us. They alter the whole balance of the book. Prayer is no longer thought of mainly as petition, and as a means to the end of the spiritual warfare, though the phrases which describe it in these terms survive in Theophan's text. Instead, we are shown how to discipline the spirit into an abiding sense of the presence of God. Perpetual prayer is set clearly before us as our aim, with the Jesus Prayer as the means to its attainment, and warmth of heart as a characteristic accompaniment of it. This fundamental idea of an abiding consciousness of the presence of God finds further expression in two other places in the *Unseen Warfare*. It enables our author to improve on Nicodemus in the chapter on spiritual communion, and to alter the balance of the chapter on spiritual dryness.

Nicodemus makes additions to the chapter on spiritual communion, but Theophan rewrites it altogether. Unlike his predecessors, the Italian and the Greek, he gives a clear explanation of what spiritual communion is, understanding the phrase in the broadest sense as a conscious realisation of the presence of Christ in the soul. Christ, he says, is always present there in fact, so long as we are not in a state of sin, but because of the distractions of daily life we do not always perceive His presence. Spiritual communion is the act of restoring this perception, so that we feel ourselves to be partaking of Christ. This perception is not ours to command; it is a gift of grace. But it is given to those who exercise themselves in virtue and in pure prayer; and to those who are pure in heart it is given as a perpetual possession. As for spiritual communion in the narrower sense, as a devotional exercise for those wishing but unable to communicate sacramentally, Theophan omits the instructions which Scupoli and Nicodemus give for this, and inserts what appears to be a warning against their views. Spiritual communion, he says, must not be confused with a devout remembrance of sacramental communion, or even with a devout longing for it; nor is it to be identified with the benefits obtained by non-communicating attendance at the Eucharist. These are real enough, but spiritual communion with Christ is more than these.

Chapter 59 of the *Spiritual Combat* contains Scupoli's teaching with regard to sensible devotion and dryness of spirit. He takes the usual modern Catholic line on the subject. He says little about sensible devotion, and seems mainly concerned to warn us against taking it too seriously. We are not to become attached to it; it is not by our feelings, but by the steady attachment of the will, that we are united with God. Scupoli has much more to say about spiritual dryness and darkness, and the assaults of temptation. These are to be endured with patience, as our allotted cup of suffering, or our Cross. They serve to enlighten us as to our sins and imperfections, and to train us in selfless devotion to God.

Nicodemus translates this chapter with one or two small additions which strengthen Scupoli's emphasis. He inserts a memorable sentence of his own: 'Do not wish to follow Jesus only when He goes to Mount Tabor, but to follow Him also when He goes to Mount Golgotha; do not wish only to perceive within yourself the divine light, and spiritual joys and sweetnesses, but also darknesses and sorrows and bitter draughts which the soul tastes from the temptations of demons within and without'. He quotes St. Isaac of Nineveh on the experience of 'darkness upon darkness, despair and fear, doubts as to the faith, and blasphemies.' assailing the soul, and how this can be met.

Theophan retains what Scupoli and Nicodemus say about aridity and temptation, paraphrasing it slightly but in substance leaving it unchanged. But he prefaces it with a long discourse on warmth of heart. This is not the same thing as the sensible devotion against which Scupoli warns us. It is a spiritual warmth, and as far removed from bodily sensations and emotional delight as heaven is from earth. It arises when we 'keep our attention within' and 'stand before God' in prayer. The attention is caught by God and divine things, and turned away from all creatures. All good and holy affections are evoked in the soul, not separately and in sequence, but all fused together in one, as the spectrum colours are fused in white light; and it is to this all-comprehending feeling for God and divine things that the name of 'warmth of heart' is properly given.

The experience comes intermittently at first, as a consequence of spiritual exercises or as a free gift of God; and no one who has once known it can fail to desire it and strive after it. It can be cultivated by cultivating detachment, inwardness, and recollection, and in the pure heart it becomes permanent. It is weakened and lost when the mind suffers distraction by becoming attached to creatures. Coolness of heart is always our own fault whether it is punitive, resulting directly from some particular act of our own, or educative, when grace withdraws in order that we may learn humility and grow in zeal. From this point onwards, Theophan reproduces or paraphrases Scupoli's advice on how to deal with such coolness of heart, when it does arise.

Perpetual prayer—the abiding sense of God's presence in the soul—spiritual warmth of heart: these are the recurring themes in Theophan's revision of this book. Their introduction restores the balance of the traditional Christian teaching, which in Scupoli as in other modern Latin authors had become disturbed. It makes the *Unseen Warfare* a genuinely Orthodox work, a worthy modern companion to the *Philokalia*, with which, both in Greece and in Russia, it has shared the same editors.